The IBM PC/XT: Making the Right Connections

MARTIN D. SEYER

The IBM PC/XT: Making the Right Connections

PRENTICE-HALL, INC.
Englewood Cliffs, New Jersey 07632

Library of Congress Cataloging in Publication Data

Seyer, Martin D. (date)
  The IBM PC/XT

  Includes index.
  1. Computer input-output equipment. 2. Computer interfaces. 3. IBM Personal Computer XT. I. Title.
  II. Title: I.B.M. P.C./X.T.
  TK7887.5.S47 1985   621.3819'5832   84-18269
  ISBN 0-13-449026-6
  ISBN 0-13-448978-0 (pbk.)

Editorial/production supervision: Karen Skrable Fortgang
Interior design: Kathryn Gollin Marshak
Cover design: Photo Plus Art
Manufacturing buyer: Gordon Osbourne

© 1985 by Prentice-Hall, Inc., Englewood Cliffs, New Jersey 07632

Chapter 2 and Appendices B, and C were previously published under the title *RS-232 Made Easy*.

The author and publisher of this book have used their best efforts in preparing this book. These efforts include the development, research, and testing of the theories and programs to determine their effectiveness. The author and publisher make no warranty of any kind, expressed or implied, with regard to these programs or the documentation contained in this book. The author and publisher shall not be liable in any event for incidental or consequential damages in connection with, or arising out of, the furnishing, performance, or use of these programs.

All rights reserved. No part of this book may be
reproduced, in any form or by any means,
without permission in writing from the publisher.

Printed in the United States of America

10 9 8 7 6 5 4 3 2 1

ISBN 0-13-449026-6
ISBN 0-13-448978-0 {PBK}   01

PRENTICE-HALL INTERNATIONAL, INC., *London*
PRENTICE-HALL OF AUSTRALIA PTY. LIMITED, *Sydney*
EDITORA PRENTICE-HALL DO BRASIL, LTDA., *Rio de Janeiro*
PRENTICE-HALL CANADA INC., *Toronto*
PRENTICE-HALL HISPANOAMERICANA, S.A., *Mexico*
PRENTICE-HALL OF INDIA PRIVATE LIMITED, *New Delhi*
PRENTICE-HALL OF JAPAN, INC., *Tokyo*
PRENTICE-HALL OF SOUTHEAST ASIA PTE. LTD., *Singapore*
WHITEHALL BOOKS LIMITED, *Wellington, New Zealand*

This book is dedicated to my wife, **Melinda,** who supplied a database of patience, encouragement, and understanding to extract from on a daily basis.

Contents

	PREFACE	xi
Chapter 1	INTRODUCTION	1
Chapter 2	BASICS OF DATA COMMUNICATION	7
Chapter 3	ASYNCHRONOUS COMMUNICATION FOR THE IBM PC/XT	19

Asynchronous environments   Intelligent modems
Board-level modems   Stand-alone modems
Acquiring RS232 interfaces   Asynchronous
Communication Adapter   Programmable
communication boards   Multifunction boards
Short-haul modems   Communication software
File transfer   Terminal emulation   RS232 in
asynchronous environments   Secondary signals
Suggested reading

Chapter 4 — SYNCHRONOUS COMMUNICATIONS FOR THE PC/XT — 57

Protocols 2780/3780 BSC 3270 BSC
Synchronous Data Link Control Protocol converters
RS232 in synchronous environments

Chapter 5 — LOCAL AREA NETWORKS — 80

Resource sharing Media Topologies
Ethernet ISO model LAN considerations
Suggested reading

Chapter 6 — CONNECTING PRINTERS TO THE IBM PC — 95

Print quality Impact printers Nonimpact printers Printer performance Interfaces Add-on options Printing techniques Graphics Reliability Printer connection DTE/DCE emulation Ground leads Data leads Control leads Hardware flow control Timing leads Serial interfacing Parallel interfacing RAM buffer Stand-alone buffer Optimization devices Printer options Suggested reading

Chapter 7 — MISCELLANEOUS IBM PC PERIPHERALS AND THEIR CONNECTIONS — 136

AC noise and spike suppressors Phone-line suppressors Backup power supplies Alternate keytops Keyboards Mouse Bar code readers Magnetic card readers Game paddles Monitors RGB monitors Color/Graphics Adapter Plotters Suggested reading

Chapter 8 — INSTALLING OTHER OPERATING SYSTEMS ON THE PC/XT — 147

DOS CP/M Unix AppleDOS
PCDOS and AppleDOS differences Apple-IBM Connection, Quadlink IBM's newest PC additions
Suggested reading

Chapter 9	OPTIMIZATION TECHNIQUES FOR VARIOUS PC/XT INSTALLATIONS	159
Appendix A	RS-232 CIRCUIT SUMMARY WITH CCITT EQUIVALENTS	179
Appendix B	RS-232 PIN ASSIGNMENTS FOR PC BOARDS, TERMINALS, AND PERIPHERALS	181
Appendix C	INTERCONNECTIONS BETWEEN THE IBM PC/XT AND PERIPHERALS	247
Appendix D	CENTRONICS PARALLEL INTERFACE STANDARD	252
Appendix E	ESCAPE SEQUENCES FOR CONTROLLING POPULAR PRINTERS	255
Appendix F	ESCAPE SEQUENCES FOR CONTROLLING POPULAR TERMINALS	268
Appendix G	ASCII CHARACTER SET	276
Appendix H	VENDOR PERIPHERAL COMPARISONS	278
Appendix I	VENDOR ADDRESSES	291
	INDEX	297

preface

Where is the PC? Is it in your possession, or does the store still have it? Having trouble deciding when to buy a personal computer? You wanted to buy an Apple four years ago but decided to wait and see if computer technology and prices would parallel the calculator's history. Four years later, you find that prices have not changed dramatically. Your neighbors, friends, and business peers are now four years ahead of you. So you go ahead and decide to purchase an IBM PC or XT. If it is any consolation, the PC really is a fine machine.

The peripherals necessary to enhance the basic PC must also be evaluated and connected properly. Many books are available on BASIC programming, spreadsheet calculating, word processing, and how to use the PC. Buyer's guides exist but do not always provide the necessary background information to aid in the selection. None exist that aid the PC/XT owner in the selection and connection of peripherals. This book has been written to aid the user in both the selection and connection to the PC of printers, terminals, modems, boards, and many other items. Communication software for both asynchronous and synchronous environments is covered in addition to local area network descriptions. This is accomplished by providing tutorials on RS-232 and Centronics parallel interfacing methods and technologies, as well as "how to" assistance. Tools, such as breakout boxes, and their use are also explained. Optimization techniques and diagrams with all necessary installation descriptions and options are included. The appendices are a source of many aids to the PC owner. Useful charts are also provided for technicians, consultants, teachers, programmers, and hobbyists in the PC world.

I searched for this information upon my acquisition of an XT. Because the search was fruitless, I have filled the void. If you have similar needs, I trust that you will find this book to be of aid in "making the right connections."

Special thanks is given to all the vendors listed in Appendixes B, E, F, H, and I who provided the information necessary to compile the text and charts for this book. Numerous references are made to specific offerings of those vendors throughout the text. Rather than confuse the reader with a large number of footnotes for the trademarks, the vendors' addresses and products are listed in Appendixes H and I. I encourage the reader to consult these and to patronize these vendors.

This work reflects the author's view only, not those of AT&T, with which I am affiliated. AT&T has recently announced the PC 6300, which is operationally compatible with the IBM PC/XT. The material presented here is applicable to this offering as well as other compatibles.

M. D. (Marty) Seyer

The IBM PC/XT: Making the Right Connections

CHAPTER 1

introduction

So, you finally decided to take the plunge! After all those trips to computer stores, many sleepless nights, a loan or two, or possibly a healthy budget allocation, your personal computer is a reality. You own an IBM Personal Computer with one drive, two drives, or possibly overdrive provided by an XT. The XT does not stand for the extraterrestrial, but it can phone home if a modem is attached. You return from your local computer store's "First Annual Going Out of Business" sale, proudly carrying your latest gadget, the computer. Hurriedly, you unpack it. Nestled between pieces of cardboard and Styrofoam lies the magic box of plastic, metal, and wires. You expected Styrofoam peanuts, but they must be reserved for the PCjr. Excitement and anticipation cause you to ignore your peers, secretary, mother, father, wife, husband, or progeny hollering in the background. You pull and tug. A sigh of relief escapes you as you lift your new personal computer from the box and find that it has no broken parts. Continuing the pulling and tugging, you remove the keyboard and monitor from their boxes. You also find the manuals that accompanied your system, the *Guide to Operations* and *Basic Reference Manual* binders. Your immediate task is to figure out which manuals must be updated. Checking the various versions and releases, you insert and replace pages following the instructions.

Upon completion of the manual updating, you are anxious to assemble your configuration. Being the technocrat that you are, or assume you are, you debate whether or not to follow the instructions for device assembly. After coming to your senses and letting your pocketbook override your ego, you proceed to read the step-by-step procedures for device assembly. The instructions are outlined in a procedure similar to the following:

1. Pop the top.
2. Scrape off the tape.
3. Guard the cards.
4. Put what you got in the slot.
5. Attach the cord to the motherboard.
6. Label the cable.
7. Make sure that the drive is alive.
8. Don't be sloppy with the floppy.
9. Switch the switch.
10. Load the code.

The actual installation procedures are outlined in the *Guide to Operations* manual. IBM offers a $100 rebate if the user uses the checklist provided. Another $50 is available if the user can determine how the cover is to be removed without consulting any documentation. (*Hint:* Check the display adapter section in the *Guide to Operations* manual for the procedure.) The rebates are a fallacy but the user really should read the instructions for proper installation. Once everything is connected, you flip the switch to run the POST, the power-on self-test, for a complete memory check. This procedure takes from 13 to 90 seconds depending on the amount of memory your system contains. You have been told by other PC/XT owners that this process can be shortened by fooling the machine. By setting the switches on the motherboard of the computer to indicate a lesser amount of memory such as 16K, the POST routine will not take as long. However, because the machine is new, you decide to leave the switches in their proper setting to ensure that all memory is good in the machine. If problems occur, use the diagnostic disk provided to analyze and correct the problem.

If all is well, you proceed to load DOS, the Disk Operating System. Upon booting the disk, you display the directory, for a catalog of available programs. Issuing a DIR, directory command, you view the long list of programs. The operator can restrict the directory entries that are displayed by using "don't care" characters. This is a joke because if the user didn't care, they wouldn't be doing it. If the keyboard does not feel good, use the flip-down knobs on the bottom to activate the tilt steering feature. If still having trouble hitting the return and shift keys, purchase from Hooleon Company full-size keys that fit over the standard smaller keys. If the monitor won't quite allow a good view of the screen from all angles, a lazy Susan may be purchased for about $5. Once the monitor is placed on this, the monitor can be rotated for any angle of viewing. This sure beats the $75 stands that vendors offer to solve the problem. Nonetheless, to view them all on one screen a DIR/W command may be issued for a wide listing. Searching for the game programs, you find that they are all hidden away in a file called "SAMPLES." Upon loading BASIC, "SAMPLES" may then be run to play music, draw graphics, calculate mortgages, and more. Alas, there are a few games to be played. It is doubtful that these will save you many quarters at the arcades. But you do get a good feeling for the machine's capabilities as you proceed to bang away at the keyboard. You grudgingly scan or read the tutorial manuals that were included with your system. You may even go as far as testing your skills at some BASIC language programming. Being a novice, the extent of your programming is loop counting from 1 to 100, adding and subtracting, printing your name on the screen 100 times, tweaking the speaker, or perhaps performing some simple graphics tricks, such as drawing lines or randomly displaying dots on the screen. After many lines of "successful" coding, you recognize that the box truly can do more than you can convince it to do. Yes, not only can this device be used to satisfy entertainment needs, but the literature indicates that it can also serve as a business tool. More than likely, the PC's application for business problems was the justification for the purchase.

For example, a teacher may have purchased the system to keep track of student grades, attendance records, major subjects, and so on. A review of computer periodicals discloses that a large number of filing programs exist to satisfy this need. An example is dBASE II from Ashton-Tate, which provides for an orderly means of computerizing your manual filing system. By entering the various records into the database management system, different reports may be generated and printed if a printer can be attached.

What about the financial wizards such as brokers, accountants, investors, and bankers who need to quickly calculate and recalculate figures and projections. The "what if" questions have never been more easily answered than with the various spreadsheets available today. Programs such as VisiCalc, MultiPlan, or Lotus 1-2-3 can save countless hours of pencil scribblings and erasures. Think of all the possible reports if only a printer were connected.

An author or clerical person can hardly survive unless some type of word processor is utilized. The editing features allow for mistakes to be corrected prior to printing. The letter-quality printer works very well when properly interfaced and optioned.

How about the terminal user who has a peripheral device called a modem or maybe an acoustic coupler connected to the terminal or microcomputer emulating a terminal. Miles or blocks away is a computer containing a variety of information just waiting to be accessed. A service bureau such as the Dow Jones data bank or GE Tymshare system can be accessed by terminals or computers, properly optioned, supporting serial communications through an RS-232 port.

Whatever the situation, as you are reading through the supporting documentation, references are continually made to computers, printers, plotters, or modems, employing serial interfaces conforming to an "RS-232" standard. Furthermore, printers may be connected to what is referred to as a Centronics parallel interface. There are plenty of reference books on BASIC programming and the use of database management systems, spreadsheets, or word processing systems. However, there are limited sources outlining connectivity issues for the PC/XT. How does the user connect peripherals to the IBM? Is there any way to optimize the use of serial and parallel ports? What factors should be considered in the selection of hardware and software? What alternatives exist for the acquisition of these ports?

The documentation indicates that an expanded set of functions are available to the user if the IBM PC supports these interface standards. Quickly you grab your manuals and skim through the table of contents to find the section on input/output (I/O). Your eyes light up when you reach the paragraph that confirms that your PC has an RS-232 serial or Centronics parallel port or at least allows a circuit board to be installed giving this capability. Even though you know that interfaces are available, you still do not know whether they are cables, pieces of software, circuit boards, or connectors. Further reading points out the existence of pins, control leads, and connectors. So you ask once again: "What is RS-232? What is a Centronics parallel port?" Very simply they are pins, connectors, control signals, timing signals, data signals, ground signals, and so on. Simplicity has just become complexity. The various ports should be simple compared with the operation of the computer. You have mastered the PC's operation but based on your reading, the connection of peripherals appears to be rather difficult. Wouldn't things be nice if

Chap. 1   Introduction

we could revert this explanation back to simplicity? The best way to achieve this is to explain the aspects of the various ports necessary to connect almost any device to the PC. Once these are understood, the user can successfully tackle just about any installation of a PC/XT, regardless of configuration.

Let's first review what an RS-232 interface is as outlined by the formal definition of the standard. The EIA Standard, RS-232-C, is the interface between data terminal equipment (DTE is typically a computer or computer terminal), and data communication equipment (DCE is typically a modem), employing serial binary data interchange. As the definition states, RS-232-C is simply a "standard." This standard outlines the set of rules for exchanging data between business machines. These business machines can be terminals, printers, front-end processors, mainframe computers, or even the IBM PC. The parallel interface contrasts with RS-232 by transferring the data bits of a character all at once instead of serially.

Why is there a need for a standard, anyway? "Once upon a time," computers and terminals tried to exchange data. These business machines were usually located in different cities or buildings. However, due to their remoteness, a problem existed because one machine did not know when to transmit characters and expect the receiving machine to get the data. Also, the characters, if not sent at the correct time, would become garbled and subsequently lost. If the characters were sent at the wrong rate of speed, bigger problems occurred. Due to the multitude of vendors supplying business machines, different connectors resulted. When two business machines, such as a computer and printer or a terminal and modem, were to be connected, they could not physically be plugged together. The size and shape of the plugs were not the same. One might say that they were not "plug-compatible" (it is hard to fit a square peg into a round hole). Beyond the physical connection, what about the electrical incompatibilities that could result? It was a "shocking" experience to connect the wrong electrical signals together. These problems exemplify the need for a standard to outline the control of when, where, and how the data were to be transferred between machines.

This book was written to explain RS-232-C and Centronics parallel interface standards in laymen's terms and to address the problems noted above. It provides a thorough description and understanding of the interfaces, and in addition, the reader will gain a detailed functional insight into the parts and interrelationships of the various peripherals that employ these connections. To provide both a layman's understanding and a technician's resource, down-to-earth analogies will be used where appropriate, together with detailed diagrams.

Once the analogies are understood, the reader will have obtained a working knowledge of the concepts of an RS-232 interface as well as the Centronics parallel standard. This knowledge, coupled with the selection and optimization factors covered throughout the text, places the user in a unique position. He or she can select peripherals that allow for both growth and flexibility in any PC configuration. What type of interface should the printer have? Should a plug-in board modem or a stand-alone modem be purchased? What are the benefits and risks of multifunction boards versus dedicated boards? Is a local area network needed in your environment?

Will enough ports be available in the PC/XT for all the desired peripherals? This book offers relief to the reader in these areas. In addition, the selection and optimization diagrams of connections involving printers, modems, protocol convertors, terminal emulators, plotters, computer boards, memory boards, monitors, a mouse, electrical power filters, and local area networks, among others, are fully explained.

The book is separated into chapters, each of which deals with a major topic, including communications, printers, and miscellaneous connections. At the end of each chapter is a list of literature to be consulted for further clarification of the subject matter. But first, let us establish a framework for communication terminology that is frequently used in serial communications, as the same concepts will be applicable for other types of connections.

CHAPTER 2

basics of data communication

This chapter describes data communication terms. If you have a good understanding of such terminology, you may skip this chapter. Recognition of the terms and acronyms presented here is important, as they are very common in the industry today. Although they are not unique to RS-232, their relevance to the RS-232 standard should be understood. The heading **Data communications** introduces technical communication definitions. These terms can easily be related to various components of the railway system mentioned in Chapter 1. Expressed in this fashion, the communication jargon will quickly become a part of your vocabulary. So, without further delay, let us get on track and start rolling!

Railroads have been exciting to people of all ages. They have been in operation for many years, yet rarely does a train crash or derail. This is even more significant when you consider that trains manage to travel in both directions on a single track without catastrophes. Sometimes there are two sets of tracks, which resolves many potential problems, but numerous single-rail systems still exist today.

What about the trains themselves? Most of them have an engine and a caboose, with the railroad cars between them. It is not uncommon to see trains with several engines and cabooses surrounding the cars. The makeup of the train plays an important role in our analogy, as you will see later.

The prerequisite for a train traveling between stations, or depots, is the construction of a railway system. There are three modes of operation on this system. The following paragraphs outline the way in which these rails can be laid.

The first case is where trains are going to be traveling in one direction only—north to south, for example. One set of rails will usually suffice. With this single track, the train can then only be traveling southbound at any time, as in Figure 2-1.

Data communications: The communication term for this mode is *simplex*. The set of rails (or, in our case, telephone lines) allowing a single direction of

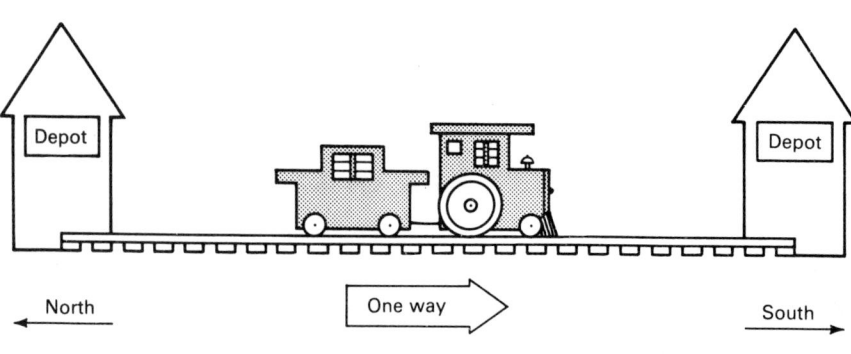

Figure 2-1

8

Chap. 2   Basics of Data Communication   9

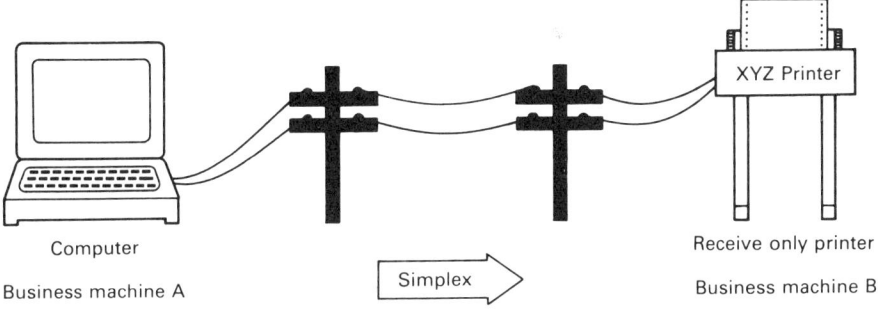

Figure 2-2

traffic can be obtained from Ma Rail (Ma Bell) or any other provider of these systems. The providers of telephone lines are commonly referred to as *common carriers*. The pair of rails in our scenario corresponds to a telephone line that is simply a pair of wires. Characters are to be transmitted only from business machine A to business machine B over these lines, as pictured in Figure 2-2. The reverse direction is not allowed in a simplex environment. *Simplex* can now be described as a mode allowing transmission of data in one direction only. This is usually accomplished by using a two-wire facility.

The second type of railway system can be constructed when trains need to travel in both directions, north and south. A single track can still handle the traffic. However, only one train can travel across the rails in a given direction at any given time (nonsimultaneously). Otherwise, a northbound train and a southbound train would collide, causing a derailment. So, train traffic can be either northbound or southbound, but not both simultaneously, as shown in Figure 2-3.

Data communications: The term for this arrangement is *half-duplex*, or *HDX*. Characters may be transmitted in both directions, but not simultaneously, over a single pair of wires, as shown in Figure 2-4. This is also known as two-way

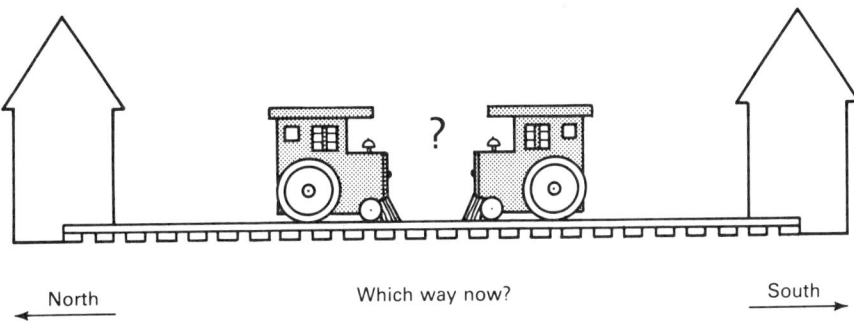

Figure 2-3

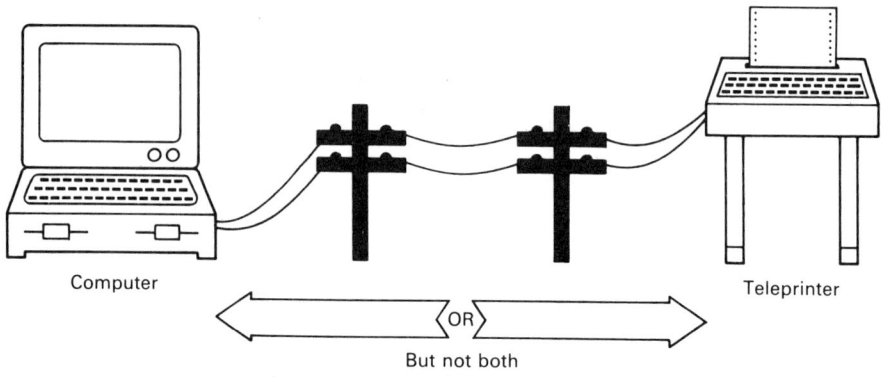

Figure 2-4

alternate transmission. The direction of traffic is alternated to utilize the single pair of wires efficiently.

Sometimes we want both northbound and southbound trains to be able to use the tracks at the same time. This is the stipulation for our third type of railway system. There are two ways of meeting this requirement. A two-track railway system can be built, with one track for northbound trains, and the other for southbound traffic. This system allows trains to travel in both directions simultaneously. The use of separate tracks eliminates the possibility of head-on collisions (Figure 2-5).

Data communications: The term for this transmission mode is *full-duplex,* or *FDX*. Characters can be transmitted in both directions, simultaneously, on a four-wire facility (two sets of tracks require four rails).

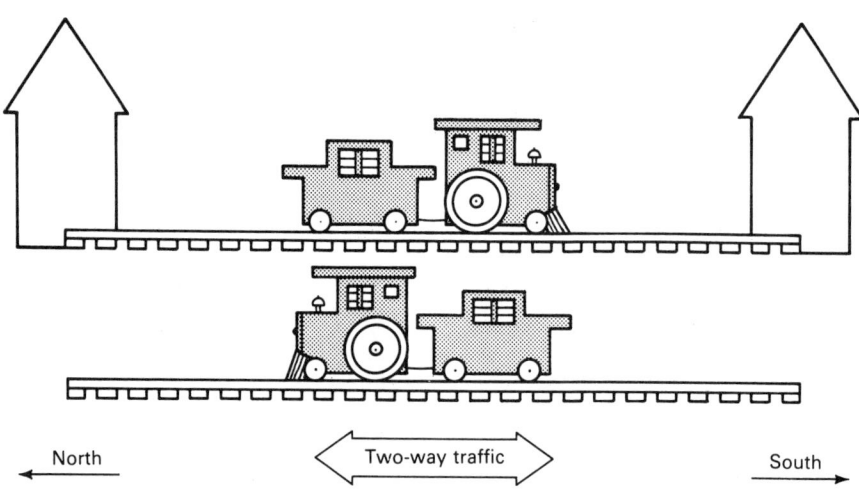

Figure 2-5

The only problem with this railway system is that the cost of buying or building the tracks can be very expensive. With a two-track system, more resources are required. The more rails the crew has to spike to the railroad ties, the greater the cost of the system for depot interconnections. Maybe this is what the common carriers are referring to when they warn that "spikes on the lines are costly"? Actually spikes on the lines are unwanted noises that cause errors in the data streams being transmitted. Usually, a retransmission of the errored data is required.

There is a way to allow data to be transmitted in both directions, simultaneously, on a two-wire facility. Because explanation of this technique is beyond the scope of this book, you are encouraged to refer to *Technical Aspects of Data Communications** by John E. McNamara for an explanation of FDX transmission over two-wire facilities.

We have described the requirements for three different railway systems that allow trains to travel between depots. It is important to realize that up to this point we haven't physically connected the depots; we have merely outlined the construction requirements. Later in this discussion we describe how we actually establish the connection of the depots that are separated by a body of water.

Data communications: *Simplex, HDX, FDX,* and *two-* or *four-wire facilities* relate to the communication modes available through the *common carrier* or telephone networks. The actual types of telephone connections are discussed in greater detail when we outline the procedures for connecting two business machines (or depots).

The goal of our train (character) is to get from station to station (business machine to business machine). These business machines could range from computers or printers to terminals. They are commonly referred to as data terminal equipment (DTE). Between the stations (DTEs) lies a body of water. To allow the trains to travel between stations, the railway system must be established. A decision must be made regarding a permanent or temporary system across the water. This decision is based on the projected number of trains that are expected to cross the water.

If the anticipated traffic load is rather large, we may elect to build a permanent railway structure across the water. The projected heavy traffic loads require that these rails be of good quality and available at all times. Generally, the quality of these tracks is proportional to their cost. The primary advantage of a permanent railway bridge is its full-time availability. The owner has use of the facility 24 hours a day.

Data communications: The technical term for our permanent railway system, or bridge, is a *private line*. Private lines, often called dedicated lines, are generally contracted for on a monthly basis from the different common carriers. The 24-hour availability of these lines allows transmission of large quantities of characters.

*Bedford, Mass.: Digital Press, 1978.

Often, the traffic volume isn't great enough to dictate the need for a permanent structure across the water. In this case, a temporary structure is available: A drawbridge will be accessible by each train station for use as needed. When trains need to cross the water, a connection is established between stations by lowering the drawbridge. This connection is broken by raising the bridge after all trains have crossed. The drawbridge will then be available to other trains. This setup is attractive because the stations pay for the use of the bridge only while it is lowered. Thus, if anticipated traffic volumes are low, a temporary facility should be considered.

Data communications: This drawbridge corresponds to the *dial-up* or *switched lines* that can be used to connect two business machines (DTEs). A call is placed between business machines using the normal telephone network and maintained as long as required for all characters to be transmitted. Upon completion, the connection is broken by hanging up the phones.

Data communications: Thus, data can be transmitted over *dial-up* or *private-line* facilities.

Both of these facilities (bridges) pass through the phone companies' switches, or central offices. These facilities are sometimes referenced as *data communication equipment* (*DCE*). The major component of DCE is a *modem*. The word *modem* is a contraction of *modulator-demodulator*. A modem is a unit incorporating a technique for placing and receiving computer signals over the common carriers' communication facility.

These modems should be viewed in our analogy as booths where traffic dispatchers, or patrolmen, reside. There is a booth at both the origination and destination locations. The dispatcher at the originating booth directs trains onto the tracks of the bridge to allow them to cross the water; the dispatcher at the far-end booth transfers the trains from the bridge to the train station.

The dispatchers also let the depots know if the bridge is available, and sometimes they provide the speed limit at which the trains can travel. The smooth operation of trains between station and dispatcher is accomplished by using common signals. Both the station and dispatcher must have a set of signals that they can generate and recognize to know when the trains can depart or arrive. The signals used to control this traffic are the major topics of the subsequent chapters of this book.

Having established that the railway system can be built in several ways and with different modes of operation, let us explore what the trains consist of and their role in our analogy. The trains are important due to the fact that they contain the cargo. After all, the cargo dictated the need for the railway system in the first place.

In order for cargo to be shipped from one location to another (depot to depot), certain types of railroad cars are needed. The most common cars used today are boxcars and flatcars. We will use these in our comparison.

At the depot, the train is put together with a combination of boxcars and flatcars. The number of cars allowed per train varies between depots. This variance

Figure 2-6

causes problems when cargo is to be shipped on these cars to another depot. The receiving depot, not knowing the number of cars to expect, will never know if the entire shipment was received. So the originator must notify the destination depot of the makeup and number of cars in the train. Knowing this, the destination depot can determine if the number of cars that arrived is the same as the number sent (Figure 2-6).

Data communications: The selection of boxcars and flatcars was intentional. These two car types allow a graphic representation of characters that business machines transmit. A character can be viewed as a specific number of 1s and 0s. The specific number of 1s and 0s representing characters is established by the machine manufacturers. Whether they be terminals, printers, or computers, this number must be consistent at both ends before data can be exchanged between two devices. Typically, these 1s and 0s are viewed as representing two positions, on and off. Pictorially, Figure 2-7 could represent a character.

Understanding what particular character these 1s and 0s represent is not important for now. There exist character code sets that determine the specific makeup of any given character. One of the most prominent is ASCII. Any given set of 1s and 0s represents a specific character. Character makeup can be derived from available ASCII charts. The important point to note is that each 1 and 0 makes up a tiny bit of the whole character. For ease of reference, we will call them *bits,* which just happens to be official name for them, though this word *bit* originated as a contraction of "binary digit."

If we assume that a boxcar is a 1 bit and the flatcar is a 0 bit, our picture would be very much the same as before (Figure 2-8).

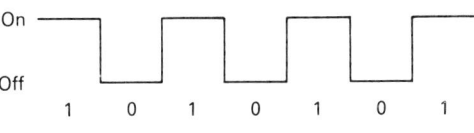

Figure 2-7

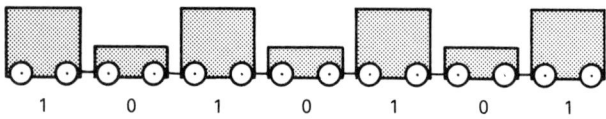

Figure 2-8

Data communications: The following discussion is unique to a communication technique termed *asynchronous transmission,* also known as *start/stop transmission.*

A train would not be complete without an engine and a caboose. When you see an engine coming down the track, you know that railroad cars are close behind. This engine signifies the beginning of the train. In our example, the engine would be followed by the specific number of boxcars and flatcars previously discussed. To signify the end of the train, a caboose is attached. The next trains will consist of the same engine-cars-caboose sequence. Often, more than one caboose and engine are attached. But for simplicity, we only will use one engine and one caboose per train, as in Figure 2-9.

Data communications: In technical terms, the engine, which signifies the beginning of the train, represents what is known as a *start bit.* The start bit informs the business machine that data bits (boxcars and flatcars) will follow. After the data bits, a caboose is attached to indicate the end of the character. This caboose is termed a *stop bit.* As you can see in Figures 2-10 and 2-11, our train (or *character*) consists of a *start bit, data bits,* and a *stop bit,* which correspond to our engine-boxcar/flatcar-caboose sequence.

Figure 2-9

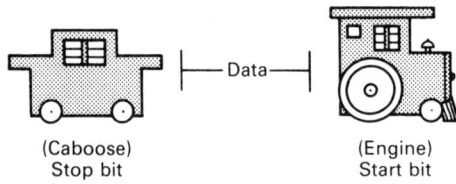

(Caboose)   (Engine)
Stop bit   Start bit

Figure 2-10

Chap. 2   Basics of Data Communication

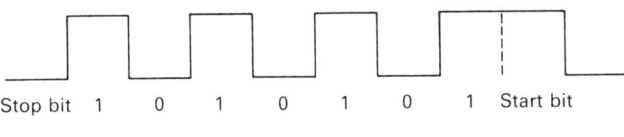

Stop bit   1   0   1   0   1   0   1   Start bit

Figure 2-11

Data communications: The fact that the stop bit may or may not be at the same level as the last bit of the character is not important. Simply keep in mind that the stop bit is a unique bit that trails the data bits.

What happens if the wrong type of cars is used in a train, if boxcars are used instead of flatcars? How does the destination depot know that some of the cars are wrong? The problem could be resolved in the following fashion: No matter how many boxcars are in the train, there should always be an odd number of boxcars. In reality, railroad cars are not arbitrarily added to keep the train to a consistent length. But, for ease of understanding, we will assume this in the analogy. The goal is to permit the depot at the destination to confirm that the proper railroad cars were received. The originator of the train makes this possible simply by counting the number of boxcars in the train. If it is an even number, the engineer adds another boxcar, making the number odd. If the number is odd, the engineer adds a flatcar. These actions not only keep the number of boxcars odd but also keep the trains the same length. As long as the receiving depot (computer or terminal) knows that an odd number of boxcars is supposed to arrive, a count can be made to determine if the correct train arrived at the depot. If the boxcar count is an even number at the final destination, the receiving depot knows that the correct cars were not received (Figure 2-12).

Data communications: This concept of keeping an odd number of bits (boxcars) in a character (train) is known as *parity*. The boxcar or flatcar that was added to keep the number odd is known as the *parity bit*. By counting the number of 1s (boxcars), the receiving depot does a *parity check*. If the number of 1 bits is even

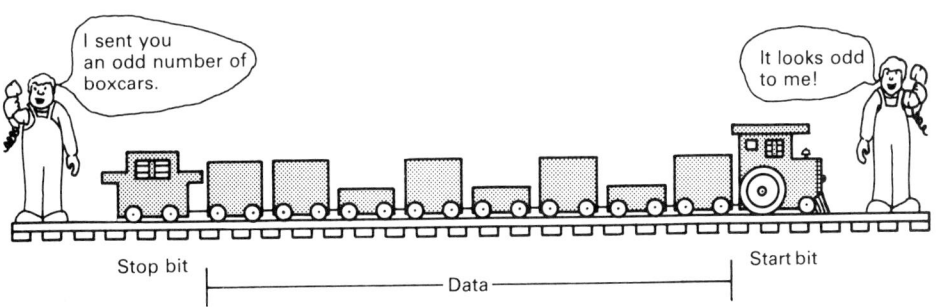

Figure 2-12

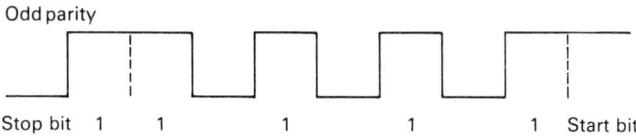

Figure 2-13

a *parity error* has occurred, making the received character incorrect. The causes of parity errors are numerous, some of the more common causes being poor-quality communication lines, power surges, and poor interface connections. Any of these conditions may cause the flipping of one of the character's bits as it travels over the communication facility. A similar scheme could just as easily have been chosen to check for an even number of 1s. This is how the terms *odd* and *even parity* came into existence (Figure 2-13).

Data communications: The concept of enclosing a character with a *start* and *stop bit* is known as *asynchronous transmission*. The start bit (engine) indicates to the receiving depot the time to start looking for the cars of the train; the stop bit (caboose) lets the depot know when the entire train had arrived. The "timing" for the beginning and end of the train is provided by the engine and caboose. Because of this, it is said that, in asynchronous transmission, the start and stop bits provide the *timing*. Each character (train) is individually *synchronized* (timed).

As the need for shipping more cargo came about, more trains were needed. However, the existing railway system wasn't adequate for these trains. What was needed was a railway system that allowed both longer and faster trains. Also, operational costs skyrocketed because one engine and one caboose were required for every train (character). Valuable time on the track was being wasted for engines and cabooses when it could have been used for more boxcars and flatcars.

So, the railway system was improved to allow faster trains and to provide a means of combining little trains into larger trains. This reduced the number of engines and cabooses required, freeing up more track time. Because of the increased speeds and sizes of the trains, a speed limit was needed for safety purposes. The decision was made to allow the railway system to establish the speed limit. The depots agreed to abide by this limit. If properly adhered to, the depots would know exactly how fast the longer trains should be traveling (Figure 2-14).

Data communications: This transmission scheme is known as *synchronous transmission*. Usually, the communications network component (railway system) established the timing (speed limit) at which the data bits would be transmitted. Better methods of determining whether the data (trains) arrived correctly were also developed. These methods are termed *protocols*. Communication protocols, having no direct bearing on RS-232, are not discussed in this book, as they are extremely complex and would complicate the discussion of RS-232. Furthermore, because the bulk of microcomputers and terminals in the market today use

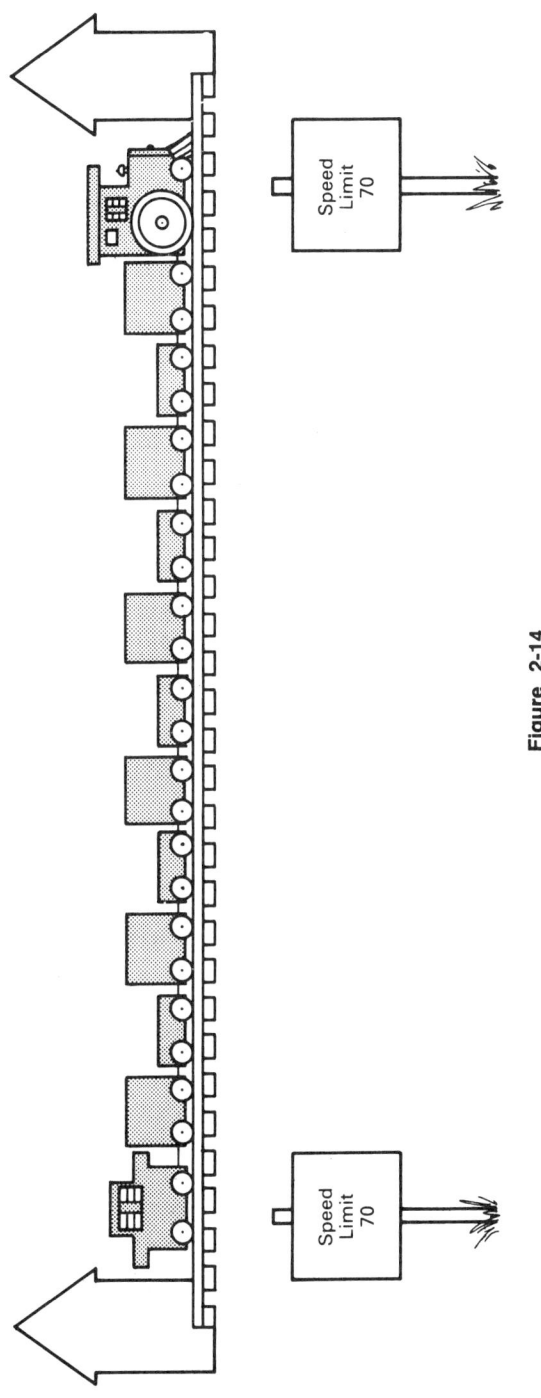

Figure 2-14

low speeds or unsophisticated protocols, we have chosen to concentrate on asynchronous transmission environments. However, synchronous transmission will be discussed again when the timing elements of RS-232 are explained. Elsewhere, unless specifically mentioned, you can assume that we are discussing an asynchronous environment.

At this point, you should have a general understanding of the *format* and *timing* of *characters* in an *asynchronous* environment. The following is a quick review of our analogy as it relates to data communication jargon.

1. The railroad tracks are the telephone lines or communication facilities.
2. *Data* transmission occurs when the trains travel along the tracks.
3. Tracks allowing trains to go in one direction only are termed *simplex*.
4. Tracks allowing train traffic in both directions but not simultaneously are termed *half-duplex*, or *HDX*.
5. Tracks allowing tracks to travel in both directions simultaneously are referred to as *full-duplex*, or *FDX*.
6. *Asynchronous transmission* takes place in an environment in which *characters* (boxcars and flatcars) have a *start bit* (engine) and a *stop bit* (caboose) to indicate the beginning and end of the *data bits*.
7. *Data terminal equipment* (*DTE*) is considered to be computers, terminals, or printers — depots and stations in our analogy.
8. *Data communication equipment* (*DCE*) is considered to be the *modems* between the computers, terminals, and printers — denoted as booths in our analogy.

Although these terms are not unique to RS-232, their understanding is a prerequisite to a true comprehension of the need for and operation of the RS-232 interface in a communication environment. Now that you are on track, let's proceed on down the rails. All aboard!

CHAPTER

3

asynchronous communication for the IBM PC/XT

With a general understanding of some basic communication terminology, we are ready for a detailed explanation of the specifics of using the IBM PC in asynchronous communication environments. This chapter will provide the reader with a complete understanding of the devices necessary to allow successful asynchronous communication with the PC. Items to be covered include modems, both intelligent and not-so intelligent, as well as board-level and stand-alone modems. The various communication ports available for the PC are discussed, highlighting benefits and pitfalls of the alternatives. The various communication software and terminal emulation software packages follow the hardware discussion. Should the reader need to know the details of interfacing these devices, a tutorial of the RS-232 interface then follows.

Asynchronous Environments: In what areas would an asynchronous dial-up environment be appropriate? A dial-up connection is normally used, for example, to access a database service, such as The Source. The information available from The Source, such as commodity and stock quotes, is to be shared by a large terminal or computer population. Typically, access to the service is for short periods of time. For example, a PC user may desire a small report once each day from the service. Over a dial-up facility, the user connects to a port, retrieves the information, logs off, and then disconnects from the port. The port is now available for other users to access. Dial-up facilities fit nicely where there are low traffic volumes per user. Many different dial-up facilities, such as Telenet and Tymnet, are available for accessing the different services. Charges for these access services generally are based on a minute of use. The cost of these facilities in conjunction with traffic volumes determines when dial-up lines are more economical to use than other facilities, such as private lines. These two major factors influence the use of asynchronous dial-up connections in the following types of service offerings:

1. Public databases
2. Service bureaus
3. Message services
4. Computer-to-computer data exchanges

Although but a few of the many areas in which the PC will use asynchronous communications, these are the ones highlighted in this chapter in our discussion of modems, communication ports, and RS-232.

Intelligent Modems: What features are necessary in a modem for it to be considered intelligent? Asynchronous modems of the past possessed very few features beyond the basic transmission requirements of modulating and demodulating. Prevalent features were items such as auto-answer, loopback tests, and lamps. Until the incorporation of microprocessors into modems, users accepted these capabilities and configured their systems accordingly. By adding the power of a computer, modem capabilities are enhanced considerably. These enhancements center around the user's interface to the modem for establishing communication links with other machines. By definition, an intelligent modem contains a microprocessor, memory, and offers enhanced dialing capabilities such as auto-dialing, keyboard dialing, mnemonic dialing, and the storage of frequently used numbers. The enhanced dialing features warrant discussion, as they offer a user-friendly interface for an otherwise complex modem. Prior to the arrival of intelligent modems, the establishment of a communication link was accomplished by lifting the handset on the phone associated with a modem, such as an AT&T 212A. The number was dialed on the rotary or Touch-Tone pad of the phone. Once the far end answered, the calling party would push a button, known as the *exclusion key*, to complete the connection. This was termed "going to data" because it would place the modem in the on-line data mode. The intelligent modem did away with the requirement for a separate handset for dialing. Dialing is accomplished by the PC operator entering the desired number directly on the keyboard. This became known as *keyboard dialing*.

Typically, a PC user with communication requirements will access the same remote computers repeatedly. Intelligent modems offer the capability of storing these frequently used numbers for ease of dialing. To use one of the stored numbers, only a single keystroke is required. The modem recognizes this and translates this digit into the desired number stored in the modem's memory. Battery backup in the modem allows the numbers to be retained even if the modem loses power or is unplugged. The tables that contain the numbers are becoming more elaborate, allowing for descriptions of the computers accessed by the numbers stored. Also, mnemonic selection of telephone numbers is appearing. This feature allows a name to be typed for dialing, instead of a number. For example, the word DALLAS might be set up in the modem to be translated into the number of the computer in that city. This eliminates the need for the user to memorize a lengthy phone number. Rather, the word DALLAS is all that is needed by the modem to establish the connection. Once the computer at the far end answers the call, the modem automatically goes into the on-line mode.

The intelligent modem can redial the last number with a single keystroke. Furthermore, the modem can be set up for repeat dialing. This feature causes the modem, in response to an unanswered call, to continue to dial a number forever or for a preset number of times. There are instances when the user does not want the modem to continue dialing an unanswered call. For example, if a user dials a computer that has more that one access number and receives a busy signal or no answer, it is desirable for the alternate number(s) to be dialed. Number linking is a feature that allows for multiple numbers to be chained together and dialed sequentially until a connection is established. If the last number in the chain is linked to the beginning of the list, continuous dialing is possible.

Another feature offered by many modems is the ability to dial a number using either Touch-Tone or rotary dialing. The telephone company determines which is the valid method for dialing. Normally, the user must option the modem to match the environment. This is accomplished either through the setting of switches or by a keyboard command. As the level of intelligence increases within modems, the ability to switch between pulse and Touch-Tone dialing can be done automatically. This feature's value is generally realized when a user has to dial several numbers to reach a computer. The use of different phone companies' services increases this possibility.

Not only must the modem deal with the different dial options, but there is also a need to detect multiple dial tones before dialing subsequent numbers. To access discount long-distance services, a subscriber must dial a number to access the service, followed by a password, and finally the desired number. Each entry requires a separate dial tone. Modems that can detect secondary dial tones allow the user the advantage of discount rates with minimal dialing aggravation. Often this can be accomplished with a single keystroke.

There are areas of the country where all dial tones are not created equal. This is evident when the customer's equipment is providing the dial tone, such as with a *private branch exchange* (PBX). A PBX is a customer's version of a telephone system. The PBX, or switch, provides a dial tone, processes calls, and connects users to the regular telephone network. Because different vendors provide these switches, dial tones from PBXs vary. Intelligent modems are used with a variety of PBXs. Consequently, the modems may not be able to detect all dial tones. Modems overcome this dilemma by providing what is known as *blind dialing*. Blind dialing allows the intelligent modem to dial a number even when no dial tone is detected.

The previous discussion dealt with the dialing aspects offered by intelligent modems. The inherent processing power offers much more in the area of interaction between the IBM PC user and the modem. Each modem has its own set of commands to be used either directly by the user or a software program that provides a simple and user-friendly interface to the PC operator. These commands offer setup procedures, dialing-directory maintenance, and "help" functions. If the user desires to issue these commands directly to the modem without a software driver intervening, they must first access the modem. For example, a Hayes Smartmodem 1200B offers a bountiful set of commands. To access these commands directly, the user may access the modem by using one of the programs provided on the DOS 1.1 or 2.0 disk. COMM.BAS is a program allowing communications to be established between the IBM PC/XT and another system. This can be used to give direct access to the Hayes modem for command issuance by using the following procedure:

1. Place DOS disk in drive.
2. Load BASIC by typing "BASIC."
3. Run COMM.BAS by typing "run "comm"."

Chap. 3   Asynchronous Communication for the IBM PC/XT

4. Select 6 from the communications menu.
5. Ensure that the caps lock key is pressed.
6. Hit the Return/Enter key three or four times.
7. Type "AT" followed by a return.
8. The "OK" response indicates that you have accessed the Hayes.
9. To dial a number, type "AT D 5551212" followed by a return.
10. Consult the Hayes *Hardware Reference Manual* for a complete list of available commands.

The COMM.BAS program had to access the modem prior to giving you control of it. This required the issuance of an address that the modem understood. The IBM PC offers two such addresses for RS-232 interfaces. These serial ports are addressable as COM1 and COM2. The program issued a COM1 command that the Hayes modem understood as its address. There is usually an option for the board-level modem to be either COM1 or COM2. If you are using the Hayes Smartmodem 1200B, the default option is for COM1. If COM2 is desired, hardware configuration switch 1 should be set off. An important consideration here relates to the COM addresses. If two devices are set up with the same COM address, neither will respond and an error message will display on the screen. So take precautions not to set up duplicate addresses. Once again, if further information is needed, consult the *Hardware Reference Manual*.

Board-Level Modems: Before being able to determine the proper address setting, the user must develop an understanding of modems and communication boards. Two types of modems are available to an IBM PC/XT owner. One is of the nature just discussed, a board-level modem. For our purposes we will assume that the modem offers a significant amount of intelligence. A board-level or expansion board modem is one that contains all the components on a single board, as depicted in Figure 3-1. This board plugs directly into one of the PC's expansion slots. An expansion board modem offers a number of benefits over a stand-alone modem. Because the modem plugs directly into a slot, no space outside the PC unit is needed for storage. This factor alone may convince you to purchase this type of modem if space is limited. Furthermore, because the modem resides within the PC, whenever you move the computer the modem is automatically carried along.

Another benefit of a board-level modem is that no special serial port is needed. Because no port is required, no RS-232 cable is required. Furthermore, no additional power outlets are needed. The modem draws its power from the slot within which it is placed. The only cable requirement is one of a modular cord to connect the modem to the telephone outlet. Since the modem is internally housed in the PC system unit, the board is not readily accessible for hardware switch optioning. Most of the options are set via software-controlled commands, which is considered a major benefit.

Figure 3-1 Hayes Microcomputer Products' Smartmodem 1200B (Courtesy of Hayes Microcomputer Products Inc.)

Although an expansion board modem offers a variety of benefits over the stand-alone version, there are a few other considerations. An expansion board modem requires a dedicated slot in the PC/XT. This implies that the modem conforms to the IBM expansion slots. If for some reason the user outgrows the PC/XT or upgrades to a different system, the modem cannot be used. The chances that the new computer system will support the expansion board could be slim. A new modem might have to be purchased for the system. The only way to circumvent this is for the vendor to offer a housing that can be used with an expansion board modem. If this is available, the board-level modem can be converted into a stand-alone modem with this acquisition. The housing will provide an inexpensive slot equivalent to the one in the IBM PC/XT. The lack of a housing accommodation is one reason the board-level modem is cheaper than stand-alones. Should this feature become available, the user must then supply an RS-232 interface as required by any stand-alone modem. This reduces the risks associated with purchasing a plug-in modem. The author predicts that these housings will start to appear in the marketplace as IBM begins to offer new personal computers. Furthermore, the loss of this dedicated slot could be costly. This is not necessarily a large concern with the XT because it offers eight expansion slots, but it could be crucial if a PC is being used. The PC, with only five slots, could reach capacity quickly with the addition of items such as a mouse, dot matrix printer, letter-quality printer, additional memory board, and other boards.

Also, use of a board-level modem does not allow for the optimization derived from sharing the modem between multiple computer types. Because an expansion-

Chap. 3   Asynchronous Communication for the IBM PC/XT   25

level modem is physically plugged into a PC, no other PC can use the modem except by moving it from one machine to another. The modem is dedicated to the PC that contains it unless some sort of local area network that offers device sharing is used. Consult Chapter 5 for technical elaboration of this technique. Also refer to Chapter 9 for more specifics on the optimization of configurations involving modems.

Stand-Alone Modems: Should the risks of purchasing a board-level modem be of major concern, a stand-alone modem is the alternative. A stand-alone modem offers the same transmission capabilities as an expansion board modem but is housed separate from the PC. This type of modem has been used with computer systems long before the PC came into existence. Because of this, some modems do not yet incorporate microprocessors to offer the features of an intelligent modem. Nonetheless, they can be used with the IBM PC. The ability of keyboard dialing is not present, so an external telephone set must be used for dialing a number. Once the computer answers, the operator must enter the data mode. There are a significant number of such modems around. For example, the Bell System 212A can be used with an IBM PC/XT. This unit requires a telephone together with an RS-232 port on the PC. The number is dialed on the phone associated with the 212A modem and placed on-line by depressing the exclusion key. The exclusion key places the modem in the data mode. The COMM.BAS program on the DOS disk may be used with this modem by adhering to the procedures outlined earlier in the section on intelligent modems.

Within the past few years, stand-alone modem vendors have incorporated microprocessors into their units as in expansion board modems. This does provide the intelligent modem features of the board-level modems. Keyboard dialing and keyboard commands are equivalent to those of board modems. Many vendors offer these modems, including those that offer board-level modems. Examples of these include the Hayes Smartmodem 1200, Ven-Tel 1200 Plus, and U.S. Robotics Passport modems. Because of the installed base of Hayes modems, most vendors now offer a Hayes-compatible mode. This mode allows the modem to accept commands normally issued to a Hayes. This is known as *emulation*. For example, the Rixon PC212A offers a Hayes emulation mode. Consult Appendix H for a comparison of individual modems and their features.

Modems of the type just described offer benefits over their board-level competitors. A stand-alone modem has indicator lights on the front panel. These lights are used for modem testing as well as providing a visual indication of the status of the transmission. Indications for send and receive data, carrier detection, and data terminal ready are generally present. Refer to the discussion later in the chapter of RS-232 in asynchronous environments for clarification of the modem tests and pin assignments.

The optioning of the modem is done by flipping switches. The switches are generally easily accessible because the modem housing design allows for this. If a modem reset is required, a switch is usually provided. If not, the modem can be powered down because it has its own power source. The heat generated by the modem does not add to that of other equipment inside the PC.

The two remaining benefits of stand-alone modems deal with flexibility. The pitfalls of expansion board modems, portability and shareability, are two of stand-alone modems' best features. Because a stand-alone modem is individually housed, it is not IBM PC-specific. All that is required for connection to an IBM PC/XT is a serial port that conforms to the RS-232 interface. Consult the section on RS-232 interfaces later in this chapter for guidance in selecting an appropriate board with this capability. Because the modem connects to a standard interface, it may be used with other computers without concern. If the user outgrows the PC/XT, the modem may be used with the new system. If a U.S. Robotics Passport modem was purchased for use with the IBM PC, it could also be used with the new system as long as a serial interface was provided. Many IBM PC plug-compatible computers are being offered today. The stand-alone modem is assured of working with these machines, whereas an expansion board modem is not guaranteed to work with these look-alikes. The portability of the stand-alone modem between different computers is a benefit to consider when faced with the acquisition of a modem.

Office environments are not necessarily limited to one PC. Often, multiple PCs as well as other types of computer systems are present. If the computers are not needed for constant communication with remote systems, a modem could be shared between two or more computer systems. The stand-alone modem lends itself to this environment. As long as the computer systems have serial interfaces, the modem can be shared. This feature allows for a substantial savings in equipment costs, as the user may reduce the total number of modems needed for multiple PC environments.

The RS-232 interface on a PC can also be shared. A single serial port may be used for multiple modems, printers, plotters, and a mouse. However, only one of these devices can be active at any given moment. The sharing of the single port to drive multiple devices is covered in Chapter 9. The IBM PC/XT currently offers a means of addressing only two serial addresses, COM1 and COM2. The ability to share a port is a means of overcoming this limitation. Recall that an expansion board modem required one of these addresses. Use of a stand-alone modem with a serial board allows for optimization of the COM1 and COM2 addresses.

If stand-alone modems allow for optimization of resources, what are the downside risks of such a purchase? Space is a consideration. A stand-alone modem requires storage space. The RS-232 distance limitation is 50 feet, so the unit must be placed somewhere near the computer. This could be of concern in an office environment where space is at a premium. Vendors are addressing this space factor by offering smaller modems that attach physically to the PC. For example, the U.S. Robotics Passport modem is three-fourths the size of normal modems. It also comes with a Velcro strip for mounting it on the side of the IBM PC. Both of these features circumvent the space problem. If the modem is attached to the PC/XT, when the PC is moved, so is the unit. Otherwise, the modem would have to be transported separately when moving the configuration.

Perhaps the biggest pitfall of stand-alone modems is that of the cable requirements. Because the modem is freestanding, a separate power source is required. The cable to the power outlet can be difficult to conceal. Furthermore, if the modem is not adjacent to the computer, an extension cord might be required. In addition to the power cord, an RS-232 cable is needed between the serial port and the modem. With this requirement comes consideration of the cable length and gender of the connectors. In most cases the PC serial port will have a male connector while the modem has a female plug. The male is often referred to as a DB25P, where the "P" stands for pins or plug; the female is known as a DB25S, where the "S" stands for socket. The pins plug into the socket. If the cable provided is not long enough to reach the stand-alone modem, as is often the case, another RS-232 cable could be used as an extension. This cable is a cord with a male connector at one end and a female connector at the other. This is the same concept as that used in a standard extension cord used in the home. The only consideration is that the distance of all cabling should be less than 50 feet to conform to the standard.

If the cable distance between the port and the modem is greater than 50 feet, there are a couple of ways to complete the connection for error-free transmission. For one way to handle this, refer to the section on short-haul modems later in this chapter. However, if the distance is less than 500 feet, special cables are available to connect the two devices. They are referred to as *shielded cables* and are manufactured with special wrapping to extend the distance. Black Box Catalog is one company that offers such a cable. Their trade name for the product is Extended Distance Data Cables. These cables have been tested to 500 feet at speeds up to 9600 bits per second (bps). Generally, the cost of such cables is based on the number of RS-232 leads that are present. When connecting a PC to a modem, the author recommends that 12-conductor cables be used. This allows for both asynchronous and synchronous operation. There is also a charge for the connector at each end of the cable. These cables can be an effective way to connect a PC and modem with a significant distance between them.

Acquiring RS-232 Interfaces: If the decision is made to purchase a stand-alone modem, a serial interface must be provided. A PC user has several options for acquiring this interface. A dedicated board providing strictly an RS-232 interface(s) can be purchased. Before rushing to make this purchase, the user needs to decide how many devices with serial port requirements will be used in the system. Refer to Chapter 9 for helpful hints. If multiple devices with serial interfaces are planned, a board or boards providing these should be acquired. Once this decision is reached, many other factors relating to multifunction boards must be considered. The various options available will be reviewed next.

Asynchronous Communication Adapter: IBM offers a board which has a single RS-232 interface known as Asynchronous Communication Adapter (ACA). The ACA (see Figure 3-2) is included with the purchase of an XT and is an optional feature with the PC. This board supports speeds of from 50 to 9600 bps. Attachment of a modem to this port is as easy as plugging it in. The COM1 and COM2 addresses are used to access the port on the board. The default option for the board is COM1. To change the address from COM1 to COM2, locate the socket on the ACA at location U15. In this socket is a programmed shunt module. By removing the shunt module, turning it upside down, and replacing it, the address is changed. While the plug is out, examine it. In one corner on the black strip is a small hole. If this hole points to the upper left corner of the ACA, the COM1 address is active. If the hole points to the lower right position of the ACA, the COM2 address is active. For the purposes of the following discussion, we will assume that the COM1 address is set. There is also a shunt plug for the port to provide either RS-232-compatible signals or a current loop interface. The latter is not used by modems and is not generally used in printers, so leave it set for RS-232-compatible signals. It is equipped with a DB25P (male) connector on the board which protrudes through the back of the PC/XT when installed. The leads that are supported by the ACA are pins 2, 3, 4, 5, 6, 7, 8, 20, and 22. For compatibility reasons ensure that the cable between the ACA and the modem provides these pins. This is termed a

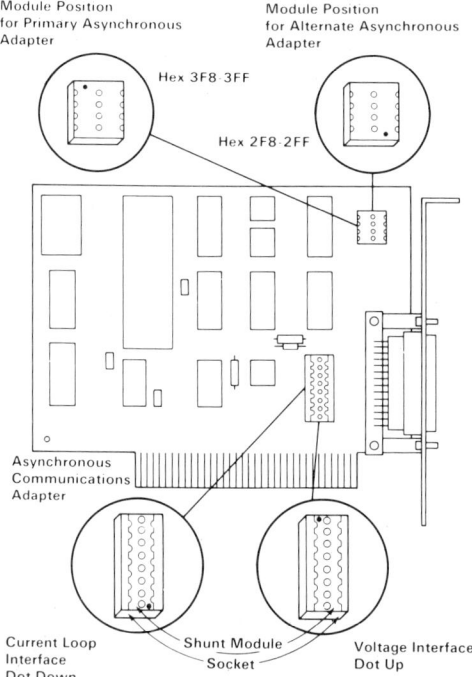

Figure 3-2 IBM Asynchronous Communication Adapter (Courtesy of International Business Machines Corporation)

straight-through cable. Refer to Appendix B for a pin description and to Appendix C, graph G12, for a graphic description of the cable required to connect the ACA to most modems.

Once the port on the ACA is set up as COM1, it must be configured for functioning with the device. When modems are involved, a software program can set up the ports. The user will be prompted for the specific attributes of baud, parity, number of data bits, and number of stop bits. The program will then translate the input into a command that the ACA understands. The command used is the MODE command given in the DOS manual. The command would be similar to the following to set up the COM1 port at 1200 bps, even parity, 7 data bits, and 1 stop bit.

MODE COM1:12

The only parameter needed in this case is the baud rate because the other parameters are defaults. However, if parameters other than the defaults are desired, they should be included on the command line as follows:

MODE COM1:12,N,8,2

These options are termed *positional parameters*. "Positional" means that no option can be omitted unless it is the last one on a command line. Each parameter can be accounted for by using a comma if it is the default setting. To option the ACA for all the defaults except speed and number of stop bits, use the following format:

MODE COM1:12,,2

The two commas set the even parity and 7 data bits as the default values. The options parameters of the MODE command should be set to match the device being connected to the ACA port. Refer to the preceding section on interfacing equipment for a discussion of each option, or protocol parameters.

A benefit of single-function boards is the cost. They are generally less expensive than multifunction boards and may be more reliable. Because of the limited functionality, they require less circuitry, which gives off less heat. The fewer the number of components, the less likelihood of failure or downtime. However, they are expensive when related to slots within the PC/XT. If multiple RS-232 ports are needed and the ACA is desired, two boards must be purchased, which would utilize two of the slots in the PC/XT. Fortunately, a number of vendors offer ACA-compatible boards that supply multiple RS-232 ports. One such vendor is STB Systems. STB's Super RIO boards offer dual RS-232 interfaces. The addition of the second port is significantly less than twice the price of single-port boards. With this product, both COM1 and COM2 are used. This board allows the use of only one slot, yet yields two serial interfaces. If a stand-alone Hayes modem is attached to a port, the same procedure may be followed as before with the Hayes expansion board modem. The prompts of the COMM.BAS program on the DOS disk for the options are translated into the issuance of a MODE command. Your input is used as the protocol parameters. Refer to Appendix H for a list of available vendors offering dedicated RS-232 boards.

Programmable Communication Boards: If you are interested in specialized programming for an IBM PC/XT in the area of communications, you should consider specialized RS-232 boards. An example of this is the AST Research Inc. CC-232 Programmable Advanced Communication Board. The CC-232 comes equipped with two communication ports. Either port can be configured as data terminal equipment (DTE) or data communication equipment (DCE). The board supports either asynchronous or synchronous operation. It can perform serial-to-parallel and parallel-to-serial conversions. The CC-232 board cannot function as the COM1 or COM2 asynchronous ports. This means that the MODE command cannot be used for optioning the ports. Switches must be set instead. In the asynchronous mode, the speed can be less than or equal to 19,200 bps. In the synchronous mode the speed can be up to 38,400 bps with the board providing necessary timing. A variety of protocol support is possible, including Binary Synchronous Communication (BSC) and Synchronous Data Link Control (SDLC) with the appropriate software drivers. Refer to Chapter 4 for a description of protocols. This board is intended for users developing unique communications software.

Multifunction Boards: The average user will not need a programmable board; however, more than just an RS-232 serial interface may be needed. If so, the PC owner should consider a multifunction board. By definition a multifunction board is a single board that provides multiple functions. These features include serial ports, parallel ports, a clock, additional memory, a monitor driver, a light-pen interface, or perhaps a game port. Figure 3-3 displays a typical multifunction board. The serial interface is used as discussed previously. But it can also be used for connection to a local printer. Another means of connecting a printer is with a parallel interface. The parallel interface is the system default for printer attachment; however, output for the printer can be redirected to a serial port. Chapter 6 discusses the connection of printers and selection of the proper interface.

Clock: A clock can be used to provide system administration features. When the PC is powered up, the operator is prompted for a date and time. Whatever is entered into these two prompts is used in DOS operations, such as a filename extension identifying the date and time the files were last written to. If a clock is purchased, software is generally provided to read the date and time from the board automatically and bypass this manual step. Battery backup is used to maintain the clock when the PC is powered off intentionally or accidentally loses power. Furthermore, certain applications are enhanced when the time and date are available automatically. Hayes Smartcom II is the terminal communication package for the Smartmodems. Smartcom II displays the time and date on the lower part of the screen. The date and time are generally skipped over by the user by merely hitting

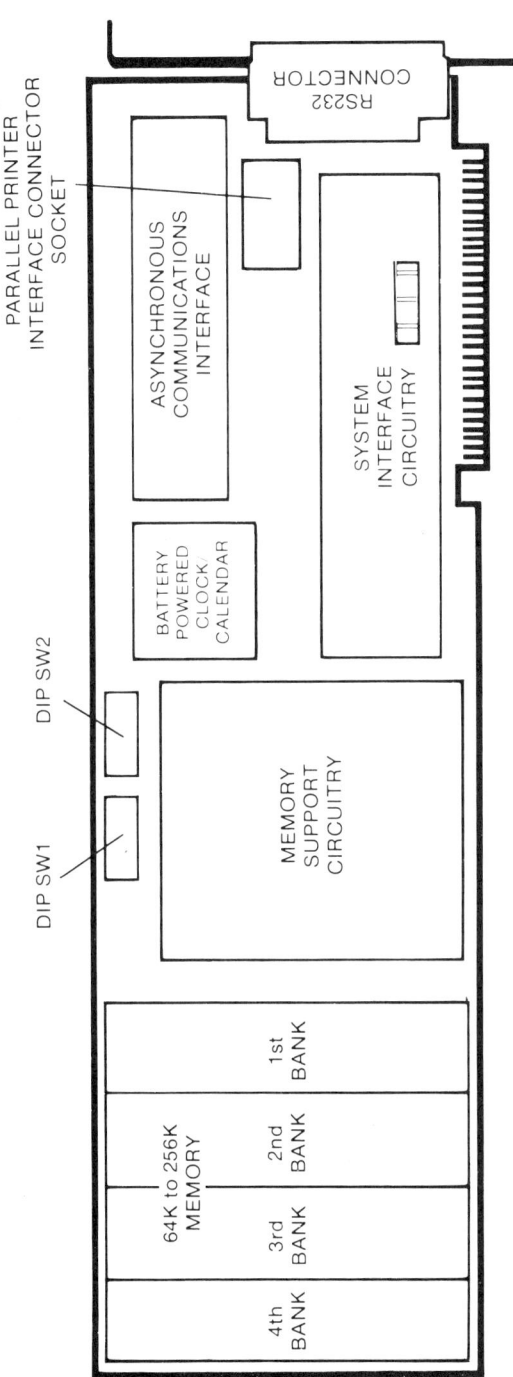

Figure 3-3 Block diagram of Quadboard (Courtesy of Quadram)

the Enter key, but is accessed automatically if a clock is installed. A clock relieves the user of many inputs because the prompts occur every time the system is reset or powered up.

Memory: Another option on multifunction boards is space for additional memory. The "plain vanilla" IBM PC is equipped with 128K of memory, while 256K is included with the basic XT unit. Many applications require more than 128/256K of memory for full functionality. If additional memory is required or desired, multifunction boards or dedicated memory boards provide for this. However, the memory on these boards might have to be transported to the PC/XT system board. The system board must be fully populated with memory chips before any memory chips may be used on an expansion board. Usually, a variety of memory amounts, in 64K increments, are available with these boards. For example, the Microsoft RAMCard is equipped with a 64K standard, allowing multiples of 64K memory to be added. The current upper limit on this board is 256K memory on the board, but other vendors provide up to 1 million bytes.

Many memory boards are equipped with software to provide a RAM disk feature. This concept evolved due to the relatively slow floppy-disk access time. The input and output associated with a PC tends to be the slowest operation in the system. The I/O can cause a serious bottleneck. If you find your PC I/O-bound, as it is termed, consider a RAM disk. The electronic disk is as fast as a hard disk would be. Because large quantities of memory are available at relatively inexpensive rates, vendors have capitalized on this. Software was written to allocate a portion of the total memory available to emulate a floppy disk. For example, STB Systems, Inc. provides a software program, the PC Accelerator, with its boards. The PC Accelerator's electronic disk feature assigns a portion of the system memory, up to 320K, to a noiseless disk-drive emulator. The command is as simple as "PCA/disk=64." Once memory is allocated for the disk emulator, a drive ID is assigned to the emulated disk. Files from a floppy disk may then be copied to the emulated disk for high-speed access. This copy routine may be part of the AUTOEXEC.BAT file, which contains commands to be processed upon system reset or startup. The memory may also be allocated for use as a spooler for the printer attached to the parallel port, not the serial port. Refer to Chapter 6 for a printer-specific implementation of the RAM allocation. Beside the basic use as additional memory, we have explored two other uses of memory. Consult Appendix H for a comparison of memory boards, both dedicated and multifunction, and the additional features that each may provide.

Color Adapter: Another type of PC/XT multifunction board is a color or monochrome adapter. These monitor boards provide a dedicated monitor adapter and perhaps also include memory upgrades, a serial port, or a parallel printer port. An example of such a board is the AST Research Inc. SixPakPlus, which is a six-function card providing memory, one serial asynchronous port, one parallel port, a clock, and a game adapter port for joystick attachment.

There are many means of obtaining an RS-232 interface for attachment of a modem. Either a dedicated RS-232 board or a multifunction board may be purchased for this capability. By combining multiple functions on a single board, precious slots in the PC/XT are saved. Furthermore, a reduction in the number of boards reduces the amount of heat produced within the system unit. Each of the functions shares board resources. Consequently, the multifunction board generally costs less per function than separate boards.

Multifunction boards do possess a couple of minor disadvantages. Because multiple functions are on a single board, the decision of what functions are needed in the PC/XT must be made up front. This implies that the user knows which peripherals will be connected to the computer. This is not always the case, as a computer system typically grows and expands as the owner's knowledge and use of the system increases. The old adage "don't put all your eggs in one basket" is applicable to multifunction boards. If all of your interfaces and memory expansion are on one multifunction board and it malfunctions, you end up with a "multi-malfunction board." Your system could be inoperable until the board is repaired or replaced. These two considerations should be taken into account when deciding on the type of board to purchase.

Maynard Electronics offers a solution to both of the disadvantages of multifunction boards with their SandStar Cards and Modules. The basic board, called the SandStar Multifunction Card, is blank with six slots. The concept is one of modularity. Modules providing the necessary functions may be added as needed. The list of current plug-in modules includes a serial port, a parallel port, a clock, and game adapter modules. Other boards offer memory or disk-drive controllers on the basic unit with slots for the various modules. With this modular approach, a PC/XT owner need not decide ahead of time the functions required for the system configuration. Modules can be added as needed. Furthermore, should one component malfunction, that module may be replaced or repaired. Provided that the malfunction is not on the main board, the user would still be able to use the rest of the system. As enhancements are brought out for the PC, they can easily be added to the board.

Short-Haul Modems: The discussion up to this point has centered around the connection of an asynchronous modem to the PC for communication with a remote computer system. Both the board-level modem and stand-alone versions satisfy the need for such communication. Furthermore, shielded RS-232-compatible cable satisfies the need for distances between two systems greater than 50 feet but less than 500 feet. However, certain configurations do not lend themselves to these two options. In particular, what is the best solution for a situation where two computers need to be connected but are more that 500 feet apart, perhaps up to 1 mile? If these computers are in the same building, the costs of intelligent modems may not be justifiable. Modems known as short-haul modems may be used instead. Short-haul modems operate in an asynchronous environment at speeds of up to 19,200 bps. They derive power requirements from either the RS-232 port to which they are attached or require a standard power attachment. They operate in pairs, one at the PC, with the other at the remote device. Assume that the remote device is another computer. The two modems are connected to one another over customer-provided twisted pairs of wires or a telephone company-provided private line. The units are simple to install and operate, as they contain no configuration switches or straps. A typical price for such a unit is $100. Gandalf Data Inc. and Black Box Catalog are two suppliers of these modems. The Black Box Catalog unit is termed the Short Haul Modem and is offered in a nonpowered version labeled SHM-NPR. The SHM eliminates the need for RS-232 cables by attaching directly into the communication port on the IBM PC. This port is provided by any of the means discussed earlier, either dedicated or multifunction boards. This in itself could save the user $100 in cabling costs if both ends are considered. The unit has four screws on one end for connection of the private-line circuit or customer-provided twisted pairs. The screw contact points are labeled tx1, tx2, rx1, and rx2. Ensure that the transmit pair at one unit goes to the receive pair at the other end. Black Box recommends at least AWG No. 24 cable between the SHMs. Each unit has dimensions of 3 × 2 × 1 inches (Figure 3-4) and thus fits in the palm of your hand. Allowable transmission speeds are relative to the distance between the pair of SHMs. The following chart relates the two factors:

Data Rate (bps)	Distances (miles)
110	18
1,200	7.5
4,800	4.5
9,600	3.2
19,200	1.2

The inverse speed/distance relations are based on the loss of signal power over distances. The bits of data become less intelligible as the speed and distance are increased, so the relation is inverse. High speeds at great distances are possible but are subject to errors during transmission. For this reason Black Box Catalog suggests adherence to the preceding chart. Because the units have no options, the speed settings in the communication port in the IBM PC and remote system determine the transmission rate. They must both be set to the same value. The SHMs support full-duplex asynchronous operation. Because they are DCE equipment the connector for plugging into the PC is a DB25S (female) plug. Pins 4 and 5, request to send and clear to send, are internally jumpered together. Pin 6, data set ready, is internally connected to either 20 or 4, depending on the unit. Data Carrier Detect actually passes over the circuit. If further information pertaining to these leads is desired, refer to the discussion later in this chapter of the RS-232-specific leads. These two units provide a private-line connection between two devices, not a dial-up connection. This example assumed two computers. These could also be used to connect an IBM PC/XT to a remote printer. The short-haul modems provide an inexpensive

Chap. 3   Asynchronous Communication for the IBM PC/XT   35

Figure 3-4 Black Box Catalog's Short Haul Modem (Courtesy of Black Box Corp.)

alternative to in-house RS-232 cabling and the more expensive, intelligent modems. Refer to Chapter 9 for other uses of these products.

Communication Software: As one can see, there are many alternatives for communicating with remote computer systems using an IBM PC/XT. Our exploration of the various modems addressed the hardware requirements of communicating systems. What applications dictated the need for this communication? In other words, what software is to be used between the IBM PC and another PC or mainframe? Perhaps the IBM PC is used to access remote databases on an IBM mainframe or Digital Equipment Corporation minicomputer. Perhaps the PC will be used to connect to The Source for retrieval of news. This could involve the collection of information from these remote computer systems for local printing or perhaps storage on the PC's disk system. Collected and edited information may need to be transmitted back to the remote system for file updates. The programs that offer these and other services are referred to as *communication software, terminal emulator programs,* or *file transfer programs.* Specialized software packages are available for each of these services. However, the trend is toward incorporating these features into one program. Communication software extends a user-friendly interface to the computer operator for an otherwise complex system environment. Without the use of these software packages, the knowledge level of the average user would have to be upgraded. However, the user is now somewhat removed from the details of communication environments. This is made possible by menu-driven software that may already have setup procedures for communicating with popular information services such as Dow Jones/News Retrieval or The Source.

```
    Smartcom II                 Hayes Microcomputer Products, Inc.

1.  Begin Communication     *.  Receive File              7.  Change Printer Status   (OFF)
2.  Edit Set                *.  Send File                 *.  Select Remote Access    (OFF)
3.  Select File Command     6.  Change Configuration      9.  Display Disk Directory  (ON)
A,B,C - Change Drive                                      0.  End Communication/Program
                                Press F2 For Help
Enter Selection: 1              O(riginate, A(nswer: O
Enter Label: A                  Phone Number: 1 555 1212

Communication Directory:

A - THE SOURCE Telenet      J - THE SOURCE Tymnet         S -
B - DJN/R Telenet           K - DJN/R Tymnet              T -
C - CompuServe              L - CompuServe Tymnet         U -
D - KNOWLEDGE INDEX TEL     M - KNOWLEDGE INDEX TYM       V -
E - Peoples Msg System      N -                           W -
F - Access (Phoenix)        O -                           X -
G - FORUM-80 (Kan City)     P -                           Y - Remote Access
H - ABBS (New York)         Q -                           Z - Standard Values
I - ABBS (Chicago)          R -

                                                     ———Smartmodem: UNAVAILABLE—
00:33:16            Tuesday January 1, 1980                              CAPS
```

Figure 3-5 Hayes Microcomputer Products' Smartcom II screen

Access to these types of services may require only one or two keystrokes, as shown in Figure 3-5.

The software that turns the IBM PC/XT into a terminal is often tied to specific modems. For example, Hayes offers a communication package, Smartcom II, which is written to work in conjunction with their Smartmodem series. PC-TALK III is a similar type of program offering similar features but designed to work with the bulk of the intelligent modems available. Regardless of the package being used, the common functions provided are transmission and reception of data. The communication software should transmit characters generated on the keyboard and display information received through the modem. This basic mode of transmission is referred to as *teletype transmission,* in which characters are transmitted and received at low speeds, typically 300 or 1200 bps. This transmission is the most popular of asynchronous modes involving 103- and 212-type modems. This minimum capability is common to all communication software. Enhancements beyond this are what separate the various communication packages. For example, the program can be as simple as that shown in Figure 3-6. Disk, monitor, printer,

```
5  CLS
10 OPEN "com1:1200" AS #1  'sets up port 1
20 OPEN "scrn:" FOR OUTPUT AS #2   'sets up screen for displaying data
30 PRINT "make the call manually or by waking up the smart modem."
35 PRINT "hit a couple of returns"
40 B$=INKEY$       'gets input from the keyboard
50 PRINT #1,B$;    'displays characters gathered from line 40
60 IF EOF(1) THEN 40   'checks for end of file indication
70 A$=INPUT$(1,#1)     'gets characters from modem
80 PRINT #2,A$;        'displays characters gathered from line 70
90 GOTO 40             'repeats above procedure
```

Figure 3-6 Dumb.Com Program

modem, and setup features are added to basic and enhanced transmission features to make these packages suitable for business applications in addition to home requirements. The next section will elaborate on the specifics of each feature. Refer to Appendix H for a comparison of vendor-specific offerings incorporating these features.

One of the key features of communication software is its ease of use with standard and intelligent modems. Most packages will work with a standard modem such as AT&T's 212A modem. This modem has no auto-dial features or terminal prompting. Consequently, the user must manually dial the remote system with the associated phone, as mentioned previously. However, because the price of microprocessor-based modems is falling rapidly, you may decide later to upgrade to an intelligent modem. Should this occur, you will not want to purchase another software package. It is better to plan for support of both modem types than to purchase separate packages.

If you purchase an intelligent modem, the auto-dial feature should be used. The software package should capitalize on this feature. Auto-redial enables the user to redial the number accessed most recently. Continuous redial enables a user's PC/XT to attempt continually to dial a number until a connection is established or until a preset number of attempts have been made. Both of these enhancements could require entry of the phone number. However, if the phone number is associated with a frequently accessed computer system, a directory of such numbers should be storable on the IBM's disk system. A directory of frequently accessed numbers allows for quick selection and connection with a remote system. The number of directory entries varies by package and is generally menu driven. Menus allow for each phone number to be assigned a letter, number, or symbolic name for quick reference. The user merely selects from the menu the system to be accessed, which will automatically setup the stored options.

The aforementioned features are generally tied to the modem attached to the PC/XT. The PC/XT and the remote system often have characteristics that don't jibe very well. The various transmission features of communication software address this potential problem. Each of the two communicating systems may output data in a different fashion, having nothing to do with the associated modems. Rather, these characteristics relate to the format and characters transmitted. For example, a remote system may transmit only a carriage return character, indicating the end of a line. If the PC receiving the data attempts to display the data, all the information will be written on the same line, with overwriting occurring. The operator will not be able to read the data received. A line feed associated with every carriage return would solve this problem. Good communication software packages offer the ability to monitor the incoming or outgoing data stream and add or delete characters as needed. In this case a line feed could be added automatically by the software package whenever a carriage return was received. Another example of the monitoring capability is in the area of control characters. Reception of these characters may cause problems for the PC. For example, when receiving information from The Source, end-of-file (EOF) characters are intentially embedded throughout the text being

```
               TE100-FT SETUP PROGRAM - Version 2.1e
               (C) Copyright 1982, 1983 by PERSOFT, INC.
                       Configuration 1:
                       SOFTKEY ASSIGNMENT UPDATE

   Shift F1:   AT_____
   Shift F2:   D 1 555 1212_____
   Shift F3:   LOG ME ON PLEASE_____
   Shift F4:   HERE IS MY PASSWORD_____
   Shift F5:   _____
   Shift F6:   _____
   Shift F7:   _____
   Shift F8:   _____
   Shift F9:   _____
   Shift F10:  _____
```

Figure 3-7 Persoft's TE100-FT function key setup

transmitted. The PC takes appropriate action when it receives the EOF character: It closes the file. To avoid this inadvertent action, a filtering function is offered. The communication software may be set up to monitor all incoming data and remove any EOF characters, thus allowing complete reception of the data. Along the same lines, certain mainframe computers may output different end-of-line (EOL) characters. Communication software allows for the substitution of the appropriate end-of-line character as needed.

In addition to the data-stream-handling capabilities offered by communication software, operational considerations must be addressed. Specifically, when communicating with remote computer systems, log-ins and passwords are required. Even when accessing discount communication services such as Telenet and Tymnet, multiple log-ins and passwords are required. The communication software should allow for storage of these strings of data. If stored, function keys may generally be used to recall them instead of entering them manually at each use. Persoft's SmarTerm/PC packages allow this, as shown in Figure 3-7. Furthermore, the package may be set to monitor the received data searching for the standard remote system prompts for this security-related data. Once received, the PC software would automatically transmit the log-in and password, freeing you of this repetitious task.

File Transfer: One other transmission-related feature deals with the transmission and reception of large quantities of data, specifically too large a quantity for the PC to act on at any given moment. This problem generally surfaces when dealing with the disk-related feature of file transfer, also known as uploading and downloading of files. If a user is logged onto The Source and is receiving important data that he or she wishes to save for later use, the software allows for the capturing of these data to disk. In order for the PC to write this information to a file on its disk system, it needs to halt temporarily transmission from the remote system. This dictates that the PC must be able to tell the remote computer when to stop the flow of data. This feature, termed *flow control,* is supported by most communication software packages. Flow control allows the PC to transmit a character, known as XOFF, to the remote system, ceasing transmission. The remote computer must recognize this character and interpret it accordingly. The PC will then have time to complete its write to the file. When ready to continue reception, the PC indicates this to the remote computer by transmitting an XON character. The computer then resumes transmission. Flow control reduces the risks of losing data because the PC is not ready to receive. With this the file transfer capability allows for the reception, or downloading, of large files from a remote computer. The same is true when the PC operator desires to transmit, or upload, a file to another PC or mainframe computer. The receiving device may have need to halt the transmitting PC temporarily, using flow control. Other flow-control techniques, such as ENQ/ACK, are covered in Chapter 6.

Specific file transfers require special attention. If non-ASCII files, known as *binary files,* are being downloaded to the PC, abnormal closing of the file could occur. Binary files are typically in assembly or machine language code. When received, some communication software may misinterpret bits for the EOF marker and inadvertently close the file. The communication software should allow for these specific types of file transfers without errors.

Capturing of files to disk is only one option for the data received. The data may be stored in memory for editing purposes. Once the changes are completed on the data in the PC's memory, the data may be retransmitted to the remote system. This allows for prompt and easy updates to information without the need to reinput the data.

Protocol: Not only is flow control necessary to avoid losing data, but a mechanism is often desired to ensure accurate reception of data. Electrical noise is possible on communication facilities. If this occurs, errors are probably induced in the data. This may not be a major concern with files to be used on a word processing system. However, with transaction-type information such as that used in accounting, where many numbers are involved, such errors are significant. To avoid this, a method of detecting and correcting errors is needed. As discussed in the data communication overview, parity identifies bad data. No corrections are made. To allow for detection and correction of errors, a protocol is used. A *protocol* is an orderly means of accurately exchanging data between two communicating computers. A protocol has sophisticated error-checking algorithms, allowing for the identification of bad received data. The receiving computer, upon detection of incorrect data, asks for retransmission of the data. One of the most widely used protocols between communication software packages on the PC is the Ward Christensen XMODEM method. The XMODEM method must be used in pairs, meaning that the communication software on the IBM PC and that on remote system must both support it. The use of this protocol is prevalent on CP/M machines and the corresponding CP/M bulletin boards. By offering the XMODEM on IBM PC communication packages, the user can be assured of received error-free files.

Printer Support: For backup reasons hard copy of the data being received may be desired. If a printer is attached to the PC/XT, the communication software should allow for a print on-line function. This enables the operator to issue a command for the printer to print all the data as they are being received. As with

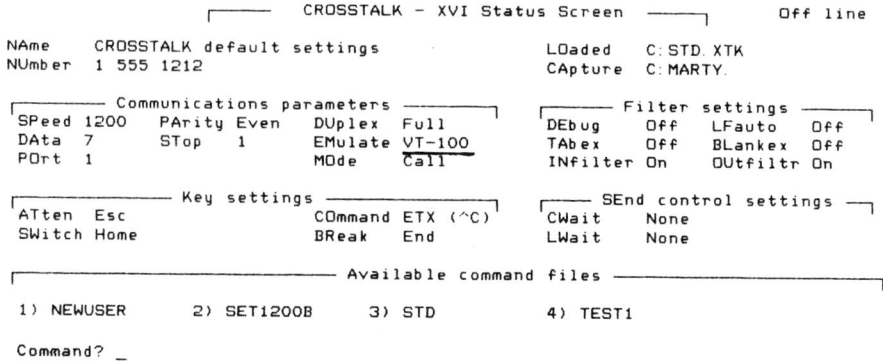

Figure 3-8 Crosstalk XVI by Microstuf

the disk access, flow control may be required when a slow-speed printer is involved. Refer to Chapter 6 for further clarification of this and other printer options. The other printer-related feature of communication software requires the filter and substitution capabilities. Some systems, including the IBM PC, often use tab characters instead of spaces in files. When printing on-line these tab characters may not be interpreted correctly. Conversion to an appropriate number of spaces may be required for proper printing or displaying of information. The communication software should be set up to monitor the data received and to substitute spaces as needed.

As one can see, communication software packages offer a significant number of options for the modem, transmission, disk, and printer features. If a user accesses the same system on a day-to-day basis, it is futile to rekey or manually set up the PC communication software with these options at each session. Ease of setup should be provided by allowing for the storage of all parameters related to a given configuration. As needed, the user would merely retrieve the saved communication parameters for easy system setup. Once called up, editing will be easy for any minor changes between systems. Crosstalk XVI is one of many packages allowing this. Its setup screen is shown in Figure 3-8.

Terminal Emulation: Software packages offering only the foregoing features generally turn the IBM PC into a teletype-like device with smart terminal features. A teletype was a device that merely received data and printed the data on paper. Because no screen was used, the device was generally called a teleprinter. Examples of such devices include the Texas Instruments TI Silent 700 Printer, the General Electric Terminet 300, and the AT&T Model 43 Teleprinter. These devices have the capability to receive one character at a time, print it, and perform a carriage return and line feed at the end of each line in the same fashion as a typewriter acts. When CRTs arrived they also used this teletype mode of transmission. The data when received were displayed on the current line of the cursor. At the end of the line a carriage return and line feed were performed.

Teletype devices, also known as asynchronous ASCII terminals, sufficed for remote communications when mere transfer of data was involved. More sophisticated applications were eventually developed requiring specific types of asynchronous ASCII terminals or CRTs. Applications of this type were developed on minicomputers such as the Digital Equipment Corporation (DEC) PDP series processors and required DEC-manufactured terminals. For example, text processors were developed on DEC minicomputers to capitalize on specific features found only on the DEC VT52 terminal. Text processors were the predecessors to today's word processors. These applications required the manipulation of text on the VT52 screen. One way to achieve this was to retransmit the entire screen of data each time a change was made in the text. At 1200-bps operation over the communication line, retransmission of a full screen, 1920 characters, would take approximately 16 seconds (1200 divided by 10 bits per character into 1920 characters). If an access charge was associated with the use of the text processor, this was an unacceptable method of making changes to text. DEC resolved this by placing intelligence into the VT series terminals. The terminals allowed for direct cursor positioning anywhere on the screen. This feature alone saved transmission time by reducing the number of characters transmitted to make a text correction. The application positioned the cursor at the location of the incorrect data, allowing the user to correct the data directly. Function keys were added to the terminal for quick action using a single keystroke. The application would interpret the reception of a typed function key and take corresponding actions. The applications were programmed to issue command strings understood by the VT-type terminal.

Other applications were written to rely on specific features of terminals. Examples include menu-driven applications, accounting applications, and data forms packages. Menu-driven applications benefited by only having to send cursor positioning characters followed by the text instead of the full screen including spaces. Accounting software derived the same benefits. Forms entry packages capitalized on the cursor positioning features to paint a form on the screen. Furthermore, the cursor could be placed in the first blank field on the screen. Once the data were entered in this field, a carriage return would be typed. The forms package would receive this and position the cursor in the next field, either on the same line or on another line. These terminals also supported features such as underlining, highlighting of fields, protected fields, hidden fields, and a nonblinking cursor. All of these allowed for clearer presentation of information to a terminal operator.

If you have used a database management system such as dBASE or Microsoft's MultiWord word processing system on the IBM PC, you have experienced the aforementioned features and may not have been aware of it. Applications such as these capitalize on the IBM's capabilities for direct cursor positioning, line deletion, underlining, and others. The commands used to perform these actions are specific to the IBM PC, just as the VT series terminals responded to their own set of commands. The DEC was only one manufacturer of a terminal that understood a specific set of commands. Others include Hewlett-Packard's HP2621, IBM's 3101, Lear Siegler's ADM series, and Televideo's 900 series. Each of these had their own unique set of commands for the various screen functions. A function as simple as clearing the screen and placing the cursor in the home position of the CRT, line 1, column 1, varies among the terminals. For example, the IBM 3101 terminal requires an ESC H sequence to be sent by the remote computer system to home the cursor. The DEC VT100 terminal requires an ESC, left bracket, and H to perform the same function. The DOS 2.0 operating system has a command, CLS, which will clear the screen and place the cursor in the home position. The differences between this and other commands become obvious when using the IBM PC to access the text processor, menu-driven programs, and forms data entry applications of both mainframes and minicomputers. The commands sent by the applications are received by the PC but are not interpreted properly. Even if the IBM is running the communication software discussed previously, these commands are processed improperly. A program is needed that will receive these terminal-specific commands and translate them into commands that the IBM PC understands. Such programs are called terminal emulator packages. Vendors offer DEC VT100, IBM 3101, HP2621, Lear Siegler ADM 3A, Televideo 900, and other popular terminal emulator software. These packages receive the commands from the remote system, such as the home command, and issue equivalent commands that the IBM PC understands. Use of terminal emulator packages on the IBM PC allows the user to access a multitude of applications otherwise not available. Generally, 95 percent of all the features found in the terminals are offered in the software programs. The features not implemented may or may not be required for your installation. For example, most TE packages emulating the DEC VT100 do not support the 132-column mode found in the terminal, smooth scrolling, split screen, reverse video, and double-high and double-wide characters. The TE software brochures usually list the features not implemented. Ensure that the remaining 5 percent of the features are not required within the applications accessed using the emulator software on the IBM PC.

Terminal emulator software allows for more powerful replacement of old terminals with the IBM PC. This benefit alone allows the IBM PC to be flexible enough to access multiple systems. If different asynchronous terminals were used to access computers running terminal-dependent software, the IBM PC is a single replacement for multiple terminals. The user merely selects terminal emulation software as needed, even if multiple packages are required. Businesses find this benefit a worthwhile investment in itself, as terminal costs may be reduced. The capabilities of terminal emulator packages offered today extend beyond basic emulation. The standard features found in a basic communication software package are also included. These features include file transfer uploading and downloading, filtering and substitution of characters, stored parameters, and functionality with both intelligent and nonintelligent modems. SmarTerm/PC is an example of a terminal emulation package offering TE and communication software capabilities. DEC VT100 or Data General Dasher emulation with programmable function keys is offered in addition to file transfer capabilities. Even the 132-column mode of the DEC VT100 is supported if a California Computer System SuperVision monitor board is used. PC/InterComm by Mark of the Unicorn offers similar features, with up to 30 function key assignments. Linkup by Information Technologies Inc. offers a communications support system offering asynchronous terminal emulation. See our earlier discussion of synchronous emulators, as this system offers communication hardware and software to include synchronous support in addition to asynchronous communication. Crosstalk XVI by Microstuf offers a long list of communication software niceties, including color capabilities (refer to Figure 3-8). Crosstalk allows the user to set the color of the characters, their background, and the status line. Furthermore, multiple terminals may be emulated with this software program, including the Televideo 900 series, IBM 3101, Adds Viewpoint, and the DEC VT series terminals.

The average user of the IBM PC in the home who accesses services such as The Source or the Dow Jones/News Retrieval networks will not require the capability of emulating specific terminals. The features of a standard communication software package will generally suffice. However, business use of the PC/XT will probably require the terminal emulation capability. An example of how the IBM PC and a communication software package with terminal emulation software would be used is that of a minicomputer offering a word processing system. Normally accessed by a specific terminal with fancy editing capabilities, the IBM PC could be used instead. Instead of the IBM PC accessing the remote system and remaining connected while a document is created, the document could be created locally on the PC for later file transfer into the system's word processor. The PC operator could optionally insert results from a spreadsheet into the text prior to uploading. The use of the PC in this environment does not tie up the main computer system as would a standard terminal. Freeing up the communication ports on the remote system could save a business an investment in hardware that could be used for additional communication ports. Furthermore, the document could be stored locally on the IBM PC. This could offload the minicomputer, especially in the case of an IBM XT, with its hearty 10 megabytes of storage. With file transfer, archiving is possible on the PC/XT. Consult Appendix F for attributes of popular asynchronous terminals. These are useful when writing software for the IBM PC that is running the emulator software packages.

RS-232 in Asynchronous Environments: This section is for the reader who desires a more complete understanding of RS-232 lead interaction when the IBM is connected to an asynchronous modem. The analogy used in Chapter 2 will be built upon to provide a thorough explanation of the RS-232 pins and their functions. Recall that the train depots correspond to the IBM PC, remote printer, or a mainframe computer, all of which are data terminal equipment (DTE). The booths equate to the asynchronous modems. The train path between these two and the signals used to control the railway facilities represent the RS-232 signals. These leads are separated by category, such as data, control, ground, and timing, for ease of learning. Our discussion begins with the data leads necessary for transmitting information.

A dispatcher knows that there are two kinds of trains at a depot, departing and arriving trains. Departing trains have a preassigned track, say, track 2. All leaving trains will depart on this track.

Once they cross the water and reach the far-end booth, the trains are switched to a different track, track 3, which is set aside for arriving trains. The dispatcher, by assigning separate tracks, can monitor each and see if any trains are departing to or arriving from the booths and drawbridge.

RS-232: In an RS-232 environment, the departing trains represent the transmitted data, and the arriving trains the received data. All data (trains) departing from the PC will go across a track called the *transmitted data lead*. A track (lead) known as the *received data lead* is set aside for all arriving trains (data) to use. In an RS-232 interface, 25 pins, or leads, are available for use by the DTE and DCE (see Figure A-1 in Appendix A). However, only a limited number of leads are used as "tracks" for data transfer. Each lead has a preassigned function. For example, the transmitted data go across pin 2, whereas the received data arrive on pin 3. By monitoring pin 2, transmitted data can be detected. To check if data are being received, pin 3 should be monitored. The tools available to monitor these and other leads are discussed in Chapter 6.

Keep in mind that at one end of the track, the train is considered to be departing, but once it crosses the bridge, it is considered an arriving train at the destination depot.

RS-232: Data transmitted at the originating PC are on pin 2 of the RS-232 interface, whereas at the receiving DTE, such as a mainframe, these data arrive on pin 3, as shown in Figure 3-9. Transmitted data are "output" at one end and become "input" at the other end.

For example, when a PC is connected to The Source, the keyboard operator's typed characters are passed to the modem on pin 2. These output data are transmitted over the communication line to the far-end modem of The Source. At this end, the received data are presented to the computer as input on pin 3.

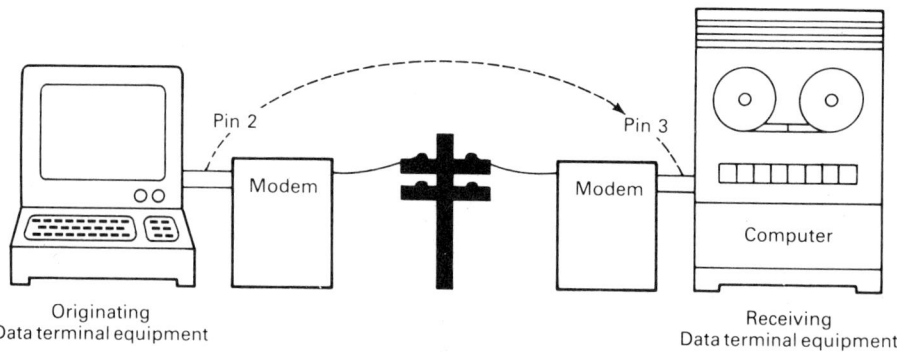

Figure 3-9 Transmit and receive data lead interaction

Chap. 3 Asynchronous Communication for the IBM PC/XT   45

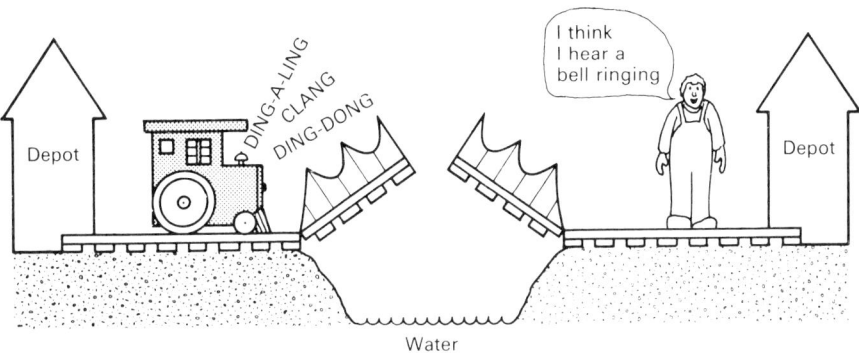

Figure 3-10 Ring indicator concept

Our bridge is a drawbridge equating to dial-up communication facilities. Control of the tracks must be maintained. The depot (DTE) must know when the bridge is in place. The booth attendant must inform the dispatcher at the station when the train (data) can be moved (transmitted) to the bridge (communication facilities). To keep our trains from going into the water, the drawbridge had better be lowered between the two depots when each train reaches it. Lowering the drawbridge corresponds to establishing a telephone connection between the PC and The Source.

As a train approaches the water it must let the other depot know that the bridge must be lowered. Each train station is equipped with a bell that produces a loud ring. Let's set up a procedure for indicating when to lower the bridge. Whenever a booth (modem) hears the ringing from the distant station, this should be interpreted as an indication that the bridge should be lowered. We will call this our ring indicator. The scenario would be similar to Figure 3-10.

RS-232: In the actual RS-232 interface, pin 22 is known as the *ring indicator*. When the telephone number associated with a modem is dialed, this lead will indicate that ringing is occurring. It will go on and off in direct correlation with the phone rings. This is an indication that a request is being made for establishment of a dial-up connection.

The booth operator at the distant end hears the ringing. However, he does not want to lower the bridge for the train to arrive unless he knows for certain that there is someone at the depot ready to receive the train. If the train arrived while the depot was not being operated, no one could receive and inspect it, and the train could get lost in the railroad yard. So, as a rule, the booth will not lower the bridge unless the station is manned.

RS-232: This signal from the depot (DTE) is termed *data terminal ready* (DTR). Pin 20 is a control lead or signal used by the mainframe or personal computer to indicate that the modem should answer the phone. Some modems are equipped with the capability to answer the call automatically if pin 20 is on. This feature, termed auto-answer, allows for PC or terminal users to establish a telephone connection with an unmanned computer site, such as The Source or Dow Jones/News Retrieval services. Although not an RS-232 term, auto-answer utilizes pins on the RS-232 interface. Generally, if the machine's power is on, DTR will be on, enabling calls to be answered for the connection to be established.

Let's assume that the train station is manned by someone who turns on a light when a request is received to signal that the booth attendant should lower the bridge. When the booth operator hears the bell ringing, he lowers his half of the bridge. At the originating station, the booth operator can tell that the remote operator has lowered his part of the bridge. He checks to see if his end should be lowered in the same fashion. If the station failed to pass him the signal, he refuses to lower the bridge. The far-end booth operator waits to see if the bridge was actually lowered. If the bridge was not lowered, after a period of time the operator raises his end so that other trains may have access to the bridge.

RS-232: This is referred to as *timing out*. Timing out occurs if the proper signal (DTR) is not present at one of the ends. The communication path will not be established. However, if the data terminal ready signals are present at both ends, the connection is maintained. To disconnect a dial-up connection, either end merely drops DTR (pin 20).

Generally, most commercially available databases, time-sharing systems, and other services are set up to support auto-answer. This allows unattended operation of the service. For example, to access Dow Jones services, you merely dial the phone number of a port on the computer. Because the port is optioned for auto-answer, DTR will be on, allowing the modem to answer the call automatically. By answering the call, the modem returns a high-pitched answer-back tone to the originator. Upon detection of this tone, the originator enters the data modem manually, or automatically if the modem can accomplish this, completing the connection. DTR determines if the connection is maintained. A good example of this interaction is detectable with a Hayes Smartmodem 1200. After the far-end 212-compatible modem answers the call, the high-pitched tone can be heard through the Hayes internal speaker. If the PC port is enabled at this time, the call will be answered because pin 20 is active on the COM1 or COM2 port. The Hayes will then automatically go into the data mode.

The Hayes modem, discussed previously, is an intelligent modem because of its on-board microprocessor. This intelligence allows features such as auto-dial, storing numbers, and counting the number of rings. But this intelligence must also access previously discussed RS-232 signals. For example, the number to be called, input on the keyboard of the PC, must be transmitted to the locally attached modem. This number, output on pin 2 (transmitted data), must be recognized by the modem as a digit to be dialed. The modem must know when all the digits are received to make a valid call. Usually, the PC operator ends the number with a carriage return, which serves as a delimiter indicating that the modem should dial that number.

Chap. 3 Asynchronous Communication for the IBM PC/XT   **47**

These digits from the PC are standard ASCII representations of numbers. The modem must translate the ASCII characters into dial pulses or Touch-Tone digits that the standard phone network can understand. This is because the telephone network has no way of knowing whether a machine or human being is placing a call. It only knows Touch-Tone or rotary-dialed pulses.

How does an intelligent modem such as a Hayes indicate that a busy condition, no answer, some other problem, or a successful call has occurred? Recall that the PC receives its characters on pin 3, received data, over the RS-232 interface. The modem must interpret the condition and pass the appropriate message to the PC on pin 3 of the COM1/2 port.

Once the call setup has taken place, the intelligence of the modem must become almost transparent and allow the modem to behave like the standard asynchronous modem. In this mode, modulation and demodulation of the characters take place as discussed in Chapter 2. The RS-232 signals now are used according to the standard.

Assume that the bridge is successfully lowered to allow trains across. To let each depot know this, each booth gives a signal to the depots indicating that the bridge is lowered.

RS-232: The term for this lead is *data set ready* (DSR). This signal is on pin 6. In a dial-up environment, DSR is asserted to the proper voltage, that is, goes high, if a communication path has been established. In our example the Hayes would raise pin 6 as a signal to the PC's COM1/2 port that the link was available for data transmission. Here is a quick review of the sequence of events.

1. The phone number is dialed.
2. The ring indicator (pin 22) is on at the distant end.
3. If the remote computer is on, DTR is on, allowing the call to be answered. This is termed auto-answer. When DTR is on and a ring indicator is detected, the call will automatically be answered.
4. Once answered, each modem will raise its data set ready lead as an indication that a line is present for data transmission.
5. The PC is on; its DTR lead is on (high), so the connection can be maintained.
6. Data may now be exchanged between the two devices.

When the transfer of information is completed, the connection is broken when either end drops DTR. The PC operator may drop DTR generally in one of four ways:

1. Manually disconnect (hang up) the call.
2. Place the PC into a mode known as the "local mode." This is contrasted with being "on-line." While in the on-line mode, DTR is on. By placing the PC

off-line or in local mode, DTR is lowered, automatically causing the modem to drop the connection.
3. Unplugging or turning off the PC. Lack of power lowers DTR, causing a disconnect by the modem.
4. Disabling the COM port. This action will also drop DTR.

The far-end computer can also generally break the connection in one of several ways:

1. If someone unplugs the computer (heaven forbid!), DTR will go off, causing the modem to hang up.
2. The program executing in the remote system, be it a mainframe or other computer system, can generally control the DTR signal and bring it down at will.
3. Often, the unit handling the communications for the computer, known as a *front-end processor* (FEP), can recognize a disconnect character from the far-end PC. Generally, in an asynchronous environment, a Control-D character sequence will be received and interpreted by the host computer or FEP as a disconnect sequence. Once this sequence is received, the FEP will drop DTR, causing the modem to disconnect.

Data terminal ready plays a major role in the establishment, maintenance, and disconnecting of a dial-up connection. In Chapter 6 the reader will see how this importance is capitalized on for control in the connection of a printer to the IBM PC through a serial interface.

For now, let's keep DTR on to maintain the line. So far, the train is right on schedule. Several types of railway systems have been discussed. One-track, one-way (simplex); one-track, two-way, nonsimultaneous (half-duplex); and one- or two-track, two-way, simultaneous (full-duplex) paths were explained in Chapter 2. For now, ignore the simplex and FDX facilities for transmitting data; we are going to focus on half-duplex (HDX).

In this mode, the bridge across the water has only one set of tracks. Things could really get messy if we did not control when and in which direction each train would cross the bridge. The booth attendants must maintain control of the situation to prevent trains from colliding and ending up in the water.

The depots, with trains wanting to cross the bridge, are in contention for the right-of-way on the tracks. When they want to send the trains (data), they should turn on the engines' headlights, signaling a request to send the trains across. The headlights can be seen all the way across the water. So if the local booth attendant sees the lights initiated by the station (DTE), he knows that the right-of-way was desired. However, the booth attendant had better check to see if the far end has the right to the track prior to giving this privilege to the local depot. Because the engines' headlights are so bright, he is easily able to see if the far end had control of the track. If he detected a light, he would not honor the request to send (Figure

Chap. 3 Asynchronous Communication for the IBM PC/XT   49

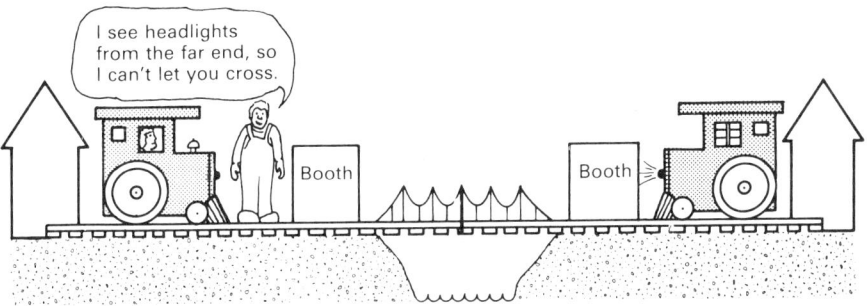

Figure 3-11 Request to send and data carrier detect interaction

3-11). However, if no light was detected from the far end, the booth attendant would give a clear-to-send signal to its station. The depot could send as many trains across the bridge as desired because it had control of the bridge.

Once all the trains had crossed the bridge, the sending depot operator would turn out the headlights as an indication that he was relinquishing control of the track. Either end could then request to send trains across the bridge and be given a clear-to-send signal by the booth attendants. Obviously, the booth attendants play an important role in controlling the smoothness of operation over the railway system.

RS-232: In a *half-duplex* environment, contention for the communication facilities exists. A typical modem found in this class is a 202 type. The 202 is an AT&T modem that operates in a half-duplex fashion at 1200 bps. Modems that operate in the same environments are said to be 202-compatible or look-alikes. Control of this two-way, nonsimultaneous path is handled by a DTE–DCE interaction. If connected to a 202, the PC raises request to send (RTS), pin 2, if it has data to transmit. This causes a signal to be passed across the telephone line, detectable at the other end on pin 8. The signal at the far end is termed *data carrier detect (DCD) or received line signal detector*. It is important to note that although separate pins are used for different functions on the interface, this does not imply that a separate communication facility for each is required. In reality, all signals

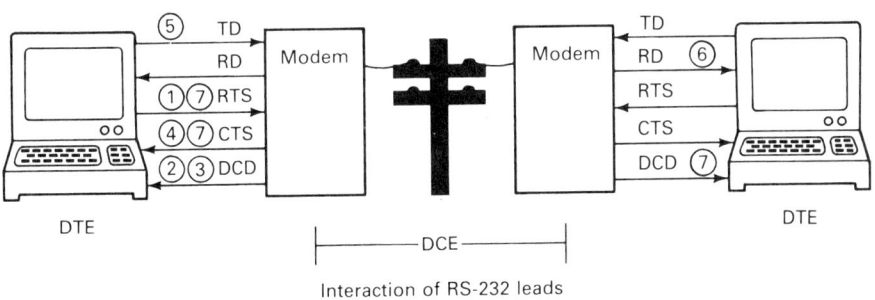

Interaction of RS-232 leads

Figure 3-12 RS-232 in half duplex environment

are passed over the same path. Locally, however, the 202 or equivalent first checks its own DCD lead, pin 8. If its DCD is not on, a clear-to-send (CTS) signal is passed to the PC COM port. The PC now has control of the facilities and can transmit data on the proper lead (pin 2). However, if the local modem detects that pin 8 is on, a CTS signal will not be given to the PC. That fact that DCD is on is an indication that the far-end DTE has control of the line. Figure 3-12 represents the interaction of the leads.

The following sumarizes DTE–DCE interaction.

1. RTS (pin 4) is raised by the PC.
2. DCD (pin 8) is checked by the modem to see if the far-end DTE has its RTS high.
3. If the far end's RTS is high (DCD is on), the modem does not give CTS. and the PC drops RTS and goes back to step 1. If DCD is off, it proceeds to step 4.
4. If DCD is off, the PC's 202 modem, after a slight delay, gives a CTS (pin 5) signal to the PC.
5. The PC then presents data on the transmit data lead (pin 2), and the modem transmits this to the far end.
6. The receiving modem puts the received data on pin 3 for presentation to the destination DTE.
7. The PC continues with RTS held high until all data are transmitted. Then it drops its RTS, which drops DCD at the far end and CTS locally, causing the line to be idle once again.
8. Either DTE can now raise RTS to obtain control of the line.

The foregoing interaction of RTS, CTS, and DCD functions the same in both asynchronous and synchronous environments. But what if our bridge across the water allows two-way simultaneous traffic? We do not have to worry about who has control of the track because each station has its own path across the bridge. To save time and to capitalize on our two-way concurrent traffic possibilities, the

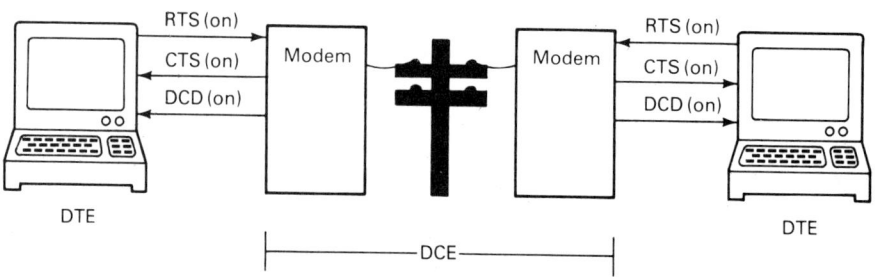

Figure 3-13 RS-232 in full duplex environment

Chap. 3   Asynchronous Communication for the IBM PC/XT   51

dispatchers should turn their headlights on and leave them on while the stations are manned. Thus each booth attendant will always give his depot a clear-to-send signal, even though he detects headlights from across the bridge. Now the stations can send traffic across a bridge without worrying about obtaining the right-of-way on the bridge.

RS-232: This is termed *full-duplex*. Several modems offer full-duplex capabilities. For example, a 103J-compatible modem operates FDX at 300 bps. A 212A look-alike modem generally offers two speeds, 300 and 1200 bps, both available in a full-duplex mode. Both DTEs have RTS held high, both modems give CTS constantly, and both modems have DCD high because the far end's RTS lead is on constantly (Figure 3-13).

The trains are really smokin' along the tracks now. But what happens if the bridge malfunctions or the operators vacate the stations? Obviously, all traffic should cease. The booth attendant turns off his CTS signal and raises the bridge. To start traffic again, the entire procedure must be repeated.

RS-232: If DTR goes off (loses power, for instance), the modem will disconnect the line. The modem will no longer have DSR high as an indication to the PC or other DTE that a connection is established. Whether the communication mode is HDX or FDX, the procedure for the dial-up connection will have to be repeated for further data transmission.

We have just described the role of several RS-232 leads in a dial-up environment. Following is a review of the interface leads, separated by function. By separating the leads into distinct functions and noting their directions, the serial interface can easily be understood. This will become more evident as we proceed into areas of cross connections.

Note two interface leads, pins 1 and 7, in the chart in Figure 3-15. These are ground leads important for electrical reasons. Pin 1 is usually a frame ground to keep people from receiving shocks in the event of electrical shorts or other problems. This is the same principle that is applied to the grounded wall outlets of your home. Pin 7 is termed *signal ground* and is used as a reference for all other signals on the interface. For example, the signal on pin 7 establishes the common ground reference potential for all the other circuits except pin 1. The principles of grounding comprise an entire science within electronics. Because of this, for easy understanding, the reader should merely accept the functions of these two leads.

Throughout the text, abbreviations are used for the various RS-232 leads. These acronyms, such as DTR, DSR⟨, and RTS, are used for ease of recognition of the leads. In practice, EIA RS-232-C and CCITT V.24, the international counterpart of RS-232, use totally different nomenclature. For example, in RS-232, the four categories of leads—ground, data, control, and timing—are referred to as the A, B, C, and D circuits. The international standard denotes the various pins by numbers such as 101, 102, 108.2, and so on. Although these standards outline the precise labeling of the leads, the industry usually refers to them either by pin

Function	Pin	Name	Direction
Data	14	Secondary transmitted data	From DTE
Data	16	Secondary received data	From DCE
Control	19	Secondary request to send	From DTE
Control	13	Secondary clear to send	From DCE
Control	12	Secondary carrier detect	From DCE

Figure 3-14 Secondary signals

assignments, such as pin 20, or by the acronyms used in this text, such as DTR. Refer to Appendix A for the precise circuit nomenclature.

Secondary Signals: One more category of RS-232 leads needs to be covered because of its importance in communication. These leads are the secondary signals of the interface. They function in the same manner as do their primary counterparts but control secondary channels of the communication facility. For example, RTS becomes secondary request to send. The same secondary nomenclature applies to clear to send and data carrier detect. In addition, there are secondary transmitted and received data channels. Intelligent modems, usually of the synchronous type, capable of tranmitting diagnostic information, use these secondary data channels for testing and trouble-reporting purposes. However, unless intelligent devices are being used, these secondary data channels are rarely utilized. Nevertheless, secondary data carrier detect, also known as secondary receive line signal detector, plays an important role in the area of transmission control. Once this concept is understood, the reader will fully understand flow control as it is used not only in communications, but also in local printer attachment to the PC. See Figure 3-14 for a list of the secondary leads on the RS-232 interface.

In half-duplex environments, these secondary signals play a key role. As you recall, when a half-duplex facility is being utilized, primary data and control signals are used in one direction at a time. Information is transmitted in a single direction with great success under normal circumstances. But what if a problem occurs at one end of the facility? What types of problems could occur? The next few paragraphs define the types of potential problems and describe their solutions using

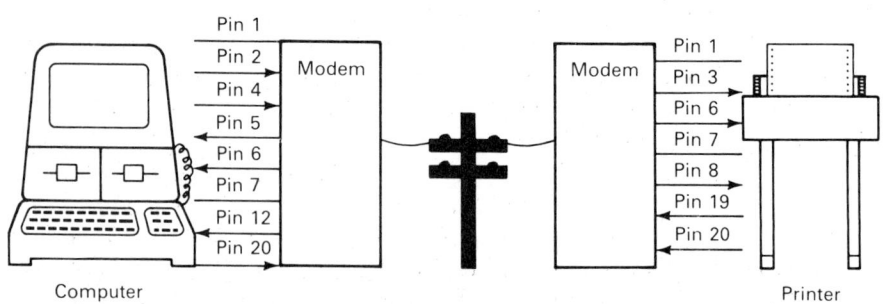

Figure 3-15 Hardware flow control depiction

Chap. 3   Asynchronous Communication for the IBM PC/XT   53

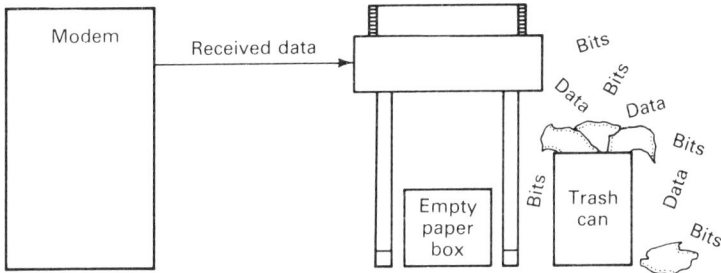

Figure 3-16   Out of paper condition

secondary signals. We will ignore our analogy and utilize pure RS-232 terminology for the remainder of this chapter.

Let's focus on a specific configuration of a computer transmitting payroll information across the communication facility to a receive-only printer over a half-duplex facility. There is no need to cover how the connection is established between the two devices, as we have been through the sequence in earlier chapters. So let's assume that the connection is established, either dial-up or private line, and that the proper signals have been exchanged to allow the computer to transmit data to the printer as shown in Figure 3-15.

Things are going smoothly until, after minutes or hours of data traffic, the supply of paper being fed through the printer begins to get a little low. As the printer continues to chug along, the last sheet of paper rolls through the printer. The problem should now be intuitively obvious to the most casual observer. The computer will continue to throw data at the printer. The printer receives the data but cannot transcribe the bits onto paper, as there is no paper. So the data are either printed on the bare printer platen or dropped into the bit bucket (Figure 3-16). This could be catastrophic, especially if the next item to be printed would have been your paycheck! Let's solve the problem so that we will not shortchange ourselves in the future.

In a half-duplex environment, the primary data path is available in only one direction at a time. However, the secondary data and control signals are available to be used from either the computer end or the printer end. We will utilize these secondary signals to control the loss of data and keep the "cards and letters" (and checks) coming.

The best way to prevent the loss of the received data is to provide a means of notifying the computer, or transmitting end, of the problem. In this case we have what is known as a "paper-out" condition. If the computer is aware of a problem at the far-end computer, it can temporarily halt data transmission until the problem is cleared up. Once a new batch of paper is threaded through the printer, the printer will be ready to crank out your check. The printing can resume after the printer gives an indication to the computer that all is okay.

Flow Control: Peripheral manufacturers capitalized on the availability of secondary control signals on the RS-232 interface to prevent the catastrophe. The solution was to have the printer, or receiving device, always give a positive indication when data could be received. This was made possible by having the printer keep its secondary request to send (SRTS) lead high. Because these secondary signals behave in the same way as do the primary signals, this caused secondary carrier data to be transmitted back to the computer. The computer was constantly monitoring its secondary data carrier detect (SDCD) lead, pin 12. As long as pin 12 was high on the interface, data could be transmitted.

Should a paper-out or other problem condition occur, the printer would drop its SRTS lead, causing no secondary carrier to be evident at the computer end. If SDCD was low, the computer would cease transmission because of the indication that a problem existed at the far end. Once the problem was cleared up, its SDCD/SRLSD pin would come back on because the printer at the far end would once again raise its SRTS signal. The computer could now print your paycheck.

Reverse Channel: Even though we are in a half-duplex environment, we can still pass these secondary signals in the opposite direction from the primary signals. This is possible because we are using a secondary channel of the communication facility which is separate from the primary channel. The technical term for this flow-control operation is *reverse channel*. Reverse channel, or *busy signal*, is used for the specific function of supervisory control.

Another frequent use of reverse channel is to prevent buffer overflow. If a device is receiving data, the bits can be placed in the device's buffer for printing at whatever speed the printer is capable of. Depending on the size, the device's buffer may fill up to the point where it overflows, or loses data. Reverse channel can be applied, in the same manner as in a paper-out condition, to prevent buffer overflow and, consequently, loss of data.

XON/XOFF: Half-duplex flow control utilizing the secondary channels, in addition to being termed reverse channel, performs what is known as a *hardware XON/XOFF function*. To understand the meaning of this function, we must revert to a full-duplex environment. With FDX, some devices, such as printers, can monitor their buffer or paper supply electronically. If either the paper is getting low or the buffer is reaching its capacity, the printer can transmit a device control character. This character is transmitted over the primary data channel to the computer, indicating that data transmission should be suspended temporarily. The printer then notifies the computer when transmission can resume by transmitting a different device control character. Full-duplex allows for this two-way communication to occur. This is often termed *software flow control*. Different combinations are possible to provide for this. One of the most prominent is XON/XOFF. To halt transmission the printer transmits an XOFF character. Once the problem situation is cleared up, it transmits an XON character for the computer to interpret as an indication to resume data transmission. Another popular technique is ETX/ACK. At the end of a grouping of data, termed a *block,* the computer appends an ETX character. The computer will not transmit more data until the printer approves by sending an ACK character. Other techniques exist but stem from the same basic concept of a character exchange between the transmitter and receiver of data. Another example is found in communication software when large files are transferred between two PCs. Periodically, the receiving PC must halt operations so that it can write data to a file. Software flow control is used to stop the transmitting PC until further notice. Upon completion of the disk operation, a character is sent to resume the data transfer.

In a half-duplex environment, data can be transmitted in only one direction at a time, limiting the printer's ability to transmit a device control character. The RS-232 secondary signals, reverse channel, are used to accomplish the XON/XOFF or ETX/ACK function. This is termed *hardware flow control* because it is handled by the RS-232 interface. Reverse channel can be used for other purposes in a communication environment, but the preceding examples demonstrate two of the major uses of these secondary control signals. Examples of software flow control were given in the communication software and terminal emulation sections earlier in this chapter. The reader will find that the same principles are applied when connecting a printer to a PC, as outlined in Chapter 6. Perhaps different pins will be used, but the reader should now have an understanding of the concepts of hardware and software flow-control methods that will be used.

SUGGESTED READINGS

Modems
1. *PC World,* "What Makes Modems Run?" November 1983.
2. *PC World,* "The Modem Market," November 1983.
3. *Data Communications,* "Modem Metamorphosis," November 1982.
4. *BYTE,* "Expanding on the PC," November 1983.
5. *IBM Technical Reference,* Publ. 6025005, pp. 1–223 and 1–248.
6. *RS-232 Made Easy,* by Martin D. Seyer, Prentice-Hall, Inc., Englewood Cliffs, NJ, 1984.
7. *Hayes Smartmodem Hardware Reference Manual.*
8. *PC Magazine,* "Battle of the Network Stars," pp. 92–104, Vol. 2, No. 6, November 1983.
9. *PC Magazine,* "Getting Hooked on PCnet," pp. 107–113, Vol. 2, No. 6, November 1983.
10. *PC Magazine,* "Getting the Net Working," pp. 123–126, Vol. 2, No. 6, November 1983.

Communication Software and Protocols

1. *DCF Series User Guide,* WALL DATA, August 31, 1983.
2. *Protocols: A Functional Insight,* by Martin D. Seyer.
3. *PC-Talk III User's Guide,* by Andrew Fluegelman of Freeware, Publ. 830806.
4. *Data Communications,* "Protocol Conversion—Product of Profusion," pp. 65–73, Vol. 10, No. 6, June 1981.
5. *Data Communications,* "Operational Characteristics: BSC versus SDLC," pp. 227–235, Vol. 12, No. 10, October 1983.
6. *Blue Lynx 5251 Remote Work Station Emulator Product Description,* Techland Systems, May 1983.
7. *Crosstalk XVI User's Manual,* Microstuf, Inc., 1983.

CHAPTER

4

synchronous communications for the PC/XT

Many applications have been developed over the years for asynchronous terminals. The reasons for using asynchronous terminals were many. The software development time for applications to support teletype-like devices was a fairly straightforward effort. Characters to paint the asynchronous terminal screen were sent one at a time, with a carriage return and line feed at the end of each line. Input back to the application from the remote device was in the same format. Programmers were readily available for this type of application development. Furthermore, the hardware to support such devices was relatively inexpensive. The individual components on the asynchronous boards and line drivers required little capital investment in the mainframe computer. Furthermore, the cost of asynchronous terminals is low compared to that of the synchronous devices that we will discuss momentarily. The average cost for an asynchronous CRT is between $500 and $1500. Also, these terminals could dial up the computer system, access necessary applications, and then disconnect, which permits the sharing of asynchronous ports on the remote computer system. These three factors alone allowed for rapid and widespread development of teletype support on mainframe systems.

Although applications supporting asynchronous terminal access are widespread, they do have a few disadvantages. Because of the dial-up nature of the network access, only one asynchronous terminal may use a port at any given moment. This is known as a *point-to-point connection*. A nonshared communication line connects the two end points. This is often viewed as an inefficient use of resources. Furthermore, the speed of asynchronous transmission is slow, typically 1200 bps. To upload one single-sided IBM PC disk to a remote computer system at this speed takes approximately 25 minutes. To calculate this quickly, divide 1200 bps by 10 bits per character, including start and stop bits, yielding 120 characters per second (cps) possible. A filled single-sided disk contains approximately 180,000 characters. 180,000 characters divided by 120 cps yields about 1500 seconds of transmission time. 1500 divided by 60 seconds per minute indicates that about 25 minutes is required to transmit the contents of the disk, an unacceptable rate in a communication manager's mind. Transmission of this many characters for such a long period offers ample opportunity for errors to occur in the form of spikes on the communication line. Unless error-checking techniques offered by communication software packages are used, errors will occur. Simple parity checking offers error detection but no error correction. Depending on the data being transmitted, this could be catastrophic. Recall from earlier discussions that communications software offering block checking and error correction through retransmission required the same software package at both ends of the point-to-point connection. Lack of error correction is generally found in these environments because the mainframe computers cannot run the same communication software as that found in the IBM PC.

Chap. 4 Synchronous Communications for the PC/XT

Although the cost is initially appealing with asynchronous transmission, the disadvantages often override this factor. A better technique may be used to overcome these objections. Synchronous transmission offers flexibilities not attainable using asynchronous transmission. Higher speeds are possible because of the timing signals used in a synchronous environment. Because both the transmitting and receiving parties are operating based on a common timing element, the higher speeds are common. Because of this, synchronous transmission does not require the start and stop bits for timing. Speeds range from 1200 bps to 56,000 bps (or 56 kbps; k means thousands) or higher. Typical modems are AT&T's 201C or 2024 operating at 2400 bps; 208A or 2048 private-line modems operating at 4800 bps; the 208B, which is the dial-up counterpart for 4800-bps operation; and the 2096 or 209 for 9600-bps operation. A character code other than ASCII may also be used. EBCDIC is an 8-bit character code, and ASCII is a 7-bit code. When 8 bits are used, more character combinations are possible. Buffers are used for temporary storage of data to be transmitted.

Protocols: Protocols were added to solve several problems associated with asynchronous transmission. A protocol is a set of rules understood by communicating parties which allows for the orderly exchange of information. The concept of a protocol is used by two parties having a telephone conversation. One party listens while the other speaks. A transmission is completed by either a question or a statement, both of which call for some sort of response. If there is noise on the line, the listening party may ask for a repeat of the last statement. Although the two parties are not consciously aware of it, they conform to a preestablished protocol, allowing for an effective means of communication. The protocols used in synchronous transmission adhere to the same general concept of orderly transmission between two parties, usually a mainframe computer with a remote device. The protocols allow for error detection and correction similar to the CP/M XMODEM concept, where an algorithm is applied to the data to compute a block check character (BCC) to be appended and transmitted with the data. The receiving party applies the same algorithm to the received data stream to calculate its BCC. The calculated BCC is then compared with the appended BCC. If they are different, an error has occurred and retransmission will be requested. Otherwise, accurate data have been received. This error detection technique allows for error correction, a significant advantage over basic asynchronous terminals. The protocols must allow for an orderly exchange of information according to the definition. The synchronous protocols do offer a means of controlling which party may transmit and for how long. There are two categories of synchronous protocols, character-oriented and bit-oriented. How all these features are accomplished depends on the protocol utilized. The details of the various protocols are not covered here, as the typical IBM PC user does not have to understand the specifics. However, we will give a short description of the most popular ones and how they are implemented to allow the PC/XT to function in synchronous environments. Two of the most popular protocols happen to be trademarks of the same vendor, IBM. IBM's Binary Synchronous

Communication (BSC or Bisync) character-oriented protocol will be covered, followed by a discussion of the bit-oriented Synchronous Data Link Control (SDLC) protocol and how to turn the PC/XT into a terminal capable of working in these networks.

Just as application software was written that required specific terminal characteristics in an asynchronous environment, many applications were written for specific classes of synchronous terminals. The protocols to allow the orderly exchange of data between these applications and terminals provided all the necessary functions. Specific functions of block checking, acknowledgment upon reception of good data blocks, and retransmission of bad blocks were provided in Binary Synchronous Communication. Special control characters were used to maintain control of the communication link. This meant that the character code used, either ASCII or EBCDIC, had to be known by both parties. Terms such as *polling, selecting,* and *contention* were used to describe the various BSC environments. Generally, control of the communication line was achieved by setting up one of the parties as the primary or controlling station, with the other(s) being secondary. If contention was used, both the primary and secondary stations had to bid or contend for use of the line. In contrast with this was polling and selection. Polling was the invitation from the primary for the secondary station to send any data it had in its buffers. Selection was how the primary actually sent data to the remote station. All of these functions were accomplished by a communications controller. At the primary or mainframe computer, the controller was known as a *communication processor* or *front-end processor* (FEP). The FEP served as a front end to the main processing system. Typical mainframes used were IBM 370s, 30XXs, 43XXs, System 34s, and System 38s. Non-IBM mainframes and minicomputers included those of Univac, Burroughs, Prime, Digital Equipment, and Amdahl. Each of these systems offered some type of BSC communications, either what is known as 2780/3780 BSC or 3270 BSC. Each of these protocols reflects the various devices they were written for.

2780/3780 BSC: When 2780 BSC is mentioned, it usually denotes a synchronous protocol written for an IBM Model 2780 terminal or equivalent that operates in a contention mode, where each end bids for use of the line. Typical software packages on the IBM mainframes supporting the 2780 or 3780 are JES2 and JES3, where JES stands for Job Entry Subsystem, and RSCS for Remote Spooling Communications Subsystem. The software driving the protocol was written in a fashion that allows for communication but also takes into account the device characteristics. Both the 2780 and the 3780 were devices used for batch input or output of data. These devices were used primarily as stations at remote sites for inputting programs, also known as *jobs,* to a central mainframe system in the form of cards. The cards were loaded into a card reader and transferred as a batch into the remote computer system. Consequently, they became known as *remote job entry* (RJE) *stations*. The cards as input were eventually replaced with disks; however, the concept remained. The software packages on the mainframe would receive the information and store it for later processing. This became known as *spooling*. Spooling, similar to buffering but perhaps on disk, stood for "simultaneous peripheral operations on-line." Scheduling of jobs occurred followed by subsequent processing. The 2780/3780 stations could not only input data but could also receive computer printouts or short messages over the communication link. Eventually, keyboards and displays were added. These stations operated with either a dial-up or a private line. The protocols for either became known as *switched point to point* (BSC 1) or *nonswitched point to point* (BSC 2). Dial-up speeds were limited to either 2400 or 4800 bps, whereas up to 9600 bps was common with private lines. Besides speed, options relating to block size and record size had to be set. Generally, because of the use of 80-column cards, the record size was 80 characters. The block size consisted of several records, with typical sizes being 400 and 512 characters. This is the amount of data to be transmitted to the host in one block. This was also an indication of how much data could be received in a block. The station then had to do something with the received block before another one could be received. By telling the remote computer system to wait temporarily, the RJE had time to clear its buffers. Individual devices at an RJE station were typically a card reader, a printer, a punch, and a keyboard and screen. For further clarification of the 2780/2780 RJEs and BSC, consult the Suggested Readings.

Because of the batch transfer characteristics of the 2780/3780 BSC, this protocol became synonomous with the high-speed batch transmission of bulk data. It was not limited to RJE stations but was also used for batch transfer of files between two computer systems. The 2780/3780 BSC was used particularly when high speed and error correction were required. The 9600-bps speed reduced the amount required for data transmission time. If, as before, we look at the transfer of the contents of an IBM PC's single-sided disk, it takes about 3 minutes compared to 25 minutes at 1200 bps. This is merely an approximation, as there is some overhead transmission time associated with BSC. Means of offsetting transmission time are also evident, in the 3780 particularly. The 3780 RJEs support space compression, which is a way of saving transmission time. Space compression allows for many space characters to be represented by only two to three characters. A count is done on the number of spaces. This number, together with a control character, is sent for interpretation by the 3780 and translation into the appropriate number of spaces. There are other shortcuts, but the important point is that computers and terminals offered a batch bisynchronous transfer of large amounts of data at high speeds.

If the IBM PC/XT is going to be used as a collection point for data to be batched into a remote system in the form of file transfer, BSC communication should be considered. Several vendors offer methods of giving the PC/XT BSC protocol capabilities or the ability to emulate a 2780/3780 RJE station. Refer to Figure 4-1 for a sample configuration. IBM offers a Binary Synchronous Communication adapter card. Used in conjunction with appropriate software, batch transfer of files is possible. One key point to consider when dealing with BSC and other protocols is that coordination is required with the data processing manager

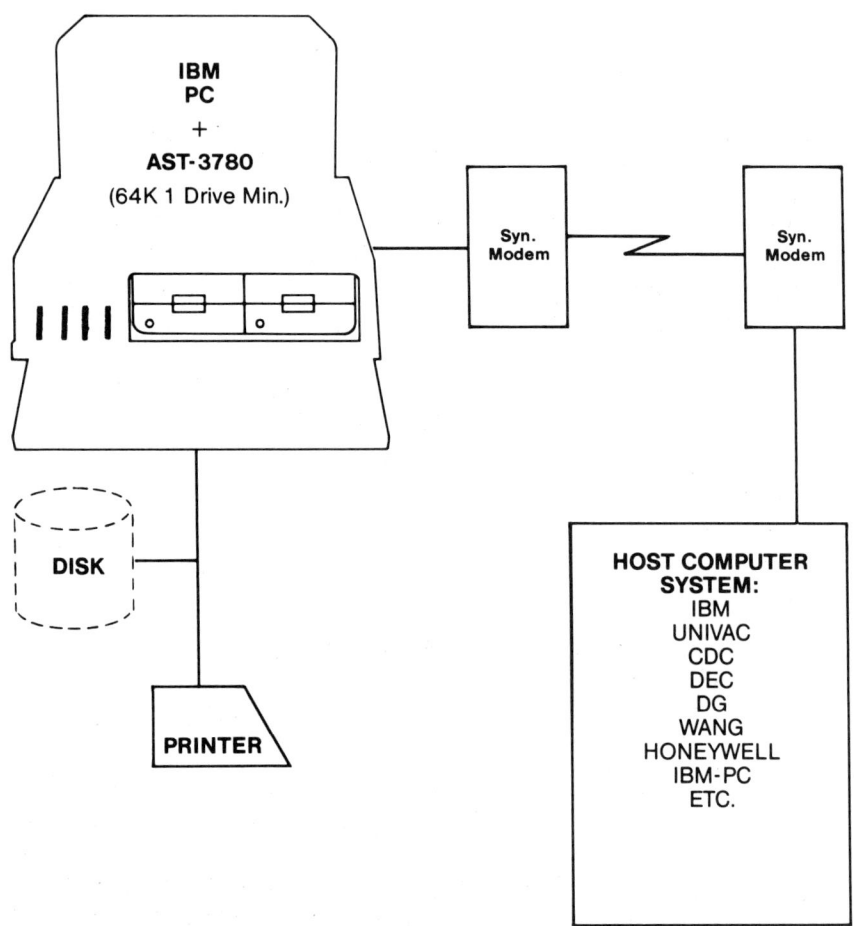

Figure 4-1 AST-3780 System Configuration (Courtesy of AST Research Inc.)

and/or data communication manager of the remote computer system. The mainframe computer configuration must be set up to support the particular device being used in the areas of addressing, speeds, log-ins, passwords, and others. Consult product manuals for assistance in this area.

Another vendor is Information Technologies, Inc. Their LINKUP communication support system consists of both hardware and software. Their single board provides multiple protocols and terminal emulations. The board provides two RS-232 ports with asynchronous speeds to 19.2 kbps and synchronous speeds up to 56 kbps. The communication software provides asynchronous terminal emulation, including the DEC VT52, VT100, IBM3101, and block-type asynchronous terminals. It also supports BSC 2780/3780 operation. In this BSC mode unattended operation is possible, allowing for automatic dial-up, log-on, job and program execution, printing, and disconnecting. A log file records date and time of connection and disconnection for tracking purposes. The features offered by this board and associated software allow easy conversion of a PC/XT into an RJE workstation. This feature, together with asynchronous terminal emulation, makes for a flexible communication system, as one board provides for access to multiple types of host systems.

AST Research Inc. offers the AST-3780 shown in Figure 4-1. This board is dedicated to synchronous communications, providing emulation for the 2770, 2780, and 3780 RJE stations together with the 3741 data entry station. The features associated with the RJE stations are provided through software. These include translation between ASCII and EBCDIC, printer control, unattended operation, speeds up to 38.4 kbps, and the expected file transfer capabilities. Should the data be scrolling across the screen too rapidly, a hold-scroll function exists for rate control. AST offers a list of the configuration parameters necessary when connecting their AST-3780 to IBM computer mainframe systems. This list should be reviewed with the DP/DC or telecommunication manager.

BARR Systems, Inc. offers the BARR/HASP, which is a hardware/software combination. HASP is an acronym for Houston Automatic Spooling Priority system. This was a popular job entry subsystem which allowed an RJE station to submit jobs for execution as discussed earlier. The JES releases and RSCS replaced HASP, but the concept remained the same. BARR/HASP allows for the creation of programs and data off-line for bulk transfer to a remote computer system running one of the spooling packages. The menu-driven software accompanying BARR/HASP provides a colorful user interface for controlling the transmission of data and reception of printouts. The software supports multiple printers. The printing may be done even while other transmissions are occurring. ASCII-to-EBCDIC translation is supported, as the HASP protocol requires EBCDIC. A nice benefit of this board is the throughput made possible by the efficient printer routines. The software provided with this system has been benchmarked against other 2780/3780 emulators and was shown to provide extremely fast output to various printers. If large volumes of data are to be printed upon receipt of file transfer to the PC, this issue becomes very important. Be sure to consider this aspect of a 2780/3780 implementation when acquiring a board.

A point to keep in mind when considering devices to support BSC communications is that the component costs are typically more expensive than for asynchronous configurations. Consequently, the fewer machines requiring BSC gear, the better. Should multiple PC/XT users require high-speed batch transfer of files to a remote computer system, thought should be given to the possibility of sharing a PC/XT configured with BSC communications. For example, if an office environment contains 10 PC/XTs, there may not be a need for dedicated BSC hardware and software in each computer. Amounts of data to be transmitted should be considered. But more than likely, sharing of one or two PCs or XTs will be possible. Each user will have files to be sent to the remote computer system. A procedure must be put in place for all the PC/XT users to transfer their files to the IBM PC/XT with the BSC capability. This may be manual delivery of disks, or if asynchronous communication exists with both machines, file transfer can occur using asynchronous terminal emulators or communication software. Once collected, the BSC-equipped PC/XT would transmit all the files collected. Furthermore, as files were downloaded from the remote mainframe system, the PC/XT operator could distribute the files to the appropriate users. Transmission time for the remote computer may be optimized by the BSC PC spooling the data to disk for later printing, as the printer speed is usually substantially slower than the communication speed. There are other ways to optimize your particular configuration. Consult Chapter 9 for alternatives.

3270 BSC: In contrast with contention-type terminals such as the 2780 or 3780, remote job entry stations are another form of BSC, known as *multipoint BSC*. Multipoint BSC allows for a primary and secondary relationship similar to that offered by contention bisync except that more than one secondary terminal is allowed, hence the term "multipoint." Typical applications were of the data entry or inquiry/response type, categorized as applications with *interactive* requirements. They were interactive in the sense that data were entered on a terminal and transmitted to a remote host, with the user expecting a response. Examples of data entry applications include order entry and data collection where forms painted on a screen were used as input. Inquiry response was typically used in conjunction with a database management system such as IBM's Information Management System (IMS). IMS allowed for queries of the files on record. Examples of this occur in the airline industry, where all available flights are kept on a database system. Reservation agents could query IMS to determine available flights. The terminals used in these environments were known as the 3270 Information Display System. 3270 nomenclature describes a family of devices. Typical CRTs in the 3270 line are the 3277 and 3278, with 3287 and 3289 being printer model numbers. These devices were attached to a controlling device termed 3271, 3274, or 3276. Depending on the controller, up to 32 devices could be connected to a single controller. This was known as *clustering* the devices. Consequently, controllers are offered that are referred to as *cluster controllers*. Although the specific features of each of these devices are significant when programming applications for them, we will cover only the basic functions of the controllers and devices necessary for connecting a PC/XT in the 3270 BSC environment.

Multipoint BSC, hereafter referred to as 3270 BSC, allows for many controllers with devices to be on the same private line (see Figure 4-2). This was accomplished by the primary station or host controlling the overall environment. The host computer systems, those mentioned earlier, controlled which terminals were transmitting or receiving and when. Control was made possible by assigning an address to every element in the configuration, including controllers, terminals, and printers. Using each element's address, the host or primary secondary would police the network. In order for a secondary station, 327X, to transmit, the host would have to ask the controller if any device associated with it had data to send. *Polling* is the term for inviting a controller/device to send data. The controller would check its buffers and respond accordingly. Data were transmitted or an indication sent that the device did not have anything to send. If the host computer system desired to transmit something to a device such as a printer, it would check to see if the printer was ready to receive. This operation of writing to a device required the selection of the specific device associated with a controller. BSC was famous for its polling and selection addresses, as each controller required one of each. In addition to the polling and selection addresses of the controller, each terminal and printer required a device address. These three addresses were important to the programmer developing applications as well as to the communication network manager responsible for setting up the network. The host with its front-end processor knew about the 3270 configurations only if these addresses were defined to them. They had to be generated in the machine's tables. The term "gen'd" was coined by IBM for defining the various parameters of a configuration such as these addresses. When a PC/XT is going to be used in these networks, the proper generation parameters must be set.

Besides the controller functions of responding to polls and selection, the devices had their own responsibilities. A 3278 CRT was a programmable device in that it understood commands and orders from the host for screen formatting. When the application program was sending data to the terminal for screen painting, various attributes had to be specified for the fields. The tubes supported features such as screen addressing. Data could be placed anywhere on the screen by direct addressing of the location. Contrast this with dumb asynchronous terminals, which did not possess this feature. *Protected fields*, which prevented data from being overwritten by the keyboard operator, were one of the features. The fields could be hidden or not displayed, highlighted, or restricted for numeric data only. These display features do not fascinate the average IBM PC/XT user because they are

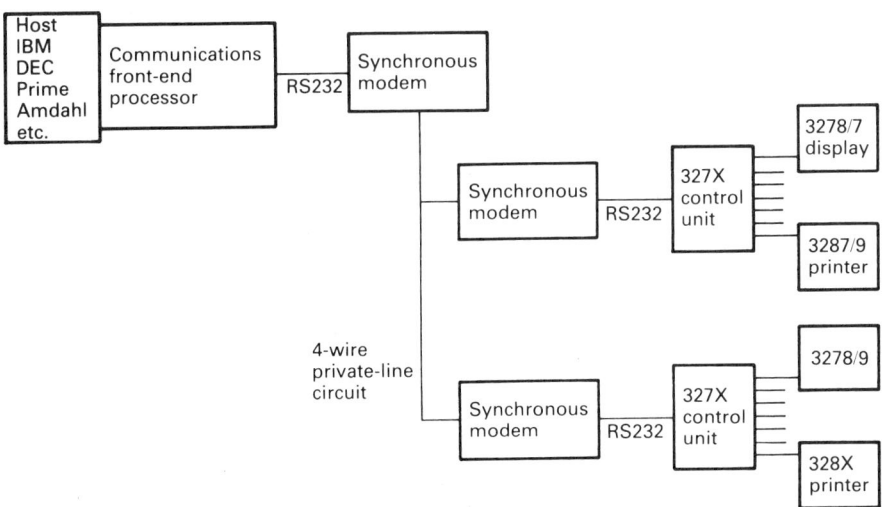

Figure 4-2 Typical 3270 BSC/SDLC environment

expected when running applications on the microcomputer in today's environments. The reader will just have to believe the author when he claims that these were neat features at the time of their debut.

Either EBCDIC or ASCII was supported by the 3270 family. Maximum speed on the multipoint private line was 9600 bps. The private-line synchronous modems were of the AT&T 209 category when 9600 bps was required. At 4800 bps the 208A was used, while the 201C allowed 2400-bps operation. These modems are used as references only, as upgrades are available from AT&T as well as many other vendors which add various levels of intelligence, mainly for diagnostic purposes. These synchronous modems are connected to the computer or 3270 with the same RS-232 interface as that used for asynchronous modems, with one exception—timing is present. For further information, consult the discussion later in the chapter of the RS-232 in synchronous environments.

The reason for discussing the basic functions of the 3270 controller and devices was to give the reader an awareness of the requirements for hardware and software that allow an IBM PC/XT to function in these networks. IBM offers communication software to be used in conjunction with its Binary Synchronous Adapter for providing the PC access to existing 3270 networks. See Figure 4-3 for a sample configuration. When implementing this on the PC/XT, the user must coordinate with the DP/DC manager to "gen" the PC with the proper speed, addresses, and device type. The software allows for emulation of different controllers as well as different terminals and printers in the cluster. Consult Chapter 9 for various ways of connecting the PC/XT to the network.

In the mode described above the PC provides controller as well as device emulation. IBM and other vendors offer software and hardware that allow the PC to be used merely as a device in conjunction with an existing IBM controller. This

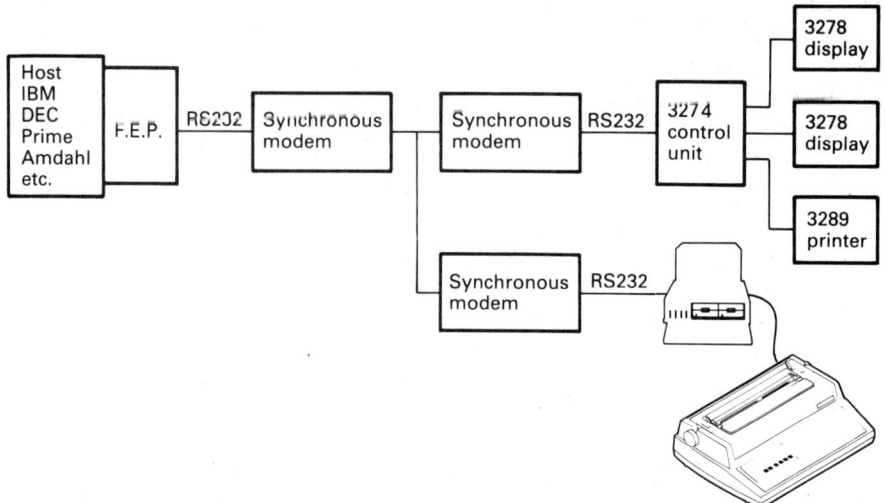

Figure 4-3 PC/XT in a 3270 BSC/SDLC environment

implies that the PC is emulating a display device only, not the controller. The connection between the PC and the controller is generally coaxial cable. This requirement dictates the need for specific hardware in conjunction with this software feature. The 3278 display stations do not normally offer storage in the form of disks. By using a PC/XT to emulate this device, the user can perform file transfer, a feature not found in normal 3270 configurations. CXI Inc. offers a product for this type of connection. Their PCOX interface allows a coaxial connection between the PC/XT and the 327X controller. Refer to Figure 4-4 for a depiction of this environment. With this product the PC can exactly emulate 3278 models 2, 3, and 4 and 3279 2As and 3As. Furthermore, menu-driven file transfer capability is available. The industry is demanding local processing with communication capabilities in their terminals or workstations.

The intelligent workstation concept is maturing to the point where this type of configuration will soon be prevalent throughout the industry. IBM's 3270 PC is a strong signal of support for this concept.

Synchronous Data Link Control: BSC is categorized as a character-oriented protocol. These protocols are viewed by IBM and other vendors as having less-than-optimal characteristics. Although widespread support exists for contention and polled bisync networks, IBM introduced a bit-oriented replacement for the BSC protocols. Synchronous Data Link Control (SDLC) is a bit-oriented protocol offered to overcome the pitfalls of BSC. IBM introduced this protocol in conjunction with a network architecture known as SNA (Systems Network Architecture). SNA is a scheme allowing corporations to build private intelligent flexible networks of host computers, terminals, and the communication gear between them. SDLC is the protocol used between the entities of an SNA environment. Before reviewing means of integrating the IBM PC/XT into an SNA environment, a basic understanding of SDLC features is required, including their advantages over BSC.

SDLC is a bit-oriented protocol. A bit-oriented protocol inherently offers advantages over its character-oriented counterpart. It is character-code-indifferent because of its bit nature. Either EBCDIC or ASCII may be used without concern for special control character functions. SDLC supports either full-duplex or half-duplex operation in point-to-point, multipoint, or loop configurations. Different terminal types may be used on the same line, whereas BSC lines are limited to one type, either 3270 or 2780, but not both. The block concept is enhanced by offering larger amounts of data enclosed in a frame. We now have frame error checking instead of block checking, including both data and control sequences. BSC error checking is limited to data transmission. The SNA controllers require only one address to support both polling and selecting. SDLC is continually evolving to provide significant improvements in communication requirements. Those described above are only a few of many benefits realized from a bit-oriented protocol.

Together with the SDLC protocol evolution came new terminal products to operate in this environment. One of them was the familiar 3270 family of terminals. They were upgraded to include not only BSC but also SDLC protocol support. The

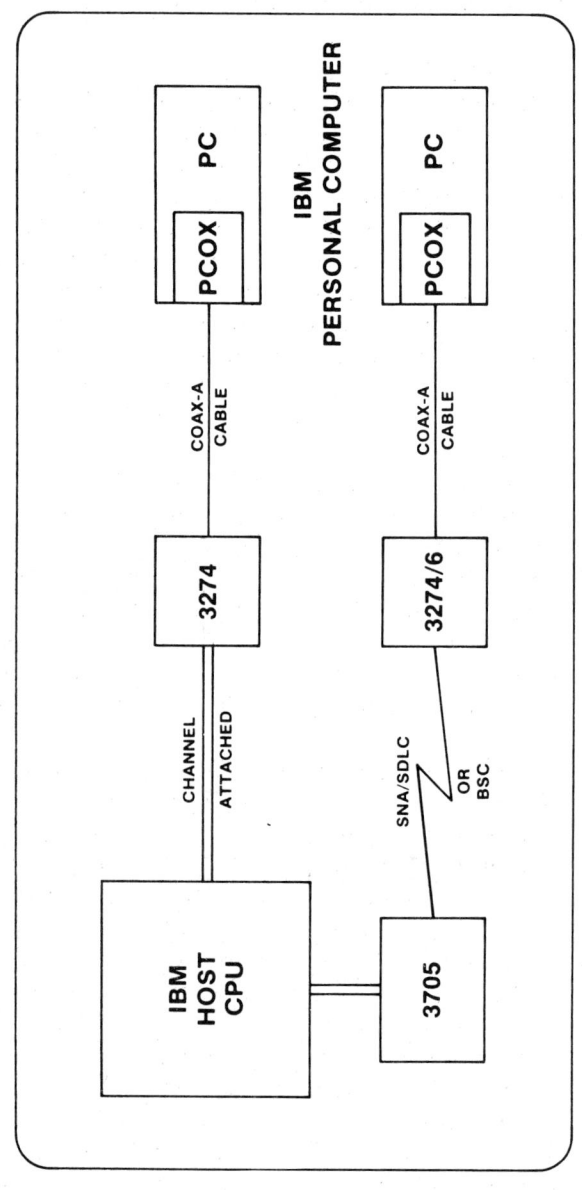

Figure 4-4 PCOX: IBM PC to COAX A-Interface (Courtesy of CXI, Inc.)

Chap. 4   Synchronous Communications for the PC/XT   69

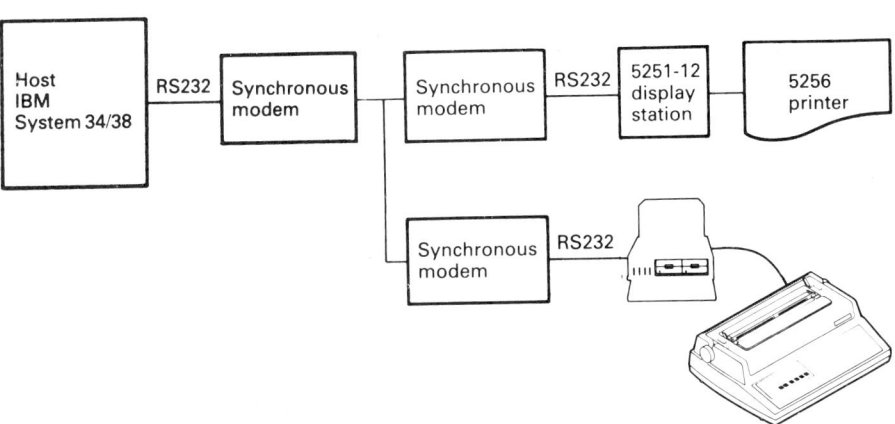

Figure 4-5   IBM PC/XT in a 5251 Display Station environment

terminals functioned similarly in both environments; however, the controller became more sophisticated to support the IBM SNA architecture. Distributed processing was a benefit of this architecture. IBM introduced several minicomputers to address this market, such as Systems 34, 36, and 38. All of these machines supported SDLC protocols. At the same time new terminals were announced. The 5251 Remote Work Station supported SDLC and became the interactive terminal associated with these systems. The population of 34s and 36s was so large that huge corporate networks supporting these terminals were put into place. How does the PC/XT fit into these environments? By now you have probably guessed it: terminal emulation.

A significant number of vendors are offering hardware and software to allow PC/XT functionality in SNA environments. Specifically, 3270 and 5251 SDLC emulator packages are available. The benefits, as before, were that processing was extended to an otherwise dumb terminal. Instead of a dumb terminal that must be on-line to the mainframe to perform significant work, the user now has a powerful microcomputer available for a wide variety of tasks. The PC/XT becomes a stand-alone distributed processor as well as an on-line terminal reducing communication line usage as well as mainframe cycle utilization.

Techland Systems Inc. offers BLUE LYNX, a System/34 and System/38 5251 Remote Work Station Emulator for the IBM PC/XT. The product turns the PC/XT into a 5251 Model 12 display station. Supporting speeds from 1200 to 9600 bps, BLUE LYNX may coexist with other 5251 terminals on a multipoint private line as depicted in Figure 4-5. The printer attached to the PC appears to the host as an IBM 5256 dot matrix printer. All of the field and display attributes are supported. With the use of IBM PC/XT disk storage, bidirectional file transfer is possible. Techland is committed to the use of the PC in the SNA environment, as they also offer a 3276 SNA/SDLC product. This product allows for 3287 Model 2 display emulation and 3287 printer emulation. File transfer is also supported. Both of these packages offer means of incorporating IBM PC/XTs into the corporate network. To obtain the look and feel of both these devices, the PC's keyboard needs to be enhanced. Hooleon Company offers keytops to be placed over certain keys for a total emulation of the devices; they are available in both 5251 and 3270 styles. These easy-to-install kits should be considered as a way of completing the emulation process.

AST Research Inc. of California offers both BSC and SDLC emulator products. We have already discussed their BSC 3780 board. In addition to this they offer 3270 SNA and 5251 terminal emulation. Both of these products offer integration possibilities. Consult Chapter 9 for various configurations of BSC and SDLC products.

Protocol Converters: The use of protocols, whether character- or bit-oriented, offers the distinct advantages of error correction, error detection, higher speeds, and multiple character codes. The PC operates very effectively in these environments with the addition of the appropriate hardare and software emulator programs. If multiple PCs are to access the applications extended to BSC or SDLC devices, each PC requires the associated hardware and software emulators. Depending on the environment, this could be a rather large investment for the corporation committed to incorporating PCs into their networks. There is an alternative for users hesitant to invest in dedicated synchronous conversion kits for the PC/XT. Just as the PC can emulate a BSC or SDLC device, boxes exist allowing asynchronous devices to fit into these environments. Through the use of equipment known as *protocol converters*, asynchronous ASCII terminals or IBM PCs emulating such devices may function in BSC or SNA environments.

A protocol converter physically sits between an asynchronous terminal and a computer requiring a specific synchronous protocol. On the mainframe computer side, modems separate the FEP from the terminal controller. The converter takes the place of the terminal controller, such as a BSC or SDLC 3276 controller. A port on the converter is connected to the synchronous modem on the line to the mainframe. This will be termed the *line side*. The other side, or *terminal side*, of the protocol converter is for connecting various asynchronous ASCII devices. RS-232 ports are available for connecting async terminals, modems, or the IBM PC.

The protocol converter should be placed in the location that best serves the users. This is important, as the amount of communication hardware required could be minimized. As indicated, RS-232 ports support various asynchronous devices. If multiple users are located within the same proximity, the converter should be placed near this congregation. If remote users need access to the applications available on the synchronous network, a modem such as a 212A should be attached to the converter on the terminal side. A possible configuration is displayed in Figure 4-6. Consult Appendix C for possible cross-connection requirements. Once a modem is in place, other asynchronous terminal and IBM PC users could dial into the converter for easy access to the applications. The use of the converter allows multiple shared access to otherwise dedicated synchronous terminal devices.

The function of the protocol converter is to translate asynchronous terminal capabilities into expected synchronous terminal operations. This implies that a dumb asynchronous terminal's keyboard must be able to generate the same keyboard operations as those of a totally different device such as a 3278 CRT. The displaying of data on the screen also poses interesting requirements. Furthermore, printers associated with the converter must be capable of printing when the mainframe makes the request. Because synchronous speeds typically are greater than asynchronous speeds, this must be accounted for. Matching of speeds involves buffering and flow control. Asynchronous devices generally use the ASCII character code, whereas IBM synchronous environments are usually EBCDIC. A method of converting from one character code to another must be available. Recall the polling and selecting functions found in BSC and SDLC protocols and the lack of these in asynchronous terminals. On the line side the protocol converter must respond to the mainframe with the proper polling and selection responses, while issuing translated commands to the asynchronous PC on the terminal side. The matching of sophisticated expectations to rather unsophisticated asynchronous capabilities is the main job of the converter.

The bulk of protocol converters are microprocessor-based, offering inexpensive solutions allowing ASCII devices access to device-dependent applications. However, the telephone companies also offer protocol conversion solutions. Manufacturers of customer premises-based switching systems typically offer voice-calling features such as those you expect from your local phone company. The difference is that these switching systems, known as *private branch exchanges*, (PBXs) are physically located on customer facilities. Features beyond basic voice services are offered in these computer-based switches. Protocol conversion is rapidly becoming available in PBXs due to extensive use of the switch for data transmission purposes. Regardless of whether a dedicated box is used or a switch provides the capability, protocol conversion is an easy way to incorporate asynchronous ASCII devices into synchronous networks.

Because of the extensive translations that must occur to map an asynchronous terminal to a synchronous terminal, the asynchronous terminal characteristics must be known. For example, if an application issues a command to clear a BSC 3278's screen and place the cursor in line 5, position 10, the protocol conversion must issue commands to accomplish the same effect on the teletype device. This is a one- or two-command operation for the 3278. For an asynchronous CRT with no cursor-addressing capabilities, this involves several steps. First, the clear screen command must be issued. Then the cursor must be homed. Once in the home position, commands must be issued to position the cursor properly. To get to the fifth line on the display, four carriage return/line feeds must be issued. Five spaces are then required. This detailed type of operation must occur for every 3278 command intercepted by the protocol converter. Depending on whether the device is a DEC VT100, Televideo 925, or IBM 3101, the commands to accomplish this will differ. Consult Appendix F for a summary by terminal of the various escape sequences that control the screen format. Generally, protocol converters will support the top-selling asynchronous terminals, using their specific cursor controls. Furthermore, the devices may be set up as a teleprinter which supports no cursor-positioning commands. Multiple fields normally found on a 3278 CRT will be sent to the hard-copy device one at a time as prompts. This allows any asynchronous device to be used.

The IBM PC may be implemented using a protocol converter in one of two manners. One of the most popular is to use the asynchronous terminal emulator package discussed earlier. For example, if Crosstalk XVI by Microstuf is used, the IBM can emulate either a DEC VT52, VT100, IBM 3101, Adds Viewpoint, or Televideo 900 series terminal. Used in conjunction with an asynchronous communication adapter or equivalent, the PC can access the protocol converter. The PC could be connected directly to one of the asynchronous ports on the terminal side of the protocol converter. Consult Appendix C for any cross-connection requirements. If remote from the converter, the PC could access it via a modem. The PC is not restricted to this network. It has access to all the normal services and computers supporting its asynchronous mode of operation. Furthermore, all the features of the terminal emulation package are available, such as uploading and downloading of files.

Because the number of IBM PCs incorporated into synchronous networks continues to surge, protocol vendors are offering direct support for the PC/XT. With this support a specific terminal emulator package is not required to access the converter. A simple communication package is provided that allows for PC/XT access to the protocol converter. The 3278 commands are then translated into ones that the IBM PC in its native mode understands. The main disadvantage of this is that to access other services, such as The Source, a separate communication software package is required. It could be more effective to purchase a single terminal emulator package that serves both purposes.

Up to this point we have referred only to 3270 environments. This is only one of many protocol conversions that are possible. The IBM PC can be used instead of 3270 BSC and SDLC devices, 2780/3780 stations, and also 5251 Remote Work Stations using protocol converters. The sophisticated converters offer multiple protocol support in the same unit with dynamically reconfigurable ports.

WALLDATA, Inc., featured in Figure 4-6, offers a protocol converter that addresses the need for interfacing the PC into otherwise asynchronous restricted environments. Their unit, called the Data Communications Facilitator, offers asynchronous, BSC, and SDLC support in the same unit. This software-based system offers fully redundant hardware and battery backup for fail-safe protection. The DCF is available with from 4 to 16 ports. Each port offers LED signals for RS-232 signals DTR, DSR, RTS, CTS, TD, and RD, visible to the user for ease of interfacing. Any of these ports can be set up as a terminal or host port as either asynchronous, BSC, or SDLC devices. Speeds up to 9600 bps are supported in either dial-up or point-to-point and multipoint private lines. The PC, when connected to this unit, has access to the applications on the synchronous communication line. Another feature, known as *asynchronous pass-through,* enables any PC with a terminal emulation package to communicate with another asynchronous device. In this case, the converter serves as an intelligent switch. This feature could be used

Chap. 4 Synchronous Communications for the PC/XT   73

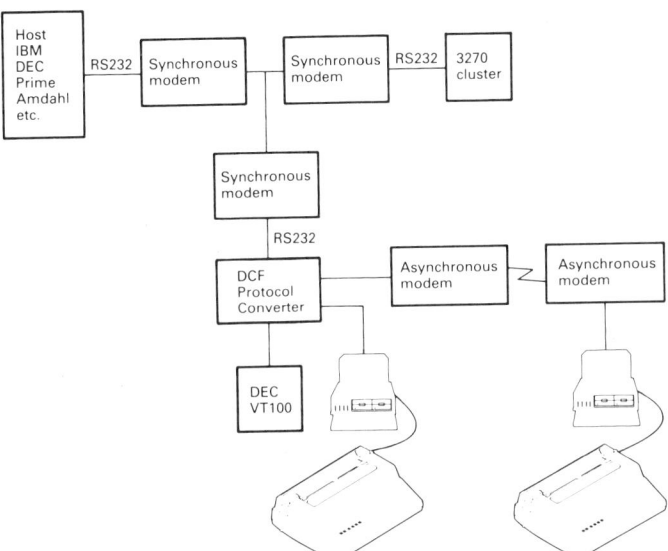

Figure 4-6 Using a WallData DCF protocol convertor to incorporate a PC into a 3270 environment. Note that the PC requires only an asynchronous port.

to access remote communication services such as the Dow Jones/News Retrieval service when not in a session with the synchronous host. Because it serves as an ASCII intelligent switch, printers may be shared by the PCs and other asynchronous terminals attached to the converter. This possibly reduces the requirement for a dedicated printer for each PC. The same rationale applies to modems, as they could be shared once attached to the converter. (See Chapter 6 for a discussion of sharing techniques using switches.) The difference here is that the switching is done through software, not by manually flipping a switch. The ports on the DCF are set up to match the attached devices, whether they be asynchronous modems, synchronous modems, or asynchronous devices. The terminal emulator software would be set up on the IBM PC as it normally would be when mere asynchronous communications is involved, matching the converter port settings. With features such as these, protocol converters are an appealing alternative to dedicated synchronous boards in each IBM PC or XT.

RS-232 in Synchronous Environments: This next section is intended for the IBM PC user requiring an in-depth understanding of the synchronous aspects of RS-232. This detail is included for telecommunication managers, data processing managers, field technicians, or the home user, all of whom want to understand the alternative to asynchronous transmission. To cover this the discussion will build on the train analogy. Up to now, the trains, consisting of boxcars and flatcars, have each had at least one engine and one caboose. The engine and caboose provided the timing of the traffic. At the destination station, once you saw an engine, you could bet that the rest of the train was following, right on time, with the caboose signaling the end of the train. Timing was on a train-by-train basis.

RS-232: This transmission scheme, known as *asynchronous transmission*, has provided the basis for the bulk of the analogy up to this point. Because of start and stop bits, each character was individually timed, or synchronized. No special timing was needed. Asynchronous transmission was used to access service bureaus, time-sharing systems, and for PC-to-PC communications. Terminal emulation and other communication software utilized this inexpensive means of communicating to enhance the IBM PC. A different transmission scheme, known as *synchronous transmission*, will now be introduced into the simile. But first, it is important to note a trend in the microcomputer field.

The use of personal computers, specifically the IBM PC, in synchronous environments is flourishing due to the communication hardware and software packages being developed by vendors. De facto standards for terminals operating in synchronous private-line environments exist. Examples are the devices mentioned earlier in this chapter, including IBM 3270 BSC/SDLC and 2780/3780 RJE stations. These terminals and others operate in a synchronous environment, involving the timing aspect of the RS-232 interface. The specific requirements necessary for the PC to emulate these devices have already been discussed. However, the additional requirements for physically connecting the PC to a synchronous environment have not. Because of this trend, our scenario will describe the elements necessary for understanding timing in these terminals, the 3270 PC, or a PC emulating one of them.

The need for longer and faster trains was discussed in Chapter 2. The basis for this need was that we had an engine and caboose for every seven or eight cars. This resulted in a lot of wasted track time. If you totaled the time on the track required for each engine and caboose, roughly 20 percent of the train was used for timing. Rather than send each train (character) out one at a time, with an engine and caboose, the Railroad Commission decided on a more economical and sophisticated method. The approach was temporarily to hold several small trains traveling to the same station and later ship them all at once as one long train.

RS-232: The communication term for this technique is *buffering*. In Chapter 6 buffers are used for the reception of data. However, with synchronous devices, characters (trains) are buffered at the originating station (business machine) into logical groupings for transmission as a single group. The need for an engine and caboose still exists, but in a different manner, as we shall see in a moment.

Once a method of buffering trains at one location was discovered, several benefits were realized. Money was saved due to the fact that fewer engines and cabooses were needed. Also, more time was available for actual train traffic because of the reduced need for engines and cabooses.

However, a couple of factors must be dealt with in this environment. The longer a train is, the greater the possibility for it to jump the track, causing garbling

Chap. 4   Synchronous Communications for the PC/XT   75

and derailment of the boxcars and flatcars. The major cause of derailment is either the track or the speed at which the train was traveling. The quality of the track is a major factor influencing the smoothness of train operation. The higher the quality, the less likelihood of derailment. A lower-quality track may collapse, causing a bit of a mess (or, I should say, a mess of bits). The tracks have already been designed by the engineers and established by the installers. So we must assume that the tracks were built and conditioned for such a traffic load. However, no one has addressed the actual rate of speed. How fast should a train be allowed to travel, and who controls this speed limit over the bridge?

RS-232:   The control of this speed limit is dubbed *timing*. Instead of individually synchronizing each character, the larger group of buffered data is synchronized by means of the timing element. In contrast with asynchronous transmission, this method is known as synchronous transmission. The engine and caboose are still present, indicating the beginning and end of the train. However, they assume a different meaning. In asynchronous transmission, the two units were start and stop bits, providing the timing for the individual characters. In a synchronous environment, the engine and caboose represent characters by themselves, indicating the start of a block of text and the end of that unit of text. They are not used for the function of timing but for the framing of a block of text. Timing is handled in a totally different fashion in synchronous transmission.

So how will timing of trains be handled when our trains are longer and faster. First, the speed limit for the tracks should be established. How fast can trains successfully travel across the permanent or temporary bridge? The speed limit should be fast enough to allow the maximum number of trains to cross the bridge, yet slow enough to allow the trains to reach their destination safely. The type and size of tracks used, for the most part, dictate the speed limit to be enforced. Based on the bridge engineers' specifications for the railroad lines, a rate will be established. Once established, enforcement of this limit is all that remains for a smooth flow of high-speed trains.

RS-232:   The speed limit is usually expressed in bits per second (bps). This rate, as with asynchronous traffic, is the number of 1s and 0s that can be transmitted in the period of 1 second. Once the speed is known, you can divide it by the number of bits per character to determine how many characters can be transmitted in a second. Typical synchronous speeds are 1200, 2400, 4800, 9600, and 19,200 bps. If the speed of a communication facility is 2400 bps and the length of each character is 8 bits, approximately 300 characters can be transmitted over the line each second. The use of protocols in synchronous environments produces certain amounts of overhead resulting in a reduction of throughput. However, this example merely provides a technique for a quick calculation of throughput. The RS-232 standard allows for speeds up to 20,000 bps. Speeds near the maximum are common in a private-line environment. In a dial-up environment, synchronous speeds of 4800 bps are more typical. However, technology is advancing to the point where speeds

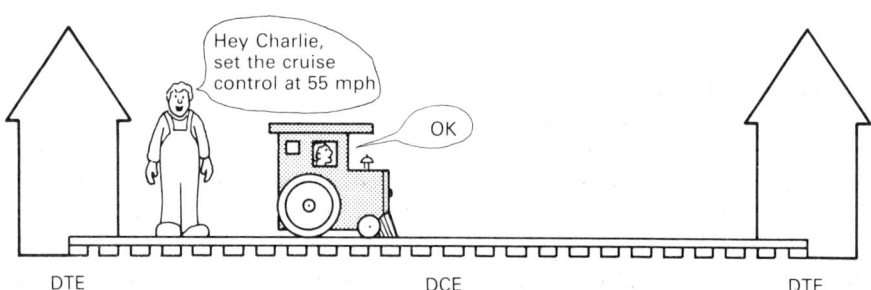

Figure 4-7 Transmit timing scenario

approaching the maximum rate allowed by the standard can be attained over dial-up lines.

Having established a speed limit for the rails, we somehow must provide for the regulation or control of the limit over the bridge. Thus trains need some mechanism for controlling how fast they should proceed down the railroad lines. Specifically, timing must be provided to control the rate at which data are transmitted and received over the lines.

The speed of the trains can be controlled at a number of different points in our bridge connection. Analyzing the various elements in our analogy, an obvious choice is the train station, because one exists at each end of the bridge. The depot at the origination site could regulate the speed of all outgoing trains. Outbound trains would be informed by the station of the correct speed at which to travel. At the same depot, the speed of the inbound trains could be monitored. The depot operator could then determine if the train is traveling at the correct speed (Figure 4-7).

RS-232: The speed control of the outbound traffic is termed *transmit timing*. Transmit timing is the clocking rate of data transmission. The characters are "clocked" out onto the line at whatever rate the transmit timing lead is providing. When transmit timing is provided by the train depot (DTE), it is supplied on pin 24. Some business machines have an option of either internal or external timing. For example, the Linkup Communications Support System from Information Technologies Inc. offers the ability to provide the transmit timing. When the PC, with this board or equivalent, is to be the source for the timing, internal timing should be selected. In this case, timing is provided by the PC on pin 24 for data transmission.

Another potential location for train speed regulation is at the booths. The booths could provide the depot with the speed at which the trains should depart from the depot and cross the bridge. Because the booths are connected directly to the bridge, they are in a better position to know the quality of the facility. Because of this, speed control by the booths is the more common of the two possibilities (Figure 4-8).

Chap. 4 Synchronous Communications for the PC/XT   77

Figure 4-8 Receive timing scenario

RS-232: The term for this is also *transmit timing*. However, the timing provided by the booth (modem) is considered to be a DCE source. A different lead, pin 15, is used to indicate transmit timing from a DCE source. In this case, if we were using the Linkup as before, the option for timing or clocking would be set for external timing. It is important to note that this could be a confusing option unless one considers the "source" of the timing. From the modem's point of view the timing is optioned as internal because the modem is providing the clock. Examples of modes offering this option are AT&T"s 201C and 208B, operating at speeds of 2400 and 4800 bps, respectively, in a dial-up environment. Their private-line counterparts are the 2024 and 2048, with the 2096 offering speeds of up to 9600 bps. In summary, if the PC is to provide the transmit timing, this timing will be provided on pin 24; if the DCE will provide it, the timing will be provided on pin 15 (Appendix A). Thus we have an option as to who is going to provide the speed limit (clock rate) of the data transfer.

At the booth across the bridge, the speed of the train could be monitored for an indication of the speed limit. Why is this required? The receiving depot must know the speed at which the trains will be arriving. This is necessary to allow the receiving station to check the train cars it received to ensure the accuracy of the shipment. To allow for this, we will let the booth derive the speed of the train as it passes by. If you have ever received a speeding ticket from a highway patrolman using a radar gun, you already understand the concept of deriving speed from moving traffic. Then the booth operator will pass the derived speed limit to the depot for proper reception of the train. When these two components, booth and depot, are working in synchronization, the trains can be properly received and analyzed (Figure 4-9).

Figure 4-9 Receive timing scenario

RS-232: This is known as *receiver signal element timing* (DCE source). For ease of reference, it is referred to as *receive timing*. This timing is found on pin 17. Typically, the modem can generate its own receive timing. However, it is often more efficient to derive the receive timing from the data being received. If the modem can extract the speed limit from the data received, this timing can be passed on pin 17 to the business machine, which uses this clock rate to receive the data properly.

At this end, we also have to allow for the transmit timing function. The fewer sources for timing that are used, the less the chance that timing problems will occur. To minimize the number of sources for timing, the following connection is possible. If the derived timing on pin 17 is looped up to pin 15 (transmit timing), synchronization is usually maintained more easily because it comes from a single source. We have also satisfied the transmit timing requirement at this end by using the receive timing. There is a single source for the timing. By looping the receive timing at one end to the transmit timing lead, there is less timing to keep synchronized. Often, in modems, this option is known as *slave timing*—the transmit timing (pin 15) at one end is slaved (derived) from the receive timing lead (pin 17). If you follow the timing all the way through the network, you can see that a single source can be used to provide both transmit and receive timing at both ends of the facility. This is the ideal environment to set up for synchronous transmission (Figure 4-10).

As we have seen, the key difference between asynchronous and synchronous

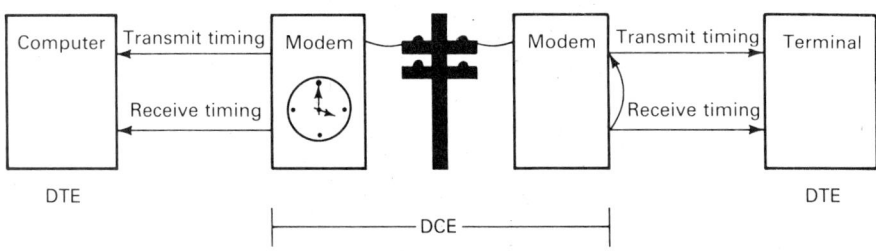

Figure 4-10 Timing in synchronous environment

Function	Pin	Lead name	Source
Timing	15	Transmit timing	From DCE
Timing	17	Receive timing	From DCE
Timing	24	Transmit timing	From DTE

Figure 4-11 RS-232 timing leads

transmission is the aspect of timing. Asynchronous transmission requires timing on a character basis. A typical example of this is teletype-compatible terminals. Each character is surrounded by start and stop bits for the purpose of timing. In most data communications over telephone lines requiring speeds greater than 1200 bps, the synchronous mode of operation will be used. With synchronous transmission, a timing signal is provided by either the DTE or DCE for synchronization of the data transmission. Special leads on the RS-232 interface have been set aside for this timing, as shown in Figure 4-11.

As a final review note, the more engineers there are trying to pilot the train, the greater the possibility of traffic problems. In a communication environment, the more sources providing the timing, the greater the chances for mismatched clock rates. To limit the potential for errors, use the fewest number of timing sources by deriving the timing (slave timing) from a single source whenever possible. The timing options should be coordinated with the telecommunication and data processing managers for the smooth installation of a PC in a synchronous network.

CHAPTER
5

local area

networks

Previous discussions have illustrated ways of optimizing the PC/XT configurations involving modems, terminals, and protocol converters. Chapter 6 indicates how to connect printers to PCs and how to share them. Each of these units is connected to the PC using either a RS-232 serial interface or a Centronics-compatible parallel interface. Certain environments do not necessarily lend themselves to these types of optimizations, particularly with regard to sharing a common file or database. Many PC users may require access to a database located on a single hard disk. The individual users may not be able to justify the acquisition of separate hard-disk units for local storage of the files because of the relatively high costs of disks. Furthermore, if separate duplicate files are used, ensuring that they are all kept current becomes a maintenance headache. Coordinating updates is barely manageable at best. Other items that may be desirable at each location but are out of the question are letter-quality printers, plotters, and archiving or backup units. How does a manager implement a configuration that is optimal but still offers each user the tools necessary for proper performance on the job?

Another option in configuring IBM PCs in communication environments is what is known as a *local area network* (LAN). A LAN is a network in which two or more devices are connected in such a fashion as to enable them to share data, programs, and hardware such as disk, plotters, printers, and other communication equipment. LANs are available in a wide variety of styles from an increasing number of vendors. A multitude of methods incorporating cables, switches, boards, and software may be used to provide a LAN and will be discussed shortly. But the typical qualities dictating needs for a local network allowing device sharing are similar in all LAN environments.

Generally, if PCs are located within the same geographic area, such as an office or campus environment, and require communication with one another, a LAN may be appropriate. Studies have proven that approximately 80 percent of data is exchanged within the same building or building complex. The characteristic of data transferred between devices is that it is bursty in nature. Large amounts of data are transferred in a short period of time. This is in contrast with the modem networks discussed earlier, where a PC running a terminal emulator package accessed a large mainframe computer for data acquisition, generally at a speed of 1200 bps. In a LAN environment, data are transferred between the devices at high speeds, and then the link for all practical purposes is idle. Physically, the link may be present, but logically the two devices are disconnected. If more than two devices are on the network, other devices could use the link.

Resource Sharing: People have different views of LANs depending on their goals. A telecommunication manager views LANs as a means of solving an otherwise expensive communication problem within a small geographic area by offering interdevice communications. This could be as simple as a number of PCs with terminal emulator software needing access to a mainframe. The LAN would offer a switching service to match users with mainframe computer ports. To a small business, the LAN is viewed as a means of reducing the hardware investment for duplicate devices. A hard disk may be shared by multiple users as if each PC operator had his or her own winchester disk storage. Furthermore, a single high-speed printer could serve many people if properly placed in the network. Regardless of the view, the common goal is to allow resource sharing.

Resource sharing is accomplished by offering device access to all on a network. A hard disk may be set up so that multiple PC users may have access to a common database stored on the winchester. For example, a telephone directory of a company is information commonly kept in some sort of database. Each PC user could keep a separate copy of this file on local floppy disks. As new or ex-employees cause necessary updates to the file, all users could make the changes if they were made aware of them. An alternative to this is to centralize the file offering public access to users on a LAN. A single update takes care of the changes, keeping the file as current as possible. This is only one example of file sharing. A single copy of an application program could be kept on the winchester disk. Anyone needing to run the program could download a copy into his or her PC for execution. This solves the updating problem but also reduces the overall storage requirements. File sharing on a LAN meets mass storage requirements without expenditures for individual storage units at each PC. Even though letter-quality printing is a requirement of each PC user, economics may restrict the purchase of multiple printers. Typically, a good letter-quality printer exceeds the cost of the basic PC itself. If a single printer is made available through the network to multiple PC users, optimization is realized.

Resource sharing through LAN communications is feasible in environments in which multiple PCs are in the same office, group of offices, building, or close grouping of offices. Benefits may be realized when LANs are used. LANs offer high-speed communications typically at millions of bits per second (mbps). A single hard disk may be divided among multiple PCs as if it were local to each user, saving thousands of dollars in storage costs. Furthermore, the number of floppy-disk drives at each PC could be reduced to one per station because the hard disk is accessible. It is even possible to do away completely with floppies at each station, depending on the environment, for the same reason. Fewer printers may be required by sharing them. With printers and plotters being a major expense item with PCs, significant cost savings can be attained.

The type of LANs available and appropriate to IBM PC users are better understood if background information about LAN technologies is discussed. This will include the various media, topologies, access and control methods, and nodes available. A discussion of each, including examples, follows. For a more complete understanding of implementing an IBM PC in a LAN environment, consult the Suggested Readings.

Media: The medium used for a LAN is generally one of three types: twisted pair, coaxial cable, or fiber optics. Each of these comprises the physical connections used to interconnect the network nodes. Nodes are the point at which a device interfaces with the network. Twisted pair is probably the most common of the three for connecting network nodes. It is the least expensive, as it consists of two pairs of plastic-sheathed copper wire twisted around one another, then wrapped with an outer protection cover. Twisted pair is also known as house-wire cabling, as it is generally used in your home as telephone cable. This same common house wire is used in office environments where PBXs are used for switching voice calls. We will see later how the PBX is considered a type of LAN, but for now we recognize that twisted pair is the medium. Speeds vary up to megabits; however, today's PBXs generally support 56-kbps or 64-kbps transmission. The attached devices generally are restricted to 9.6- or 19.2-kbps operation even though the medium may allow higher speeds.

Coaxial cable is another medium offering unique advantages. Use of this medium has plummeted as a result of the widespread use of Ethernet, one of the pioneering LANs which dictates the use of coax. Coaxial cable generally costs 30 to 60 cents per foot. It is 75-ohm, like the TV cable for services such as HBO or MTV. It supports half-duplex operation with speeds only up to 50 mbps. Typically, however, speeds are in the range 3 to 10 mbps with a very low error rate.

The medium receiving the bulk of attention these days is fiber optics. Still in its infancy, fiber optics is rarely used but is gaining in popularity as technological advances continue. Fiber-optic cable consists of a center core of glass or plastic, surrounded by shielding. Each fiber provides a single unidirectional transmission path. Speeds up to 50 mbps have been achieved up to 6 miles without having to boost the signal through the use of repeaters. This will be a popular medium, as, unlike twisted pair and coaxial cables, it is unaffected by electrical interference, noise, crosstalk, power outages, and short circuits. Its cost, presently $7 per foot, will restrict the use of fiber optics as a medium until lower prices are achieved.

Topologies: The way in which the various devices or nodes are connected conform to a certain structure or pattern referred to as a *toplogy*. Three different topologies are used today: star, ring, or bus architecture. A *star topology* derives its name from the fact that the main node is in the center, with the outlying nodes connected directly to the main node. For this type of network, control is centralized in the main node. The outlying nodes have point-to-point connections to the controller node. All of their transmission must go through the controller, which serves as a traffic cop and routing vehicle. This node is considered a critical node in the sense that if it is out, the LAN is inoperable.

Typical examples of LANs using this topology include intelligent switches and PBXs. An intelligent switch may be used to connect two devices as needed to transfer data. Advanced Systems Concepts, Inc. offers various switches capable of physically connecting end points for a session. For a relatively small investment,

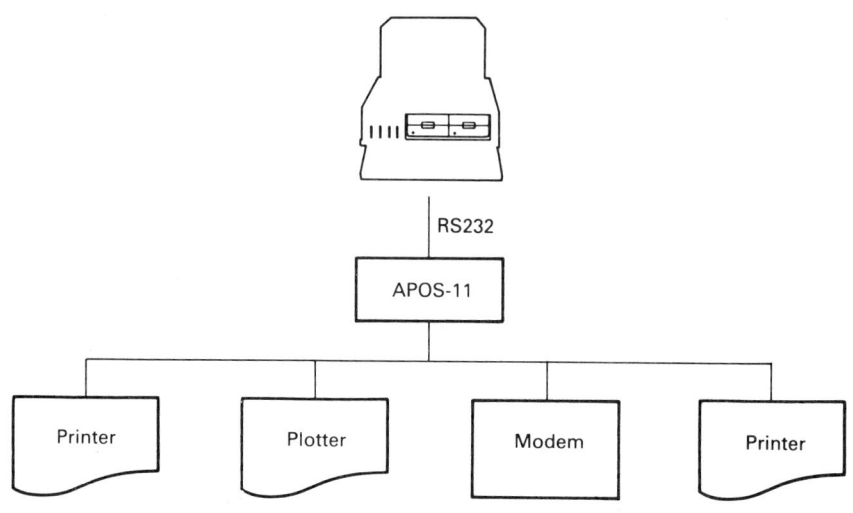

Figure 5-1 Intelligent switch

resource sharing is attainable. Their AQS and APOC series switches allow as many as four devices to be shared by a single IBM PC, or conversely, a single device to be shared by four computers. The connectivity is through RS-232 ports or Centronics parallel connections if desired for printers. Consult Chapter 6 for a more detailed explanation of connectivity issues. An IBM PC could have two printers, a plotter, and a 212a modem available to it through a switch requiring only one ACA or equivalent in the IBM. This is illustrated in Figure 5-1. Control characters are transmitted by the PC to select a device. Consult Chapter 9 for various configurations and associated cabling and optioning. Through the use of a model API, four IBM PCs could share a single letter-quality printer. Once a control character was issued by a PC getting control of the printer, all other requests by the other three devices are denied until printing is completed. This type of LAN is feasible for small installations when devices with RS-232 or parallel interfaces are used. Sharing of hard-disk systems on XTs are generally not feasible in these environments unless file transfer programs are used between the XT and the PC using asynchronous communications. In other words, direct access to the hard-disk system is not possible through the issuance of standard DOS read and write commands. Communication software must be used.

Another configuration offering a star configuration is the PBX. Recall that the PBX is a switching system located on a customer's premises which processes calls in the same fashion as the central office does for your home phone. These computer-based systems are universally being heralded as local area networks. They certainly conform to the LAN description of a community of users in the same geographic area needing to share data or peripherals. Originally conceived for switching of voice calls, they are evolving to support high-speed data traffic. The PBX serves as a central switch establishing circuits between devices or nodes (see

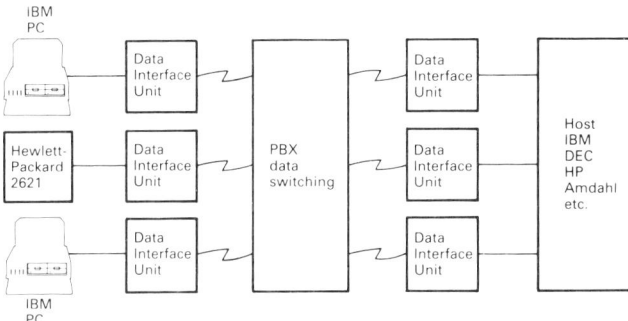

Figure 5-2 Star topology with a PBX

Figure 5-2). A PC would attach to a line on the switch through either a modem or a digital equivalent interface unit. The number of the other party is dialed, usually through the keyboard, and transmission occurs through the switch. Upon completion, the call is disconnected as a modem-type connection would be. This is known as circuit switching, as the controller maintains access by establishing a circuit between two devices as needed. The medium is generally twisted pair with point-to-point wiring between the switch and the end point. Even though modems may be used, switches are now supporting total digital transmission. In light of this, interface modules are used instead of modems, as no conversion from analog to digital and back to analog is required. RS-232 interfaces are required on the PC for connection to these interface units, imposing the same file-sharing restrictions as the intelligent switch just discussed. Speeds of up to 64 kbps are possible but are generally limited by the PC or devices attached to the switch. The PBX is generally sold as a competitor to LAN products. In the future coexistence will be possible between these two products using *gateways*. Gateways allow for two different networks to be connected. Necessary protocol and speed translation occurs between the two LANs. A hybrid of PBXs and other LANs will be prevalent in the late 1980s, blending various topologies.

Another topology is the *ring network*, in which the nodes are connected by point-to-point links arranged to form a closed circular configuration (see Figure 5-3). Each node plays a critical role in controlling the network. This is especially true for nodes connected between two communicating nodes. These middle nodes serve as active repeaters for messages not directed to them. They merely relay them. There is virtually no end to the number of nodes possible on a ring network, constrained only by address space. However, the age-old question "Will the circle be unbroken?" applies. If one of the nodes fails, the network could crumble. The method of controlling the network requires a closed loop or ring. *Token passing* is the round-robin passing of a control token from one node to the next. The token must be acquired before a message can be transmitted. Once obtained, a node has a specific amount of time to remove the token, accept or add a message to it, and relay it. Token possession offers exclusive use of the network. All other nodes are in the listen mode for their address with the message. Once successful transmission

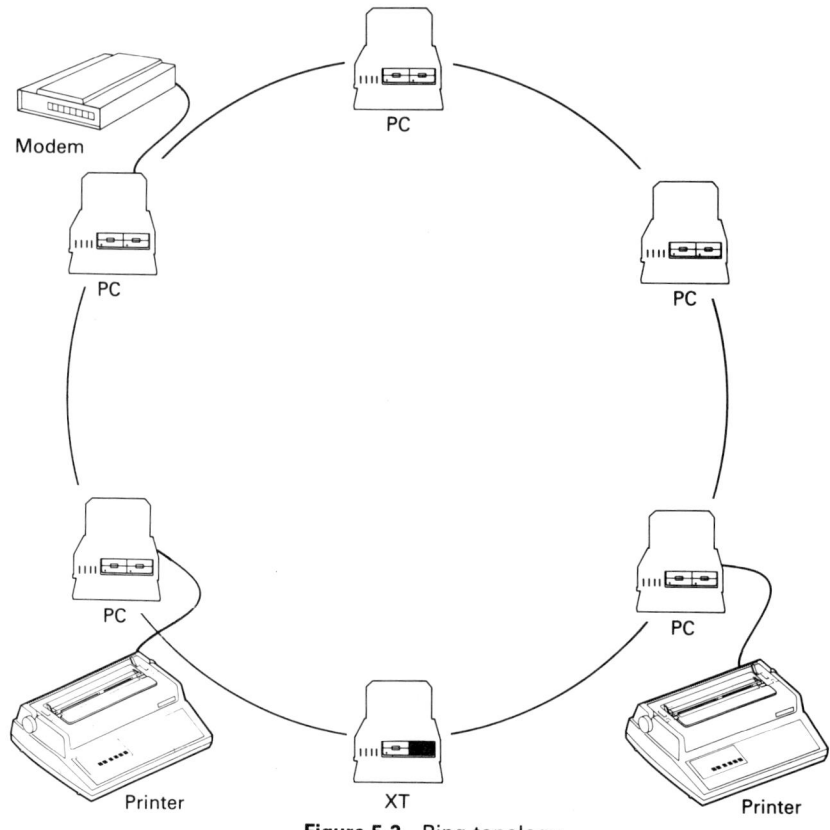
Figure 5-3 Ring topology

is complete, the token is passed to the next node. One can see that each node is a critical node. Means of overcoming the possibility of network downtime is accomplished by additional circuitry in the nodes. This logic changes the node to a passive mode where only relaying is performed when the main node processor is malfunctioning. Ring-type networks have not been utilized much in PC environments but should be more prominent within the next few years, as IBM is expected to announce a LAN incorporating the ring topology and token-passing control method.

The final topology to be discussed is that of *bus networks,* depicted in Figure 5-4. With bus structures, nodes in the network receive all transmissions and must listen for their addresses. However, they do not have to do any routing or regeneration of messages, minimizing the single-point-failure problem. Control of the network may be either decentralized or centralized. If decentralized, control is via a contention technique known as *carrier-sense multiple access with collision detection* (CSMA/CD). Each node listens on the network to determine if another node is sending a message. This is called *carrier sensing.* Any node may transmit its message upon sensing that the channel is free, a process allowing multiple access.

Chap. 5   Local Area Networks

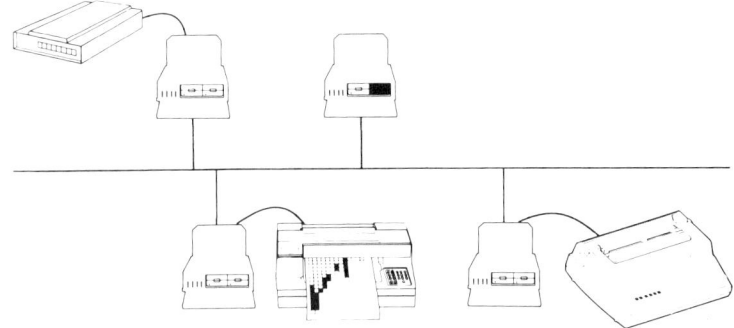

Figure 5-4 Bus topology

A transmitting node continues to monitor the channel while it sends its message. If more than one node begins transmitting simultaneously, a collision will occur. Because it is listening, each node will hear something different from that which it transmitted. Consequently, collision detection allows the node to refrain from transmission temporarily for a random time period, then listen and start the process again.

Ethernet: Bus topology is used in Ethernet networks. Ethernet is a local area network standard evolving from a project funded by Xerox, Intel, and Digital Equipment Corporation, announced in 1979. We will review a specific Ethernet-compatible network but first, what comprises an Ethernet LAN? What does it mean to be Ethernet-compatible? Ethernet allows for up to 100 nodes on a given segment. The nodes must be at least 2.5 cable meters from one another. Repeaters located at nodes are used to connect multiple segments. Segment lengths may be up to 300 meters. Coaxial cables between nodes within a segment must be less than 1500 meters without repeaters. The maximum end-to-end network length is 2800 meters with a maximum of 1024 nodes. The access control is CSMA/CD. Transmission speed is limited to 10 mbps. Ethernet-compatibility implies that the connectivity specifics adhere to the foregoing restrictions and support the same protocol.

ISO Model: Recall that a protocol is a body of rules allowing the orderly and reliable exchange of information between devices in a network. The protocol is a subset of a model proposed by the International Standards Organization (ISO). This layered protocol, known as the *OSI* (Open Systems Interconnection) *architecture,* offers seven layers. The layers are as follows:

Layer 1: Physical control
Layer 2: Link control
Layer 3: Network control
Layer 4: Transport end-to-end control

Layer 5: Session control
Layer 6: Presentation layer
Layer 7: Process control

For a further clarification of each layer's function, consult the Suggested Readings. It is important to note that layers 1 and 2 are defined by the Ethernet standard. It is these two layers that must be supported to be Ethernet-compatible. Ethernet compatibility allows addition and expansion to an existing network as new products evolve.

Ethernet offers a form of distributed control of the LAN. Centralized control of bus networks has not yet been used much. However, AT&T Labs has issued papers describing bus networks with centralized control. A separate bus is used for contention of the network and another for the transfer of data. The determination as to which contending node gets the opportunity to send its message is resolved on the contention bus. The node that wins contention has exclusive use of the data bus to transmit and receive messages. AT&T has recently announced their LAN offering, known as Information Systems Network (ISN), which incorporates this technology.

LAN Considerations: The implications of incorporating PCs in LANs using an intelligent ASCII switch or PBX for circuit-switching-type local area networks are fairly straightforward. Considerations in the areas of nodes, media, topologies, and access rules have been discussed, aiding in the decision process for acquiring a LAN. What are the considerations when implementing IBM PCs and XTs in message-switching local area networks such as Ethernet-compatible networks? The best way to understand the factors is to categorize them as either network-related, disk-related, or printer-related. Once these concepts are understood, the reader will understand the specific vendor offerings reviewed in this book and will be equipped to review future offerings.

Several network-related factors must be considered when acquiring and setting up a network. Each network generally requires the addition of both hardware and software. The hardware comprises a board offering network access and is known as a *network adapter, bus interface unit,* or *transporter.* The physical interface is neither RS-232 nor Centronics parallel, but rather a serial interface for high-speed communication. Its connection is generally dependent on the medium. Software accompanies the hardware to provide network setup for network servers, shared PCs, or user PCs. The software generally includes a software patch for DOS to allow enhanced features of file sharing and locking, print queueing, and remote operation on PCs. The attempt is to allow standard non-LAN applications to be run in a LAN environment. Although not all applications are compatible yet, this is a common goal of the vendors.

Server: A common component of LANs incorporating PCs is what is known as a *server.* A server can be any device that allows a peripheral to interface to the

LAN. The server can interface either nonintelligent or semi-intelligent devices to the network. Generally, there are four types of servers: network, file, communications, and printer servers. Servers may be either dedicated devices for this function or shared PCs or XTs. For example, the network server is an interface device that controls the network. EtherLink, a LAN offered by 3Com Corporation, utilizes a dedicated general-purpose microcomputer as a network server. This computer is not used as a workstation as are the PCs attached to the network. The network server houses mass storage units, tape units, or printers to be shared by PCs on the network. In contrast with this arrangement is PCnet by ORCHID Technology, which allows an XT to be shared, providing equivalent server functions as well as an active workstation. If the PC/XT is to be shared, then other PCs, referred to as *user PCs,* can access files on the shared computer while it simultaneously performs other functions. Restrictions can be placed on access to the shared system through the use of network IDs and passwords. The administration of the LAN can become quite complex, depending on its size. It is often desirable to assign someone as network administrator with responsibility for server setups, assignments of IDs, and file maintenance functions, including archiving.

File Server: The network administrator will play a key role in the disk-related factors of PC LANs. If a PC's storage system is to be shared by others on the network, the PC must be set up as either a dedicated server or a shared PC. Either of these functions allow for network access to files on the storage medium. The XT in Figure 5-4 could be set up as a file server to itself and other PCs on the network. The media could include hard disk, floppy disks, tape backups, or RAM disks. RAM disks are electronic counterparts to the normal platters in a hard-disk system or to floppy disks. Files are loaded into the computer's memory, running a disk-emulator package. This software emulates a disk drive on the PC, providing instant access to files in memory. They do not have to be loaded from a disk when accessed, as they are already in memory. Access time is minimal. A hard disk on the XT offers a capacity of 10 megabytes. Other systems range from 5 to 72 megabytes. These disk systems may be shared by partitioning them into smaller segments available to users. Access to files in a shared environment must be controlled to avoid conflicts. For example, if one PC user on the network is reading from a file, no other PC should be allowed access to that file. If they could write to it, the PC reading the files could retrieve conflicting information or the file could arbitrarily be closed by another user. The local PC user on the shared system could also erase a file without the on-line user's concurrence. The means of controlling these conflicts is through file locking. File locking is a function provided by the operating system or software patch. Once a file is accessed by a PC user, all other access attempts are denied. This locking may be at different levels: the drive, volume, file, or even the record level. DOS does not provide this yet, but could possibly evolve to include this when multiuser or multitasking capabilities are added. The network administrator would be responsible for configuring the system to allow for desired access and locks as appropriate.

Archiving: Another key function for the administrator is archiving files. *Archiving* is the process of removing old or unused files from the disk system. These files may not be accessed frequently enough to reside on the expensive and precious hard-disk space but do not deserve to be purged or erased forever. Archiving allows for backing up selected files on a periodic basis to either floppy or tape for possible later use. This frees more space for users. The administrator should establish a schedule for short-term backups and archiving. Some networks, such as Corvus's Omninet, allows for an archiving station to be attached to the Corvus LAN. Their Mirror product uses a standard video tape recorder to make backup copies of files. Other networks suggest archiving on floppy disks. Printing a hard copy of the information is another method for archiving. Regardless of the method used, archiving is a necessary function in LANs and should be implemented carefully and consistently.

Communication Server: A communication server allows for the sharing of communication equipment such as modems, protocol converters, and perhaps other LANs. These servers are not yet widely available on LANs but will be within the next few years. If modems, for example 212s, can be shared within a LAN, communication equipment costs can be lowered using similar techniques as the disk sharing access. Chapter 9 offers various solutions to switching a modem between multiple PCs. However, the PCs have to be colocated for manual switching. The only way around this is the ASCI switch discussed earlier. Both of these methods required stand-alone modems with their RS-232 interfaces. In a LAN both of these obstacles are overcome. The communication servers will allow remote access to the modems through the network. Furthermore, board-level modems can be used in a shared PC as hard disks are shared today. The modem in Figure 5-4 could be shared by other PCs if communication servers are supported. A gateway will offer access to other LANs. Gateways allow similar or dissimilar networks to be connected. Resources on each will be available to all if gateways are used. Necessary speed and protocol translations will soon be commonplace in communication servers. Today, however, few LANs have communication servers.

Printer Server: The final type of server is the print server. This server allows multiple PCs to request output to be dumped to a printer on the network. The printer may be too costly to be located at each PC, especially if they are plotters, letter-quality printers, or laser printers. Consequently, a single printer may be purchased and strategically placed in the network to handle all requests for hard copy, as shown in Figure 5-4. The primary concern when sharing a printer between multiple PC users is contention. If the printer is in use and another PC issues a print command, the print server must deal with the request. Different methods of handling the contention are available. One technique is outright denial of the request should the printer be busy. This is generally indicated by the server sending a message back to the originator of the print command. Basically, the user must try later and hope that the printer is free. Another method of handling multiple simultaneous requests is to queue or buffer them. The server maintains a queue of requests in the order in which they are received: first in, first out (FIFO). From this queue the print server schedules the printer. The print server must indicate to the originator the status of these jobs. This makes efficient use of the expensive print resource by keeping it active as requests arrive from the PCs on the LAN. If the print server is part of a dedicated server system, RS-232 serial interfaces are generally required on the attached printers. This could require the purchase of another printer if yours has a parallel interface. A serial interface can probably be installed in the printer as an option to overcome this potential problem. In any case, a print server can save costs in the overall design of a network.

When all the foregoing concerns abound when acquiring and implementing a LAN, a standard procedure should be followed by the administrator prior to actual installation. Representing the network layout graphically is often beneficial. Once items such as devices, users, and files comprising the network are identified, actual installation of the network becomes significantly less of a burden. The following is a suggested step-by-step guide to assist the network administrator.

1. Define the network graphically.
   a. Inventory the PCs to be attached, establishing a profile of each.
   b. Assign a physical address to each PC or workstation.
   c. Assign any mnemonic address.
   d. Compile a list of users and desired log-in sequences for each.
   e. Determine the devices at each PC that will be shared.
   f. Determine which files and applications are to be shared.
   g. Determine the file access requirements.
   h. Represent the network pictorially for ease of reference.
2. Install the necessary hardware.
   a. Set the physical address on the adapter board.
   b. Install the board.
   c. Install the cables.
   d. Make the connection to the network if not done in step 2c.
   e. Test the hardware and network.
3. Define the network software based on the step 1 and 2 configuration.
   a. Use the vendor-provided programs to set up databases defining the network.
   b. Set up the user database.
   c. Set up file access privileges.
   d. Test the software.
      (1) Retrieve the directory of shared disks from different PCs in the network.
      (2) Change the access privileges on different files on the local PC and attempt to access them remotely.

(3) Download BASIC through the network from a shared file system and execute it.

(4) Access remote devices such as printers or modems from different PCs.

(5) Perform any vendor-supplied tests to confirm a successful installation.

(6) Make a backup copy of the software programs and network definitions.

(7) Make another one and store it at your grandmother's house or other safe place.

4. Implement a procedure to track network usage patterns for fine tuning.

5. Update master records from step 1 with the latest network layout.

Although LANs can be quite complex configurations, a methodical approach similar to that outlined above allows for smoother installation and easier updates to the network.

In the next section specific local area networks are discussed, highlighting their features. These few provide a good representation of the LANs presently available. However, they are evolving to incorporate changing requirements for PC installations. Furthermore, the reader should understand that each of the LANs offers its own unique methods of physically connecting the adapter boards to the network. For example, XNET by XCOMP, Inc. uses nine-pin connectors, known as "D" connectors because they look like the letter "D." PCnet by ORCHID Technology utilizes the standard BNC connectors at the PC with "tees" for connection to the network. Because as yet there is no de facto standard, consult the installation guide included with each network package for the particular hardware interface requirements. However, to connect peripherals to PCs in the network, consult the appropriate sections of this book, as the standard RS-232 and parallel interfaces are appropriate.

XNET: A popular local area network for an IBM PCs is XNET, offered by XCOMP, Inc. XNET is a combination of hardware and software enhancements used in conjunction with DOS 2.0 to allow a distributed local area network. Up to 255 PC/XTs can be connected using twisted pair as the medium. If you are a programmer, you quickly determine that 8 bits are enough to address a network physically. The PCs are daisy-chained together using D connectors. The maximum distance between two nodes is 600 feet without repeaters, allowing a transmission speed of 2.5 mbps. The board for each PC has a male and a female connector for easy installation. The network loop must be closed by using terminator plugs on the PCs at the two extreme ends of the network. A starter kit is available which contains the boards, connectors, terminator plugs, cables, and software necessary to connect two PCs. The protocol or control is the CSMA/CD technique. Through software provided, a network administrator or superuser defines physical and mnemonic addresses, users' log-ins and passwords, and devices available at each node.

Chap. 5   Local Area Networks   93

File and record locking are available to ensure data integrity. An extension to DOS provides for a directory listing with associated access notations for each file. Macros may be used to circumvent lengthy commands necessary to access shared devices. A thorough understanding of the path feature in DOS is required of the administrator. For example, a command stream to remotely access BASIC stored on a drive at another node requires a path stream 10 to 20 characters in length. To avoid these lengthy inputs, macros are used. Macros are a frugal person's method of programming or issuing commands to set up paths to other devices on other nodes. With the use of macros, the command above could be reduced to five characters or less. Each user has the capability of defining his or her own macros as well as setting up file control. Access privileges or denials are set up by the owner of the files using a protect command. Once the network is started by a single command, the network is secured by enforcing log-ins and passwords for each user. Servers are not required in this network, as control is distributed to each node. Disk systems, printers, plotters, and modems are available to anyone on the network if set up for shared access.

PCnet: PCnet is another LAN offered by ORCHID Technology. This network is technically capable of addressing up to 64,000 devices. CSMA/CD is the access protocol over the 75-ohm coaxial cable link. Distances between 5000 and 7500 feet have been successfully installed carrying signals up to 1 mbps. The BNC connectors are easily installed together with the network adapter card. A DOS software extension handles the file sharing as well as a feature known as *remote execution*. Remote execution allows commands to be entered remotely and executed as if entered directly on a PC's keyboard. This allows for the sharing of devices such as printers, plotters, and modems. Plug-compatible IBM computers such as the Compaq, Columbia, and Corona computers have been successfully implemented in PCnet. ORCHID also guarantees compatibility with Tallgrass, Tecmar, Corvus, and Davong hard-disk drives. An optional Electronic Mail package allows PC-to-PC file transfers.

If Ethernet compatibility is desired for larger non-PC network integration, 3Com's EtherLink should be considered. If different personal computers are to share the printer, modem, and disk resources, Corvus's Omninet can be used. In addition to IBMs, Apples and other computers are supported on the same network. These networks are but a few of the LANs supporting IBM PCs. Furthermore, other network offerings did not evolve from the PC networking requirements but rather from terminal and host system requirements. Vendors in the latter category include Ungermann-Bass, Datapoint, Digital Equipment Corporation, Sytek, and Intecom, among others. These networks will be extended for specific PC support due to the proliferation of PCs in a corporation's communication network. Whether a LAN is a dedicated PC network or shared by other computers and/or terminals, local area networks offer opportunities for significant cost savings if properly selected and implemented. To optimize the potential savings and take future expansion into consideration, assign a network administrator to analyze, design, implement, and review LAN designs.

SUGGESTED READINGS

1. *Local Area Networks: Selection and Evaluation,* by James S. Fritz, Charles F. Kaldenbach, and Louis M. Progar, Prentice-Hall, Inc., Englewood Cliffs, NJ, 1984.
2. *Communications and Networking for the IBM PC,* by Larry E. Jordan and Bruce Churchill, Prentice-Hall, Inc., Englewood Cliffs, NJ, 1983.
3. *PC Magazine,* "Battle of the Network Stars," by Bill Machrone, pp. 103–158, Vol. 2, No. 6, November 1983.
4. *PC Tech Journal,* "PCnet—for the IBM PC," by Bruce Churchill, pp. 92–113, Vol. 1, No. 2, September–October 1983.
5. "Local Area Networks," a white paper by Don Gray of AT&T Information Systems.
6. *Introduction to Local Area Networks,* Digital Equipment Corporation, Order No. EB-22714-18, 1982.
7. *PC Magazine,* "Getting Hooked on PCnet," pp. 107–113, Vol. 2, No. 6, November 1983.

CHAPTER 6

connecting printers to the IBM

To this point the tutorials, how-tos, and optimizations were oriented toward environments where the PC required communications. With the increasing population of PCs in office environments, their requirements for communications will grow rapidly. Paralleling this growth is the need for hard-copy devices associated with each PC or shared in a network. For example, suppose that the author of this book has projected the number of books that must be sold for his wife to purchase a Mercedes (please tell your friends to buy this book). He creates the projections on Multiplan and wants to print a copy to show his wife. He may also desire a printout of all the vendors that supplied products for review in this book from a dBASE II file. Using Microsoft Word, a letter is composed thanking each of them for their contribution. Each of these needs can be fulfilled by connecting a printer to the PC. Furthermore, communications software packages invite the use of printers attached to the PC. For a quick copy of the contents of the PC screen, DOS offers commands for dumping it to a printer. Each of these exemplifies the need for connection of a hard-copy device. What should be one of the easiest connections turns out to be the biggest problem that a personal computer owner faces. To reduce the headaches associated with the selection, connection, and optioning of printers, this chapter offers a printer tutorial section followed by a discussion of connection and optimization techniques.

Print Quality: Before a printer is purchased, the user should determine the quality level(s) required for their installation as many printers are available offering a multitude of features. One of the first decisions to be made involves the quality of print necessary. The possible output includes data processing, draft, correspondence, near-letter, and letter-quality appearance. Different printers offer varying qualities of print, with some offering more than one type. For example, the NEC Spinwriter 3500 series offers letter-quality printing. The Okidata Pacemark 2410 offers three printing modes: correspondence, draft, and data processing qualities. Refer to Figure 6-1 for a comparison. The data processing quality output is of minimal quality for people who truly do not care what the output looks like. This descriptor arose from data processing shops, where massive amounts of output were generated of which little was actually read. Draft quality is a step above data processing quality but significantly more readable. A single pass of a dot matrix printhead, to be covered later, generates draft-quality print. Next in quality is correspondence printing. This is generally decent enough to send to someone in an office environment, but the reader will be able to distinguish the letter from one generated on a typewriter. If you desire to fool the reader into thinking that the letter is true typewriter letter quality, demand near-letter-quality printing capability. This is the next best thing to the top output, letter quality. Letter-quality printing is accomplished in the same manner as a typewritten letter. Fully formed characters

```
THIS IS DATA PROCESSING MODE PRINT
so is this but in small letters.

THIS IS DRAFT MODE PRINT
so is this but in small letters.

THIS IS CORRESPONDENCE QUALITY PRINT
so is this but in small letters.
```

Figure 6-1 Different print qualities, printed on the Okidata Pacemark 2410 printer

are generated by typewriter-like balls, daisywheels, or thimbles. The output is undistinguishable from typeset print. The choice as to quality of print will generally be inversely proportional to the speed of the printer for most PC printers. Laser printers may be an exception but are generally out of the price range of the average PC user. Many of these qualities may be acceptable to you or the recipients of your output. One of the safest ways of judging the quality is to compare samples of the paperwork currently used in your environment with the output of various printers before making your decision.

Impact Printers: To achieve the different qualities of print, a variety of technologies is used. Generally, printers are divided into two categories, impact versus nonimpact. Impact printers utilize some sort of typing element with a letter or piece of a letter which is hammered against a ribbon onto the paper. The two types of impact printers discussed here include full-character impact and dot matrix impact printers. The *full-character* uses the same principle as that of a typewriter. A ribbon sits between the fully formed character of an element and the paper. A hammering device causes the image on standard types of paper. The noise of these letter-quality printers is similar to that of a typewriter. However, cabinets are available to enclose these printers, reducing the noise. These devices use daisywheels, thimbles, or balls like the IBM Selectrics, allowing multiple copies to be printed. Different elements, easily installed, are available to accommodate different printing requirements. Examples of full-impact printers include the NEC Spinwriter series, the Qume Sprint series, and Diablo Systems 600 series letter-quality printers. Impact printers offer speeds ranging from 10 to 75 characters per second and are constantly being improved.

The other type of impact printer is the *dot matrix*. On these machines the letters are generated using tiny dots that approximate the shape of a character instead of forming them fully. The term "matrix" is used due to the grid, array, or matrix of dots or pins available for hammering against the ribbon and ultimately the paper. The size of the matrix and the number of dots determine the legibility of the characters. Printheads generally have seven or more pins in a vertical column. As the printhead moves across the paper, the hammers hit the pins as necessary to form the characters (see Figure 6-2). The IBM printer is an example of this type of printer. The characters being printed on this machine can be shrunk, compressed,

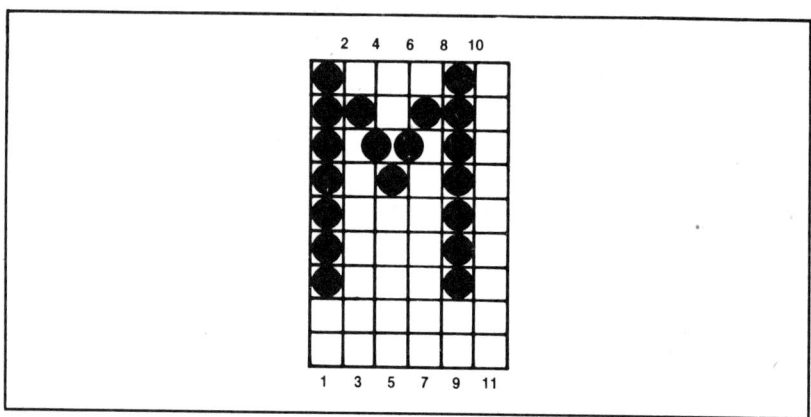

Figure 6-2 Dot matrix printing technique

italicized, or double-struck, all under control of the PC. Descenders, which are the parts of the letters g, j, p, q, and y that descend below the print line, are printed. Typical speeds of dot matrix printers are between 100 and 200 characters per second. These types of printers are very popular with personal computer owners. Specific vendor offerings are described later in this chapter.

NonImpact Printers: Nonimpact printers do not strike the paper at all. Hammers are not used to get the print on the pulp. A thermal printer, a good example of this type, requires special heat-sensitive paper. Although these printers are less expensive than their impact counterparts, the paper is more expensive and potentially more difficult to obtain than is standard paper. Other technologies in this category involve electrosensitive, light, photographic, and light techniques. Ink jet printers are becoming increasingly popular. They contain nozzles used to spray dots of ink onto the paper. Laser printers use the same principles as a photocopying machine, offering speeds significantly faster than those of impact printers. Laser printers output is generally paced according to the number of pages of print per minute, with a range of 20 to 50 ppm. At the current pace of technological improvement in printer technology, ink jet and laser printers could soon be affordable by the average PC owner.

The features offered by a printer may be the determining factor in purchasing a particular output device. These features can be categorized as follows:

1. Performance
2. Interfaces available
3. Add-on options
4. Printing characteristics
5. Graphics capabilities
6. Media-supported

Chap. 6   Connecting Printers to the IBM

7. Format controls
8. Proven reliability

Printer Performance: A printer may offer a variety of print speeds depending on the printing method enabled. For example, if the data-processing-quality mode is invoked in a printer offering different modes, the output rate may be very high. For example, the Okidata Pacemark 2410 is capable of printing 350 characters per second (cps) in the data processing mode. This printer also offers a correspondence-quality print at a rate of 85 cps. To achieve these high throughput rates, bidirectional printing is used as well as logic seeking functions. *Logic-seeking functions* are optimizing routines that force the printer to take shortcuts to increase throughput. If a short line is printed, there is no need to print spaces filling the remainder of the line. The printing of spaces is generally done to position the printhead at the end of a line for printing the next line right to left. Logic seeking allows a carriage return line feed to be performed, saving valuable time and consequently improving print speed.

Interfaces: Generally, two interfaces are used for connecting printers to the IBM PC: serial and parallel. Another, 20-milliampere current loop, is available but is decreasing in popularity. RS-232 and Centronics parallel interfacing will be covered in depth later in this chapter, but here we will say only that it is important to determine which is to be acquired in the printer. Furthermore, consideration should be given to future expansion. If a parallel interface is standard on the printer, is a serial interface option available for easy installation later? For example, the Epson FX-80 printer comes standard with a Centronics parallel connector. Practical Peripherals, Inc. offers a user-installable serial interface in the printer. These interfaces are mutually exclusive but offer extreme flexibility as a system expands and evolves.

Add-On Options: Add-on options are available with many printers. As the printer is generally the slowest device in the PC configuration, a means of making the PC available while the printer is chugging along is desirable. Buffers of different sizes are available for most printers. Generally, 2000 (2K) or 4K increments are possible in the printer itself. The computer then quickly dumps the data to the buffer and may proceed to another task. The buffer feeds the data at the printer's operational speed. Often, multicolor ribbon support is available. If single sheets of paper are to be used, sheet feeders may be a required option for the printer. Single- and dual-bin-cut sheet feeders are generally the two options. A dual bin feeder allows both plain paper and letterhead paper to be loaded into the printer automatically. If the printer is using single sheets of paper, *friction feed* is the technique used to roll the paper around the platen. Often, a *tractor-feed* option is available. Also known as *pin feed* or *sprocket feed,* mechanisms allow for paper with holes on the sides to be used. This paper is generally continuous with perforations between sheets for easy separation. Tractor-feed operation may either be an option or come

Normal Print:

- Superscripts and Subscripts QWERTYUIOP[]ASDFGHJKL;'~<>,.?/\!!@#$%^&*()_-+=1234567890
- Condensed Font (16.7 cpi) - ABCDEFGHIJKLMNOPQRSTUVWXYZ1234567890abcdefghijklmnopqr
- COMPRESSED FONT (12.5 CPI) - ABCDEFGHIJKLMNOPQRSTUVWXYZ123456
- Standard Font (10 cpi) - ABCDEFGHIJKLMNOPQRSTUVW
- Correspondence Font (10 cpi) - ABCDEFGHIJKLMNOPQ
- Elongated Font (10 cpi) - ABCDEFGHIJKLMNOPQRSTUV
- Expanded Font (5 cpi) -
- Expanded, Normal, Superscripts and Subscrip
- ELONGATED AND EXPANDED

Bold (Double-strike) Print:

- Superscripts and Subscripts QWERTYUIOP[]ASDFGHJKL;'~<>,.?/\!!@#$%^&*()_-+=1234567890
- Condensed Font (16.7 cpi) - ABCDEFGHIJKLMNOPQRSTUVWXYZ1234567890abcdefghijklmnopqr
- COMPRESSED FONT (12.5 CPI) - ABCDEFGHIJKLMNOPQRSTUVWXYZ123456
- Standard Font (10 cpi) - ABCDEFGHIJKLMNOPQRSTUVW
- Correspondence Font (10 cpi) - ABCDEFGHIJKLMNOPQ
- Elongated Font (10 cpi) - ABCDEFGHIJKLMNOPQRSTUV
- Expanded Font (5 cpi) -
- Expanded, Normal, Superscripts and Subscrip
- ELONGATED AND EXPANDED

Emphasized (Shadow) Print:

- COMPRESSED FONT (12.5 CPI) - ABCDEFGHIJKLMNOPQRSTUVWXYZ123456
- Standard Font (10 cpi) - ABCDEFGHIJKLMNOPQRSTUVW
- Correspondence Font (10 cpi) - ABCDEFGHIJKLMNOPQ
- Elongated Font (10 cpi) - ABCDEFGHIJKLMNOPQRSTUV
- Expanded Font (5 cpi) -
- Expanded, Normal, Superscripts and Subscrip
- ELONGATED AND EXPANDED

Figure 6-3(a)   Different print pitches, printed on the Printronix MVP 150B printer

Chap. 6   Connecting Printers to the IBM   101

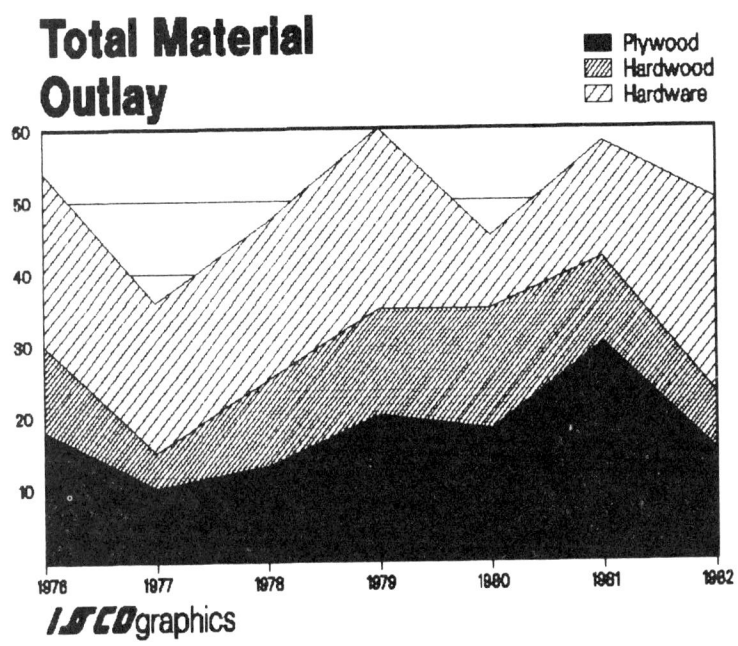

Figure 6-3(b)   Sample graphics printed on the Printronix MVP 150B printer

standard with the printer. If tractor feed is used on the printer, ensure that the printer supports variable-width paper. This means that the sprockets are adjustable to support different-size papers.

Printing Techniques: The actual printing characteristics vary from printer to printer. The matrix size may vary depending on the quality and size of print. One of the most popular features of a printer is *condensed* or *compressed printing*. This is the ability of a printer to alter the size of the characters being printed. The standard output is 10 characters per inch (cpi) horizontally. With compressed/condensed print, up to 17 characters may be squeezed into an inch of space. In this mode a printer can squeeze 132 characters into the space normally available in 80-column printers. Refer to the sample printout in Figure 6-3(a) with 132 columns available, or 13 inches, over 220 characters are possible. This allows for large spreadsheets to be printed. It may be desirable to do the opposite and reduce the number of characters per line by *expanding* the print. This is useful for headings on documents. If an item needs to stand out in text, *double-striking* and/or emphasized printing is available to print bold lettering. Superscripts and subscripts may also be desirable. *Proportional spacing* as used by typesetters is also available on many printers. Most if not all of these features are operable under computer control. Commands in the form of control or escape sequences are used to set up the different modes of printing. These characters are received and acted upon but not printed. Many programs, such as VisiCalc, offer printer setup sequences. The control and escape sequence may be entered for desired printing results. Consult Appendix E for a list of popular printers and their control commands with respective functions. Should these printing modes always be desired, switches may be set to enable them permanently.

One final printing characteristic is printer *emulation*. Because of the widespread use of some printers, such as Texas Instruments 800 series, Printronix, Qume Sprint series, and Epson printers, support for their control codes are inherent in certain applications. Other printers offer emulation modes allowing them to be used in these environments and perform just as the emulated devices would. Some printers go a step further by offering the ability to download a character set to the printer from the PC, allowing for personalized application development.

Graphics: Graphics is another desirable feature for dumping images from the IBM to a printer. Either block-mode or bit-mapped graphics may be supported. *Block-mode graphics* offers simple horizontal and vertical lines as well as shapes such as squares, circles, and rectangles to draw pictures. If better resolution for pictures is desired, *bit-mapped graphics* is the choice. Generally, the printer vendor will publish the number of points that are addressable in the form of dots per inch. The greater the density, the better possible the picture. Figure 6-3(b) offers sample graphics available on dot matrix printers.

The medium supported by the printer determines whether pin-feed paper or single-feed paper is usable. Furthermore, multiple copies may be allowed. If single sheets are fed by a sheet feeder, forms control should be an option. This allows for the top of the form to be set and automatically aligned for subsequent sheets if the form length is properly set. *Horizontal and vertical tabbing* are also desirable format controls, as they can reduce actual printing time and may ensure compatibility with software packages that rely on them.

Reliability: The final feature to consider, but perhaps the most important, is the reliability of the printer. Because it is largely a mechanical device, a printer is subject to breakdowns because of the moving parts. Vendors generally set forth rigid requirements for printer testing, as they realize the importance of uptime for these systems. The measurement for reliability is generally expressed as MTBF, *mean time between failures*. This is the amount of time between successive failures on a printer. Furthermore, downtime should be considered as how long it takes to repair the machine. This is expressed as MTTR, *mean time to repair*. These should be prime considerations if the printer will be used heavily.

Printer Connection: To this point the discussion has centered around selection criteria for the printer of your choice. This section focuses on the practical aspects of actual printer connection to your PC. The discussion will include the building of null-modem cables, the use of breakout boxes for both serial and parallel interfaces, optimization techniques, and associated optioning. The bridge scenario of previous sections has provided an excellent foundation for a thorough description of a data communication environment. The train depots and booths stood for DTE and DCE, respectively. Between the two booths was the bridge, which represented the telephone lines for communication facilities. Recall that the bridge could be of a permanent or a temporary nature, allowing for the distinction between private and dial-up lines. For the printer discussion the bridge and booths will be excluded, as no communication facility is required between the PC and the printer. In its place the proper interface cable must be constructed and implemented. Where possible, the analogy will be used to reinforce key points for serial interfacing. However, a separate example will be used for the Centronics parallel interface, following the RS-232 discussion.

The first point to realize is that because of the removal of the communication facility, DCE is no longer going to be present. Specifically, the modems and telephone lines are not needed to connect the PC to the printer, plotter, or other local device, provided that they are sitting side by side, or at least within 50 feet of each other as allowed by the RS-232 standard. Keep this in mind when locally connecting two devices with serial interfaces.

Even though the communication facility, or bridge, is gone, the local connection must have the capability of handling the trains as if they were crossing the bridge. So the same "handshaking" must occur for the depots to operate as normal stations would, even though we are in a different environment. The tunnel must be built in such a fashion that the depots do not have to change their procedures for train traffic. In short, the local interface connection must emulate the booths and the bridge. This is a requirement to allow the standard stations to be built to operate on either a bridge or a tunnel type of facility.

DTE/DCE Emulation: Business machines such as the PC allow for serial interfaces that normally conform to the RS-232-C standard. If the standard is adhered to, RS-232 leads (pins) should be similar for any DTE. This also implies that these business machines are set up to expect the standard RS-232 signals normally provided by the DCE. Specifically, a modem would supply the proper signals to allow the PC to function properly during its data transmission. When a port is configured to expect the signals normally provided by a mode, that port is said to be emulating data terminal equipment. While it is expecting to receive these signals, it will also generate signals such as request to send and data terminal ready, which are output signals from DTE. The ACA is a good example of this and is covered later in this chapter. If, on the other hand, the port is emulating data communication equipment, leads such as data set ready, clear to send, and data carrier detect are output signals generated from the port. When either of these categories, DTE or DCE, is being emulated, the proper output signals should be generated and the corresponding input signals can be expected. Recall from earlier chapters that these standard signals fall into four categories: ground, data, control, and timing. When connecting these leads to allow local connections between machines (without modems), all four categories of leads on the RS-232 interface must be crossed to emulate a communications environment, as if modems and lines were present. Because the cross-connections cable is used when no modems are present, we generally refer to it as a *null-modem cable*. The following discussion describes the cross connections required to build this type of RS-232 cable. The reader will find that the direction of the leads, input or output, becomes very important. Because of this there is a general rule that should be followed at all times. An output signal will be connected to an input signal, and vice versa. Never connect an output signal to another output signal; always pair output with input and input with output. This will become evident in our discussion of the data and control categories of leads. The leads and their directions are outlined in Figures 6-4 and 6-5. But first let's discuss the straightforward leads.

Ground Leads: The first and easiest category is ground. Because these signals are present for protection and signal reference, merely allow for them in null-modem cable. Protective ground (pin 1) is electrically bonded to the machine or equipment frame, while signal ground (pin 7) establishes the common reference for all other interchange circuits except pin 1. So in a null-modem cable, merely provide these two pins straight through from PC to printer. No crossovers are required (Figure 6-6).

Data Leads: This category includes the data leads (pins 2 and 3). Pin 2 is used for transmitted data and pin 3 for received data. Both are normally present at both ends. The exception might be pin 2 at the printer end. Why? You guessed it: Printers do not usually transmit data; they receive only. Only when software flow control is used, as discussed in Chapter 3, will pin 2 on the printer's port be used. Data are transmitted over pin 2 from the PC and received on pin 3 at the printer. To allow for proper data transmission and reception at both machines, cross pin 2 at one end with pin 3 at the other end. This conforms to the general rule of connecting an output signal to an input signal. Repeat this at both ends, as represented in Figure 6-7.

Pin	Function	Direction
2	Transmitted data	From DTE
4	Request to send	From DTE
11	Reverse channel (SRTS)	From DTE
19	Reverse channel (SRTS)	From DTE
20	Data terminal ready	From DTE

Pin	Function	Direction
3	Received data	To DTE
5	Clear to send	To DTE
6	Data set ready	To DTE
8	Data carrier detect	To DTE
12	Secondary DCD	To DTE

Figure 6-4 and Figure 6-5 RS-232 leads from an IBM ACA viewpoint

Chap. 6   Connecting Printers to the IBM

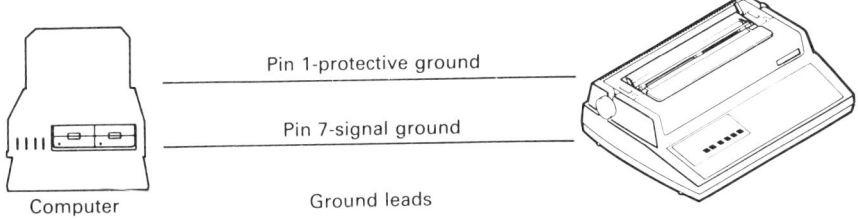

Computer   Ground leads

Figure 6-6   Ground leads

Control Leads: So far we have accommodated both ground and data leads in the interface—50 percent of our null-modem connections. All that remain are the control and timing leads. We must allow for actual DTE leads as well as emulated DCE leads in the cross-connection cable. Data-terminal-equipment-provided signals are all that are present in a null-modem cable used between the PC and a printer or a plotter. This limitation forces us to provide DCE signals with available DTE signals. Specifically, the DTE signals (RTS and DTR) must be used to provide or emulate the DCE-provided signals (DSR, CTS, and DCD) that would have existed in a normal telecommunications environment. We will see once again that the general rule holds true: output to input, and vice versa.

If you consider the configuration, two DTEs are to be locally connected with merely a cable between them. Business machines, built for a communications environment evidenced by DTE-compatible ports, are expecting the standard RS-232 control signals usually received through the modem. We will now explain how the DCE signals can be emulated by the available PC and printer signals DTR and RTS.

Data terminal ready (pin 20) is ordinarily provided by the printer to indicate that power is on and provided by the PC's COM port when it is enabled. This is used to maintain the connection in a dial-up communication environment. For an indication that the line is established between the two devices, the DCE normally gives a signal on pin 6 (DSR). As long as DSR is on, one can assume that the DCE, both modem and line, is available for data transmission. If pin 6 is not present, the line or connection is not available. To emulate DSR at both ends, we strap the DTR signal at the PC device across to pin 6 at the printer. The same strapping is done in the other direction. By strapping pin 20 across to pin 6, whenever DTR is high, the other end will get an indication that the transmission line is available, even though there is no actual transmission facility between the two. If

Function	Pin	Pin	Function
Transmitted data	2	2	Transmitted data
Received data	3	3	Received data

Figure 6-7   Data leads

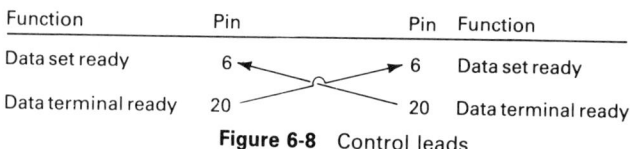

Function	Pin	Pin	Function
Data set ready	6	6	Data set ready
Data terminal ready	20	20	Data terminal ready

Figure 6-8 Control leads

power is off, the other end will not have DSR, indicating that the communication path is not established. The pins should be crossed as shown in Figure 6-8.

The other element of the control function on the interface is path control. Three leads were necessary for this function (Figure 6-9). RTS was the headlight on the train, turned on by the depot. This light was seen at the far end on pin 8, data carrier detect. CTS was the indication from the booth (modem) that a depot had control of the tracks and could send trains across the bridge. When only a single track was available on the bridge (half-duplex), path control was extremely important; when two-way traffic was allowed simultaneously (full-duplex), this concern was somewhat relaxed, but the signals were still present.

In a null-modem cable, the same track/control signals must be allowed for. The booth/modem signals are not present. We must provide these by utilizing available signals from the depot's point of view. Of the three signals necessary for train path control, only one is available at each end. This signal is the headlight indication of a request to send a train to the other depot. How are we going to get three signals from only one? Believe it or not, this can be accomplished rather easily.

We must once again cross-connect certain leads to achieve this. We will apply the concept of mirroring the RTS signal back to the originating machine. RTS (pin 4) is normally generated by the DTE, that of both PC and printer. For data transmission to be allowed, CTS (pin 5) must be received by the PC. So we loop the RTS signal back to the PC by wiring it back to pin 5 (CTS). Pictorially, this is represented as shown in Figure 6-10.

Whenever the PC COM port raises RTS, it immediately receives a CTS signal indicating that data transmission is now possible. As for the need of the receiving device to have an indication that data will be arriving, we must provide for DCD (pin 8) to be derived from the same source, RTS. Thus we also connect RTS (pin 4) at the PC port to the data carrier detect lead, pin 8, at the printer, as shown in Figure 6-11. By making these cross connections, not only will a CTS signal be given but when RTS is raised, the other end will receive its DCD signal, indicating that data transmission is possible. Repeat these connections from the printer's perspective to allow two-way transmission. Whether the terminals are set up for HDX or FDX, path-control requirements have been met in the null-modem cable.

Function		Pin
Request to send	RTS	4
Clear to send	CTS	5
Data carrier detect	DCD	8

Figure 6-9 More control leads

Chap. 6 Connecting Printers to the IBM   107

Function	Pin
Request to send	4
Clear to send	5

Figure 6-10 Keeping CTS on with RTS

Hardware Flow Control: These control leads satisfy standard null-modem connections. However, if hardware flow control is to be used, different cable configurations are required. In Chapter 3 we discussed the need for a printer to notify the computer at the distant end of an alarm condition. Specifically, the secondary control signal (reverse channel) was used to indicate that a paper-out condition had occurred. When modems are not used, as in the local attachment of a printer to the PC, the same concept is often applied. So different cross connections may be required for printer control functions, specifically involving the control category of leads. Specific examples of these will be discussed later in this chapter, but first the theory should be understood.

To cross-connect properly between the PC and the peripheral, the technical specification for the serial ports must be reviewed. First, determine which lead is held high by the printer to indicate that the printer is functioning properly—with no paper-out condition or buffer problems. Usually, this lead is a secondary request to send (pin 19 or 11), but on a printer, pin 20 (DTR) or pin 4 (RTS) often provides this function.

Whichever is used, this lead will still function in the same manner. However, the lead must be cross-connected to a lead at the PC end that is required before the computer can transmit.

At the PC end, a lead(s) must be found that is important enough that the computer can transmit data if and only if it is on. If it is not on, it must prohibit the computer from transmitting data. Secondary data carrier detect is sometimes used for this function, but not on the IBM PC-compatible serial ports. Depending on the board supplying the port, pin 5, 6, or 8 may be monitored by the PC for regulating when data can be transmitted. To be safe, connect all three of these leads to the lead at the printer end used for printer control, hardware flow control. Once connected, the computer and printer behave in a normal fashion, as if there were modems between the devices. Figure 6-12 illustrates this connection. Assume that pin 19 is used for this purpose. Connect pin 19 from the printer to pins 5, 6, and 8 at the PC. Do not connect pin 20 of the printer to pin 6 at the PC as discussed previously. If you were to do so, pin 6 would not fluctuate, defeating the purpose of the cross connection for hardware flow control.

Should software flow control be used instead of hardware flow control, many cross connections are possible. Figure 6-13 outlines some possibilities.

The particular null-modem cable used depends on the signals required and

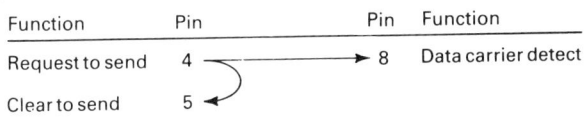

Function	Pin	Pin	Function
Request to send	4	8	Data carrier detect
Clear to send	5		

Figure 6-11 Crossover of control leads

IBM ACA	Pin		Pin	NEC 3500
Clear to send	5 ◄─┐	────	19	Secondary request to send
Data set ready	6 ◄─┤			
Data carrier detect	8 ◄─┘			

Figure 6-12 Hardware flow control leads

provided by the data terminal equipment to be connected to the PC and is affected by flow-control leads. Consult Appendix C for further possible cross connections.

Timing Leads: The preceding section has taken care of 95 percent of the local peripheral attachments to the PC, as they use asynchronous serial interfaces. However, the timing category of leads remains. Recall that the only situation in which timing was required was in a synchronous environment. If the null-modem cable is being built for an asynchronous PC-to-peripheral interconnection, the reader can ignore this section and proceed to the next. However, if timing is of the essence, read on.

The first question to be answered is whether the board in the PC or the peripheral can provide the timing. Recall that an option usually exists on PC boards for either internal or external timing. This is a key option, as a null-modem cable cannot be built if the PC or peripheral cannot provide the timing. If the board cannot provide the timing, it always depends on the modem (DCE) to provide the clock. Because there is no DCE when connecting two devices locally, a separate unit must be placed between the devices. This unit is often termed a *synchronous null-model device* or *synchronous modem eliminator*. It eliminates the modems as the standard null-model cable does, yet allows the essential timing element. Not only are the ground, data, and control leads taken care of, as described previously but timing is also provided by the box (Figure 6-14). An example of such a unit is Black Box Catalog's SME-3. This unit eliminates the need for two modems and the communication facility between the PC and the other computer or peripheral. This unit supports both BSC and SDLC environments with speeds up to 19,200 bps.

However, what if at least one of the DTEs can provide the timing? If the synchronous PC board can supply the clock, we can go back to the null-modem

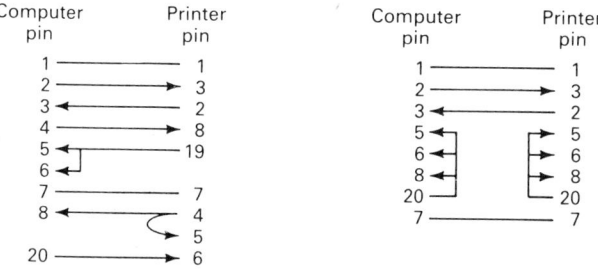

Figure 6-13 Typical null-modem cables

Chap. 6   Connecting Printers to the IBM

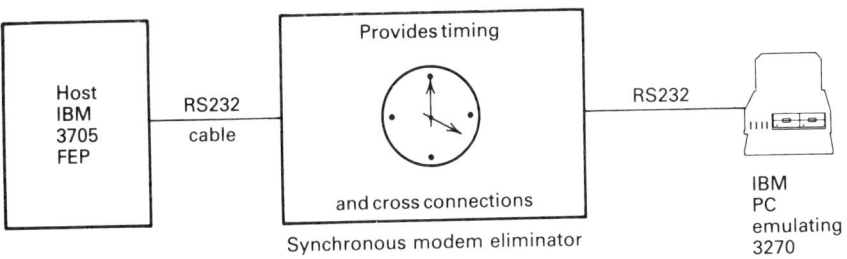

Figure 6-14   Synchronous modem eliminator

cable. There is need for only a single source of timing. If both the PC and the device to be connected have this capability, decide which will be optioned to provide it. Once optioned, the timing will be provided on pin 24, transmitting signal element timing (DTE source). This is the timing that will be used for both devices, whether transmitting or receiving. Satisfying the need for timing at both ends is rather simple. Because a single source of timing is supplied, merely connect all the associated timing leads, both transmit and receive. Connect pin 24 to pins 17 and 15 at one end, and connect one of these leads across to pins 15 and 17 tied together at the other end. The fashion in which pins 15 and 17 are connected really does not matter as long as both sides are eventually connected to the timing source on pin 24. This is depicted in Figure 6-15.

Now that all timing leads are connected, synchronous transmission should occur successfully. In fact, pin 15 on the DTE side, which provides the timing, does not need to be connected at all. The source DTE is providing its own transmit timing; it will ignore whatever timing is presented to it on pin 15. We have built a synchronous null-modem cable whereby one of the DTEs is providing the timing. This may be used in situations where the PC is emulating a BSC or SDLC device and is colocated with the mainframe with which it is communicating. Figure 6-16 summarizes a standard asynchronous null-modem cable. To work in a synchronous environment with the DTE providing the timing, add the lead connections shown in Figure 6-15.

Serial Interfacing: Several tools exist that aid in the connection of peripherals such as printers and modems to the IBM PC. Such tools as breakout boxes, RS-232 lead monitors, device-sharing switches, buffers, and standard null-modem cables reduce the installation time required. Some of these devices are discussed in Chapter 9 but merit discussion for proper selection for your particular environment.

Function	Pin	Pin	Function
Transmit timing	15	15	Transmit timing
Receive timing	17	17	Receive timing
External timing	24		

Figure 6-15   Timing leads in a null-modem cable

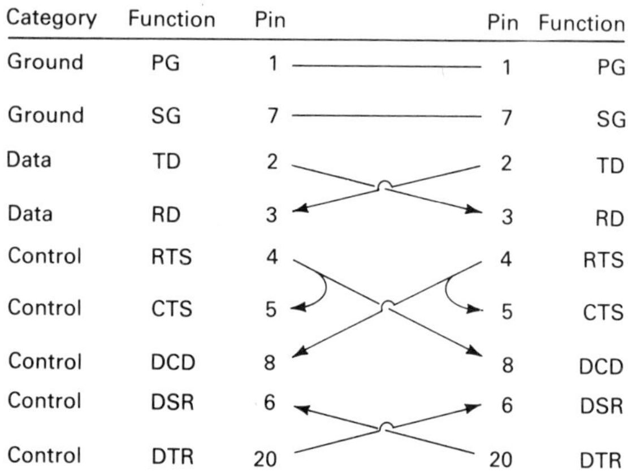

Category	Function	Pin		Pin	Function
Ground	PG	1 ———————		1	PG
Ground	SG	7 ———————		7	SG
Data	TD	2	╲╱	2	TD
Data	RD	3	╱╲	3	RD
Control	RTS	4	╲	4	RTS
Control	CTS	5	╳	5	CTS
Control	DCD	8	╱	8	DCD
Control	DSR	6	╲╱	6	DSR
Control	DTR	20	╱╲	20	DTR

Figure 6-16 Standard null-modem cable

Serial Breakout Boxes: One of the most useful devices when working with RS-232 environments is a breakout box. This unit offers the ability to watch the interaction of the leads in an RS-232 environment. Specifically, data, control, and timing leads may be viewed to determine if each port is set up properly. By determining which leads are high or low, the viewer can determine whether the port is configured as DTE or DCE. Furthermore, jumpers are available for crossing leads to satisfy individual port requirments. Some of these units require a battery for operation, whereas others draw their power from the RS-232 lines themselves, known as *line-powered*. The price of these units ranges from $40 to $500, depending on features included with the box. For example, Jaxon, Inc. offers the line-powered OWL-1, allowing the monitoring of eight leads, pins 2–3–4–5–6–8–20. This provides monitoring capabilities sufficient for most home PC installations. Should additional capabilities, such as jumpering, disconnection or opening of leads, and voltage to be supplied on certain leads be desired, a more complex breakout box should be considered. A multimeter may be used for detection of the dc voltage level of RS-232 signals. With the ground probe of the meter connected to a ground reference, touch the other probe to one of the control leads to cause a reading on the meter. The dc level setting should allow between +3 and +15 volts to determine which leads are on. This is not as effective as a breakout box but can be used in its absence.

The usefulness of a breakout box will be highlighted in the next section. For discussion purposes we will use the Black Box Catalog SAM+ RS-232 Tri-State breakout box, with SAM denoting a status activity monitor. This unit is pictured in Figure 6-17. One of the key uses of the unit is to determine if a printer port is set up to emulate DTE or DCE. Most printers offer DTE interfaces, implying that request to send and data terminal ready, pins 4 and 20, respectively, are on if the

Chap. 6 Connecting Printers to the IBM   111

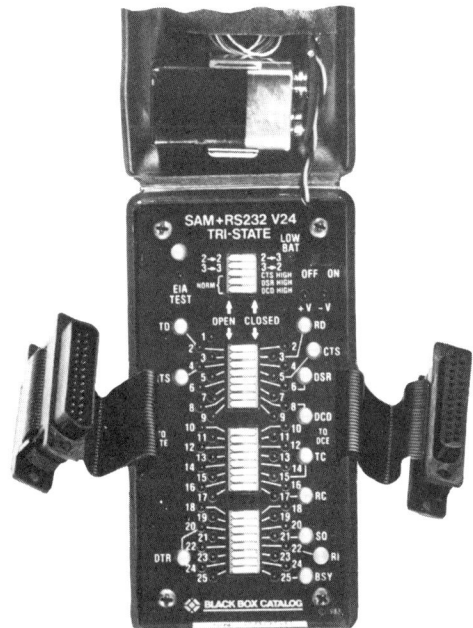

Figure 6-17 Black Box Catalog's SAM+ Tri-state break-out box

printer is on-line. A general rule, meaning as sure as this is printed it will be contradicted, is that ports configured to emulate DTE have a male or DB25P (pin) connector. This usually gives the first clue. Placement of the SAM+ directly on the port in question confirms this. Pins 4 and/or 20 should be on if the port is configured as data terminal equipment. This means that a modem or DCE device is to be connected. However, if the lamps for pin 5, 6, or 8 are high, this port is set up as data communications equipment, ready for direct connection to a DTE port such as that provided by an Asynchronous Communication Adapter (ACA).

Another use of the breakout box is actually at the computer port. The ACA was just mentioned as having a DTE connection. This is listed in Appendix C but could have been determined just as easily in the same manner as the SAM+. Enabling and testing the port, we find that request to send and data terminal ready are on, indicating that the port is set up for DTE. This means that a modem such as a Hayes Smartmodem 1200 can be connected directly to this port with a straight-through cable. Furthermore, a null-modem cable is needed to connect a printer also set up for DTE. (See the explanation elsewhere in this chapter for specific null-modem configurations.) But what if you do not have the modem or printer set up and you merely want to test the port on the board. The SAM+ may be used, as it offers the ability to hold clear to send, data set ready, and data carrier detect high as a modem or null-modem cable would. This is done by flipping three switches on the breakout box. Now a simple test can be performed to check the RS-232 port. With the DOS disk in the current drive, enter the commands MODE COM1:96,e,7,1,p and MODE LPT1: = COM1, each followed by a carriage return. This sets COM1 to 9600 bps and redirects the printer output to it. Now depress the Shift and PrtSc keys simultaneously and watch the transmit data lead on the SAM + . It should flicker correlating to the 1s and 0s of the data being transmitted. If data are being sent, all the port control leads are satisfied. If clear to send, data set ready, and data carrier detect are not on, the PC will not transmit the data. This is exactly what the computer store technician does to run diagnostics on the serial ports. She or he uses a wrap plug to accomplish what we just did with the breakout box except that the DCE-derived signals are provided with request to send and data terminal ready. Furthermore, pin 2, transmit data, is looped back to receive data so that all output data are also received as they are transmitted. A breakout box can also be used strictly for viewing the interaction of leads to determine if features such as flow control are working properly.

Another useful device is a box allowing various pin configurations to be tried before a cable is wired permanently. Also called a breakout box, this unit offers no monitoring capability. It is used only for constructing many variations of cables until the appropriate connections are found. The final lead configuration is then duplicated in a real RS-232 cable.

Let's review a specific installation using tools such as the breakout box. For our purposes we will use the Okidata Pacemark 2410 printer with the RS-232 serial interface. A connection is desired to the ACA serial port for use as the system printer. A step-by-step procedure follows, making the assumption that the printer has been set up, including installation of the ribbon. Furthermore, the printhead must be freed for use, as it was tied down for shipping purposes. None of the switch settings will be changed; the default options will remain as shipped from the factory. Consulting the documentation the reader will find that these defaults include 9600 bps, no parity, 8 data bits, 1 stop bit, and hardware flow control. Hardware flow control is going to be used, implying that pin 11 will be high/ready when the printer is on-line and no alarm condition exists. Ensure that paper is in the printer before attempting this exercise. This approach is equally applicable to other serial printers except that the flow-control lead may be different together with other control leads supported, but the same technique can be applied.

ACA Interface: As stated in the preceding paragraphs, it was determined by using the SAM + that the ACA offered a DTE interface because pins 4 and 20 were high when the port was activated. These leads are turned on once the printer

Pin	Direction	Status
4	Output	On if port is active
20	Output	On if port is active
5	Input	Must be on for transmission
6	Input	Must be on for transmission

Figure 6-18 ACA control leads

Chap. 6 Connecting Printers to the IBM 113

output is redirected to COM1 and the Shift and PrtSc keys are depressed. However, until pin 5, 6, or 8 is high, data will not be transmitted. Actually, pin 8 is not monitored by the ACA logic but is included for completeness. Keep this in mind, as these leads will be used for hardware flow control as discussed earlier in this chapter. Figure 6-18 lists the ACA and equivalent port pins. The general rule of a DB25P (pin) connector emulating DTE holds true with the ACA and equivalent ports. The direction of pins 4 and 20 from the PC/ACA confirmed this. Our redirection was accomplished by typing the commands MODE COM1:96 and MODE LPT1: = COM1, each followed by a carriage return. The other settings of the COM1 command assume their default settings if not included in the command line. The defaults of even parity, 7 data bits, contradict the default printer options mentioned above, but are specified to demonstrate how the installer can detect such problems should printer documentation not be available.

Printer Interface: The next step is to test the Okidata printer. Consulting the printer documentation may be easier but may not always be available. In lieu of this, the SAM+ should be plugged into the port on the printer, which happens to be a DB25S socket. According to the general rule, a socket connector would imply a port emulating data communication equipment (DCE). However, with the printer on-line pin 20, data terminal ready is high, indicating that the port is configured for DTE. In reality the RS-232 standard actually calls for the rule to be followed. Connecting two DTE ports requires the use of a null-modem cable. How this cable is to be built will be determined next.

Building the Cable: Consulting either the charts in Appendix C or the printer documentation, the user will be able to build a null-modem cable allowing for transmission of data and proper flow control. Separating the leads into the four categories of timing, ground, control, and data as discussed earlier will ease the installation. The easiest categories in a cross connection or null-modem cable are the ground and timing leads. The author has never seen other leads for ground besides pins 1 and 7 for protective and signal ground, respectively. Because of this these pins should be connected between the computer and the printer for straight-through connections, 1 to 1 and 7 to 7. Because the ACA is asynchronous, as is the printer, no timing leads are required, so ignore pins 15, 17, and 24. The two remaining categories are the most important and, you guessed it, the most difficult.

The control leads should be tackled next. Recall that the control leads include data terminal ready, request to send, clear to send, data set ready, data carrier detect, and possibly a separate flow control lead. Because flow control is extremely important, the first step is to determine which lead from the printer is used if

Pin	Direction	Status
20	Output	On if printer is online
11	Output	Hardware flow control lead
8	Input	Must be on to receive data

Figure 6-19 Okidata Pacemark 2410 serial port pinout

hardware flow control is to be used. Generally, pin 20, 19, 11, or 4 is used for flow control, as they are DTE-generated signals. If documentation is not available, the breakout box may be used for assistance. If the printer is on-line, plug the SAM+ into the Okidata printer port. Pin 20, data terminal ready, is on but pin 4, request to send, is not. From this we cannot conclude that DTR is the hardware flow control. Pins 11 and 19, secondary request to send, should be tested to see if they are on. The SAM+ has an EIA test position to check any of the 25 leads on the interface. Jumper pins 11 and 19 to this test pin one at a time to see if they are on. Should one of these leads be on, it is generally the hardware flow control lead. If neither of these is on, probably pin 20 is used or no hardware flow control is supported. This would leave software flow control to ensure proper data transfer. Should this be the case, double-check the documentation to see if hardware flow control is supported. As pin 19 is tested on the Okidata printer, the breakout box indicates that it is off. Pin 11 is on, however. Watch the lead and take the printer off-line. Pin 11 goes off in conjunction with this action. This is our flow control lead, as listed in Figure 6-19. This is the lead that should be connected to the ACA control leads, which must be on for the PC to transmit data. So jumper pin 11 on the printer port across to pins 5, 6, and 8 of the ACA port. This allows for hardware flow control.

The ACA is now capable of outputting data, but can the printer receive the data? Generally, printers offering DTE ports also require pins 5, 6, and/or 8 to be on before data reception can occur. The Okidata must have pin 8 on to receive data, unless the default option is changed. Furthermore, pin 5 must be on for the printer to transmit data. The only time the printer would need to transmit something is if software flow control is being used. To be safe, make sure that all these leads are on/high. This may be done by connecting to them a lead that is constantly on. Pin 20 from the Okidata is on when the printer is powered up and on-line. Connect this by looping it back to pins 5, 6, and 8. Now all the control leads are taken care of allowing both the PC to transmit and the printer to receive.

But how should the remaining category of data leads be connected between the PC and the printer? There are only two options. Either pin 2 at the ACA is connected to pin 2 or it is crossed over to pin 3 at the printer port. To determine this, connect pin 2 straight through between the devices. With the printer output redirected to COM1, depress the Shift and PrtSc keys. If the printer attempts to print something, the pins are to be straight-through. If not, cross the ACAs pin 2 to pin 3 on the printer. Once again, dump the screen and the printer should begin printing. Consulting the documentation, the reader finds that the ACA outputs information on pin 2 while the printer accepts data on pin 3. Pin 2 of the printer should be crossed to pin 3 of the ACA in case software flow control is to be used. If XON/XOFF is use for flow control, the XOFF character will be output on pin 2 of the printer and must be input into the ACA on pin 3. So pins 2 and 3 should be crossed between both devices for flow-control flexibility. The finished test cable should be duplicated according to the configuration on the SAM+, summarized in Figure 6-20.

Chap. 6 Connecting Printers to the IBM

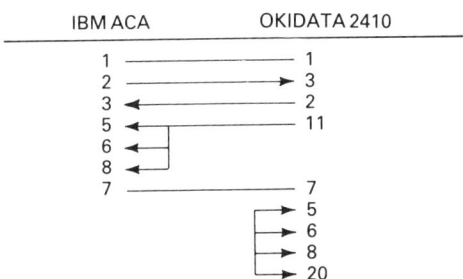

Figure 6-20 Completed cable

The printer may have attempted to print but did not print exactly the contents of the screen. This has nothing to do with the cable but rather with the options of the COM1 port or the printer options. Either the speed, parity, character length, or number of stop bits is the problem. If none of the characters is legible or match what is on the screen, the speed option could be the culprit. Reissue the mode command for the COM1 port, trying different speeds. If this does not solve the problem, reset it to 9600 bps. In this test, some of the characters were legible. Generally, this is an indication that character length and/or parity is mismatched. With the four options of speed, parity, character length, and stop bits, many combinations are possible. The user can either try different combinations of these or check the printer's default settings. Recall that the printer was optioned for 8 bits, no parity, and 1 stop bit. By merely issuing the MODE COM1:96 command, the defaults of 7 bits, even parity, and 1 stop bit were set. The heart of the problem has just been found. Issue the command MODE COM1:96,N,8,1,P to match the ACA properly to the printer. Redirect the I/O to the serial port with the command "MODE LPT1:=COM1." Once the PC output is redirected to COM1, issue the Shift/PrtSc to test the interconnection. It should work. If not, the ACA is probably not functioning properly. Check to ensure that it is set up for RS-232 and not for current loop signals. Furthermore, ensure that it is configured for COM1, not COM2 operation. Then check the printer options to ensure that they were set up as the earlier assumptions indicated.

Other Aids: The breakout boxes are ideal for the procedure described above, especially when hardware flow control is to be used between the PC and a printer. If software flow control is to be used, the same technique may be used by ensuring that the control leads are active between the two. This would be a standard null-modem cable. There are devices that make this interconnection even easier in reference to the cable. Jaxon, Inc. offers the LBS, Loopback Switch. This plug-in unit is inserted in-line between the PC and the printer's straight-through cables. The LBS switch automatically crosses appropriate control leads to keep them enabled. The unit allows for pins 2 and 3 to be either straight through or crossed for data and flow control by a mere throw of a switch. This unit allows a quick interconnection.

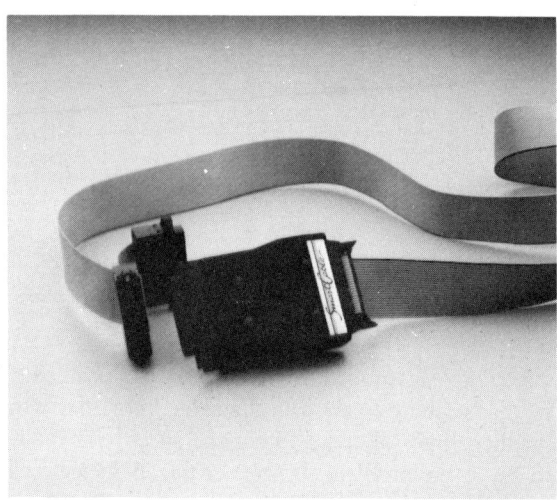

Figure 6-21 SmartCable by IQ Technologies (Courtesy of IQ Technologies Inc.)

Another such device is the SmartCable by IQ Technologies, Inc., pictured in Figure 6-21. The SmartCable offers flexible and versatile device connections with minimal operator assistance. The unit consists of a module with an extruding cable. The module is plugged into the PC port with the cable then connected to the device, such as the printer. Two switches and lamps are available to satisfy the connection requirements. A maximum of two or three throwings of the switches is required to complete the connection. This unit is different from the preceding one in that it does offer a matchup for hardware flow control. The unit has several patterns that it draws from to provide the flow-control connections. The lamps are used to direct the user through the setup. Once properly set up, data transfer is possible.

Neither the LBS nor the SmartCable solves the option setup requirements but certainly solves one of the most difficult areas of connecting peripherals to the PC. These units generally work better in environments where software flow control is used, as they do not necessarily take into account all the different hardware flow-control leads. However, the Smartcable vendor is constantly updating the unit as new cable configuration possibilities are discovered.

Other tools that assist the user in the interconnection of the PC to peripherals are items such as gender/sex changers, which convert female plugs to male plugs. Other units exist to match the genders, allowing a female connector to connect to another female connector. Pin extractors are useful to pull the different leads out of a DB25 connector. They can also be used to insert them. Another device provided in the IBM dealer diagnostics kit is the *wrap plug*. This plug crosses leads to allow a port to be tested. The pin configuration is as follows:

1 to 7
2 back to 3
4, 5, and 8 connected together
20 to 6

These crossovers fool the port into believing that a modem is connected and on-line. Any data sent out of the port will be looped back into the IBM computer. The software then reads the incoming data and compares them with the transmitted data.

The truth breakout boxes allow for the temporary testing of different cable configurations prior to actual cable construction. Breakout boxes allowing the monitoring and/or jumpering of leads are available. Standard null-modem cables can be purchased for most cross connections. These boxes range in price from $40 to $1000 depending on the features included. For example, Jaxon offers a breakout box with monitoring capabilities affordable by the average home PC user. B & B Electronics, Inc. offers an RS-232 Wiring Adapter for jumpering leads. Black Box Catalog offers an array of all the devices in this paragraph. For available products, consult the vendor addresses in Appendix I and order vendor catalogs for a complete selection of devices that make the PC-to-peripheral(s) connection both easy and economical.

From the preceding examples you can surmise that one of the first factors to consider when interfacing equipment using RS-232 ports is whether a port or terminal is configured to emulate DTE- or DCE-provided signals. The best way to determine this is to review the device documentation. Consult the user's manual for this information. Ordinarily, the manuals that are provided with the equipment contain the information necessary to determine the direction and functions of the RS-232 leads. The breakout box was another means of obtaining similar information. If neither the documentation nor a breakout box is available, consult Appendixes A and B. The pin assignments with their corresponding directions are listed for a multitude of devices. From the direction of the pins, a determination can be made as to how the device is configured. Should all these sources fail, consult the dealer or vendor who markets the product.

Parallel Interfacing: The default printer with the PC is the IBM 80 CPS Matrix Printer or the Graphics Printer. These printers are manufactured by Epson for IBM and come with a Centronics parallel interface. This interface is different in many ways from the RS-232 serial interface. The greatest difference is the manner in which the bits of each character are transmitted. Other areas of difference include flow control, error condition and reporting, and number of ground leads. As with RS-232, the best way to understand the interface is to group the leads into the four categories of data, ground, control, and timing. Each of these areas will be discussed to give the reader an appreciation of the advantages and disadvantages between parallel and serial interfacing. The explanation that follows centers around the most common parallel interface, the Centronics parallel interface. Centronics, Inc. is a printer manufacturer that offers a 36-pin parallel interface in their printers. The actual connector on the port is an Amphenol connector, allowing a maximum distance of 5.5 yards. This interface was copied by many printer manufacturers to become eventually the default standard for most printers. As with RS-232, this is merely a standard. The degree of adherence to it is left totally to each vendor. However, the introduction of the IBM PC is helping to force conformance. References to parallel interfaces throughout this text are to the Centronics parallel standard, as discussed in the following sections.

Data and Ground Leads: Recall that in serial transmission the bits of a character were transmitted one bit at a time. The receiving machine had to know character length, start/stop bits, speed, and parity to decipher the characters for proper handling. The serial interfaces could be used for either printer or modem connections, as they allowed two-way communications. The parallel interface contrasts with the serial by allowing the PC to transmit all of a character's bits simultaneously instead of one at a time to the printer. Picture the runners in a 100-yard dash. They all start at the same time and if all goes well, all arrive at nearly the same time. The data bits are transmitted in a similar fashion. The IBM PC parallel port, addressed as LPT1-LPT3, outputs all the bits of each character to be received by the printer. IBM DOS 1.0 and 1.1 support only one parallel port addressed by either LPT1 or PRN device names. However, DOS 2.0 supports LPT2 and LPT3 in addition to PRN and LPT1, allowing up to three parallel devices to be connected directly to the PC/XT. RS-232 offered a single lead, transmit data, for the passing of the data bits serially. To transmit all the bits at once requires eight separate data leads. The Centronics standard sets aside pins 2 to 9 for data transmission. Another difference between RS-232 and parallel is that data transmission is unidirectional. Actual data bits can be transmitted in only one direction, from the PC to the printer. Each of the data leads has a corresponding ground lead for signal-level reference. Whereas RS-232 sets aside only one lead, pin 7, for this, the Centronics interfaces uses pins 19 to 27 as a ground reference for each data lead. Pins 1 and 19 are a pair, as pins 2 and 20 are, and so on. Refer to Figure 6-22 for these pairs. Other ground leads for each lead will be seen as we cover the

Pin	PC to printer Function	Ground lead
2	Data bit 1	20
3	Data bit 2	21
4	Data bit 3	22
5	Data bit 4	23
6	Data bit 5	24
7	Data bit 6	25
8	Data bit 7	26
9	Data bit 8	27

Figure 6-22 Parallel interface data leads

Chap. 6   Connecting Printers to the IBM   119

remaining 20 leads of the interface. The protective or chassis ground for prevention of shocks is pin 17. The logic ground lead which is tied to the other paired signal ground leads is found on pin 16. As with the RS-232 interface, ground leads have no direction.

Control Leads: Data and ground leads account for two of the four lead categories, leaving only control and timing signals. The control leads of both interfaces are used to control the transmission of data between the two devices. Direction of transmission is not important as it was in the serial interface. Rather, control functions must allow for conditions of paper-out, printer in off-line mode, and other printer error or fault conditions. Furthermore, flow control must be maintained so that the PC knows when data may be transmitted. Pins 10 to 14 are used to provide for control functions.

How does the PC know when a character may be transmitted? The LPT port must monitor several leads. Pin 10 is an output signal from the printer indicating to the PC that a character has been received and that the printer is ready to accept another character. This lead is known as the *acknowledge lead* and must go off before more data can be received. If this lead is on, the PC should refrain from transmitting data until it goes off or low. Pin 28 is the signal ground for the acknowledge pin.

If the printer cannot receive any more data, it must indicate this to the PC. Sound familiar? It should, as this is the flow-control portion of the interface, similar in concept to the serial counterpart. RS-232 supported either hardware of software flow control. Full duplex was required for software flow control, using XON/XOFF or ETX/ACK as physical characters were transmitted by the printer back to the PC. Because the parallel interface is unidirectional or simplex, only hardware flow control is possible. Pin 11 is used for this function. As long as pin 11, known as the *busy signal,* is off/low, data may be transmitted by the PC if the acknowledge lead allows it. A busy condition causes the printer to turn on pin 11 as an indication for the PC to cease transmissions. The signal becomes high if the printer is off-line, in an error condition, or if the printer buffer is full and the printer needs to catch up. Once the printer is placed in on-line mode or the error condition clears, this lead goes off/low, signaling the PC to resume transmision. Pin 29 is the ground return for the busy signal. The busy lead functions exactly as the hardware flow control in RS-232. The only difference is the polarity. Pin 11, 19, or 20 in RS-232 was generally high as an indication to the computer that data could be transmitted. The Centronics parallel busy lead is low, as a positive indication to continue transmission. Other than this, they are functionally equivalent.

The printer has a special lead that it uses to tell the PC that it has been selected and is on-line. If pin 13 is on/high, the PC can be assured that the printer is on-line. It is also referred to as the *select lead*.

Should the printer run out of paper, an indication is passed to the PC. Found on pin 12, the PE signal is a paper-out signal from the printer. If this lead goes high, the PC should halt transmission to prevent loss of data. As with RS-232, this could be catastrophic if the printer is printing your paycheck. Once paper is threaded through the printer mechanisms and the printer is on-line, pin 12 will turn off, indicating the clearing of the condition. If the printer is malfunctioning for some reason, pin 32 will be turned off by the printer until the condition occurs. Even if paper-out is the reason for the malfunction, this lead will also go out in addition to pin 12. Once the malfunction is cleared, pin 32 returns to its high state.

If the IBM PC desires to reset the printer to its original mode, a special pin is used. Pin 31 is on/high unless a reset is desired. A reset may be used if the printer has been set up for compressed print, double-strike, italics printing, or other software-controllable features. If the PC lowers this lead, the printer will return to its standard mode according to the hardware switch set options. Also, the data in the buffer of the printer will be lost if this reset is used. Lowering of this lead is equivalent to powering the printer off and back on again.

Although the bulk of printers do not use pin 14, the IBM printers interpret this lead for carriage control. If this autofeed signal is turned off by the PC, the printer sees it and advances the paper one line after printing. The IBM printers have an option to set this lead permanently low to allow for automatic line feed after the printing of a line. Another lead not commonly supported by printers other than the IBM is pin 36, select in. This lead is an input to the printer and should be low to allow data entry from the PC. As with the line-feed option, a hardware switch setting allows for a permanent low setting. Many printers will not use these leads, or reserve them for use as a signal ground.

Timing Leads: All that remains is the timing for the data transmission. RS-232 had separate transmit and receive timing leads. The Centronics standard offers only a transmit lead, as the interface is simplex. Pin 1 or the strobe lead provides for the synchronization necessary to receive data. This is an input clock for the printer and allows for reading of the parallel data bits. The strobe is of short duration, about 0.5 microsecond. Once a character is read in, the strobe goes off for a short duration and then goes low again to receive the next character. Speeds of up to 1000 cps are possible with this interface.

IBM Parallel Connector: Now that all the leads are defined and the reader recognizes that the RS-232 and the Centronics interfaces are different, we will show how they are the same. IBM gets all the credit for this, as their physical port offering a Centronics parallel interface uses the same connector as an RS-232 interface. Yes, a DB25 connector with 25 pins is used for a parallel port. This means that some of the 36 pins are not used or shifted around. More important, though, is the cord-plug-compatibility issue. Most printers with parallel interfaces use an Amphenol-type connector. This is also termed a *champ connector*. Even with a shoehorn you cannot plug a DB25 connector into a champ receptacle. Because of this physical

Chap. 6 Connecting Printers to the IBM   121

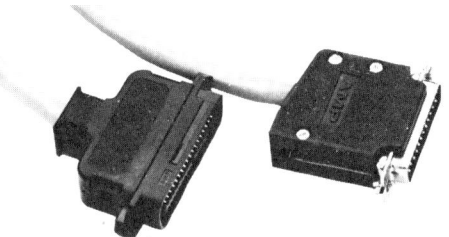

Figure 6-23 PC to printer convertor cable

incompatibility, a conversion cable must be purchased. At one end of the conversion cable is a DB25 connector. At the other is the Amphenol connector most printers are used to being cabled with (see Figure 6-23). The gender of the DB25 connector on the conversion cord is male. This means that the port on the PC is a female or socket plug. This is useful to know when multifunction boards are used in the PC. Many of the boards discussed in Chapter 2 provide among other things both serial and parallel ports. A quick way to determine which is parallel is to find the female plug. The RS-232 port will almost always have a male plug or plug with pins, as it is emulating DTE. Consequently, the conversion cable will require a male DB25 plug for connection to the PC port. Many companies, such as Black Box Catalog, offer these conversion cables. The purpose of these cables is to allow a standard printer to be connected to an IBM PC parallel port. The pin assignments at the DB25 connector on the port are shown in Figure 6-24.

From this you can see that the pin numbers of the DB25 do not equal the pins laid out in the Centronics standard discussion. Consequently, these pins will have to be connected to the appropriate leads at the other end of the cable within

DB25 Pin #	Function
1	Strobe
2	Data bit 0
3	Data bit 1
4	Data bit 2
5	Data bit 3
6	Data bit 4
7	Data bit 5
8	Data bit 6
9	Data bit 7
10	Acknowledge
11	Busy
12	Paper end (out of paper)
13	Select
14	Auto feed
15	Error
16	Initialize printer (reset)
17	Select input
18-25	Ground

Figure 6-24 IBM parallel port pinout

```
DB25                    Amphenol
 1  ─────────────────  1
 2  ─────────────────  2
 3  ─────────────────  3
 4  ─────────────────  4
 5  ─────────────────  5
 6  ─────────────────  6
 7  ─────────────────  7
 8  ─────────────────  8
 9  ─────────────────  9
10  ───────────────── 10
11  ───────────────── 11
12  ───────────────── 12
13  ───────────────── 13
14  ───────────────── 14
15  ───────────────── 32
16  ───────────────── 31
17  ───────────────── 36
18  ───────────────── 33
19  ───────────────── 19
20  ───────────────── 21
22  ───────────────── 25
23  ───────────────── 27
24  ───────────────── 29
25  ───────────────── 30
```

Figure 6-25 Black Box PCPA cable configuration

the Amphenol connector. The Black Box Catalog cable is termed PCPA (Personal Computer Printer Adapter). The crossover of the pins in the cable are laid out in Figure 6-25. Different lengths of cable are available between the DB25 and Amphenol connectors, which must be specified when ordered. Consult Appendix D for a complete list of the Centronics interface with associated lead functions and directions.

Printing Operations: Once the printer is cabled to the PC, the printer may be accessed by application programs using appropriate LPT addresses and commands under DOS. The operator of the PC may activate the printer in one of two ways directly under DOS commands. In the lower right-hand side of the IBM keyboard near the Enter key is a key labeled PrtSc. When held down in conjunction with the shift key, this key causes the printer to print whatever is on the screen at the time. Even if the printer cannot be heard or seen, the operator can watch the screen as an underline character travels across and down the screen, indicating that the data are going out the port for the printer. If this underline character is not present, chances are that something is wrong at the interface. Should continuous printing be desired, hold the PrtSc and Ctrl keys down simultaneously. This causes a print on-line action, where anything entered on the keyboard will be printed once the enter key is depressed.

Parallel Breakout Box: Should the user desire to monitor the interaction of the pins in the Centronics parallel interface, the Black Box Catalog offers a tool for this known as the SAM+Centronics. This Status Activity Monitor is a breakout box which is also very useful to the technician who is attempting to connect any printer to an IBM LPT port. The SAM+, also available in an RS-232 version, allows for viewing the individual leads of the interface. This breakout box offers lamps for important leads in three of the four interface categories: data, control, and timing. With these lights the lead interaction may be monitored for a complete understanding of the interactions necessary for data exchange from the PC to a printer.

The unit, pictured in Figure 6-26, has two Amphenol sockets together with a parallel cable for placing it in-line betweeen the computer and the printer. The SAM+Centronics requires a power supply of +5 volts (V) on pin 18 for operation. This means that either the IBM or the printer must have a lead outputting this voltage. The parallel port on the IBM Monochrome Display and Printer Adapter does not supply a 5-V power supply on the interface, so the printer documentation should be checked when using the breakout box in this PC environment. For example, the Toshiba P1350 and Printonix MVP 150B printers both supply +5 V on the interface for powering such devices. The ground leads 14, 16, and 17 may need to be tied together for proper operation of the debugging tool. Should neither the PC nor the printer supply +5 V, an alternative power source must be used to provide the current. A short-term solution could be to connect a 9-V battery to the breakout device. The positive voltage goes to pin 18 while the return post of the

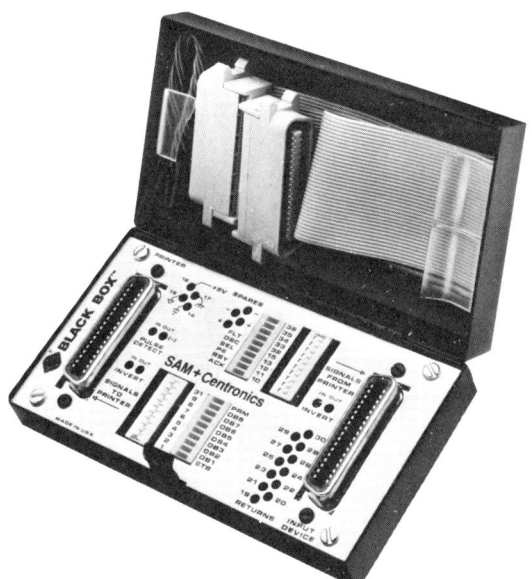

Figure 6-26 Black Box Catalog Centronics break-out box

battery should be connected to pins 16 and 14 on the breakout box. Other variable power supplies may be used to provide +5 V connected in the same manner. The unit will then display the status of the activity on the interface.

If the proper leads are present between the PC and the printer, the interactions will be viewable. The interaction between the IBM 80 CPS Dot Matrix printer and the IBM PC was monitored for the lead statuses. When the printer is in the idle state or not receiving data, the strobe (1), acknowledge (10), select (13), prime or reset (31), and fault (32) lamps are lit, indicating that they are high. Once data transmission starts, the printer accepts one line of data, then raises the busy signal (11) to halt the PC's transmission temporarily while the printer prints a line of data. Then the busy lead is lowered, allowing the PC to transmit another line of data. Games can be played with the interface by shorting out various control signals. Connecting pin 17, ground, to the reset lead, pin 31, will cause the PC to stop transmitting data. Grounding out pin 10, the acknowledge lead, for greater than 5 microseconds will also halt transmission. This is important to know for nonstandard parallel implementations. If pin 10 is not provided on the printer, select the lead that temporarily goes low to indicate that data have been received or a lead that remains high/on until an error condition has occurred. Jumper this lead to pin 10 for your flow-control mechanism. Should experimentation of lead jumpering be required, a separate unit such as Black Box's BOB Centronics or BOB-PCPA should be purchased. Either of these units allows the experimentor or technician to try variations of a cable until a working version is perfected. Once obtained, a matching permanent cable should be constructed to correspond to the final pin configuration and crossovers. Both of these units allow for building of specific parallel cables, with the PCPA having one Amphenol and one DB25 connector instead of two Amphenols, as included with the BOB-Centronics. These tools are very useful for learning or implementing the Centronics parallel interface of the PC and associated printers. They can save many hours of frustration. If a battery was used to power the SAM+ unit, disconnect it when finished, as the unit will eventually drain the juice.

Acquiring Parallel Interfaces: Parallel ports may be acquired in a number of ways. Acquisition of the IBM Monochrome Display and Printer Adapter or the California Computer Systems Supervision's 132-column display board provides a single Centronics port in addition to monitor functions. Dedicated parallel printer adapters are also available, but more popular are multifunction boards, providing among other facilities a parallel printer interface. An example of this is the AST SixPakPlus Memory Expansion and I/O card. In addition to a parallel printer port, a clock-calendar, a RS-232 serial port, additional memory, and a game adapter port are also available. Another offering is the Quadram Corporation Quadboard, which contains an RS-232 asynchronous port, up to 256K of memory, a clock-calendar, and a Centronics parallel interface port. These are only a few of the popular multifunction boards offering parallel interfaces. Consult Appendix H for a list of many more such boards.

A word of caution: Many of these boards were developed in the DOS 1.0 and 1.1 time frames. The significance of this stems from the fact that only one parallel port could be addressed under these operating systems. With DOS 2.0, two more ports are available. If more than one parallel port is planned, ensure that the port address on the board is switch-selectable. If this option exists, the user has the flexibility of increasing the number of parallel attached devices to a single PC. Refer to Chapter 9 for alternatives to this limitation. However, the user should be aware of this potential conflict.

RAM Buffer: Most of the multifunction boards offering additional memory for the PC include a disk containing useful utility programs. Emulation of a hard disk is possible by RAM disk programs that turn some of the PC's memory into an electronic disk for high-speed access. Of more importance to the printer, however, is the inclusion of software spooling or buffering packages. In the printer option discussion the use of buffers as an add-on piece of hardware allowed for improved throughput. This improvement was possible because the PC dumped the data to the buffer at the fastest rate practical. This freed the PC for other tasks while the printer chugged away at its own pace. The add-on option is not the only method of obtaining buffers for the printer. Multifunction boards offering both increased memory space and a parallel interface also provide a solution to the slow printer problem. A software program usually accompanies the board, allowing the user to allocate a certain amount of the extra memory as a buffer for the printer. This print spooler uses the PC's main memory, RAM, to store data temporarily and feed it to the printer at whatever speed the printer can accept it. These spooling packages are often limited to the parallel port, disregarding the possible use of a serial printer. However, some of these software packages are quite elaborate. For example, SuperSpool from AST Research is a program included with the SixPakPlus discussed earlier. SuperSpool provides buffered output to either the serial or parallel port with user-defined buffer sizes. In addition to the basic buffering function, keyboard commands are offered to stop and restart printing, print the previous page, and alter the number of lines per page. The setup of this spooler is straightforward via programs on the disk. For example, the SUPERSPL LPT1/U = 128/M command spools printer output to LPT1, reserving 128K for the PC. All remaining memory is used, as for the spool buffer. This must be configured each time the system is powered on. The easiest way to accomplish this is to enter this command into the autoexec.bat file on your disk. Consult the DOS manual for methods of creating the autoexec.bat file, which executes automatically when the disk is booted. For it to function, however, you must include the SUPERSPL program on the same disk as the autoexec file. Programs such as this included with multifunction boards are an efficient means of increasing the throughput of the PC by freeing it up.

Standalone Buffer: In addition to the PC's RAM print spooler and the built-in printer buffer, a stand-alone unit may be purchased to provide this function. Many of the RAM spoolers of the multifunction boards do not support serial printers. These stand-alone boxes overcome this disadvantage by supporting either serial or parallel interfaces. They may accept parallel input from the PC and transfer the data to the printer through a serial interface, or vice versa. These buffer boxes are flexible in that they may be shared between multiple PCs and printers. Furthermore, they grow with the user when the computer or printer must be upgraded, as they are not an integral part of either. Black Box Catalog offers such a unit, called the Mini-Print Spooler (MPS), shown in Figure 6-27. This spooler is microprocessor-controlled with memory expandable from 16K to 64K. Because of the inherent logic, it is control-panel-operated, allowing reprinting of a page, multiple copies, and a temporary halting of printing. Multiple speeds are selectable if using one or more serial interfaces. Furthermore, the serially interfaced port(s) support XON/XOFF or ETX/ACK protocols in addition to hardware handshaking, with each port independently selectable. If the PC is using a serial interface with the printer supporting a Centronics interface, the busy, acknowledge, and fault handshaking signals are supported on the parallel side. Refer to the earlier parallel and serial sections for clarification of the various flow-control techniques. This unit may be connected between either the COM# or LPT# ports of the IBM PC and a printer with either a parallel or a serial interface. If the same interfaces are used on the PC and printer, with the buffer box to be positioned between the two units, ensure that the printer

Figure 6-27 Print Spooler

can transfer data directly to the printer before placing the spooler between the two. This aids in the installation of the box by immediately isolating any potential problems. Refer to the optimization section below for specific uses of such units in both serial and parallel environments.

Optimization Devices: The connection, optioning, and setup of printers, modems, and networks has hopefully given the reader a better understanding of aspects associated with connecting the IBM PC to peripherals. This section will equip the reader with several alternatives for optimizing various configurations.

Many of these optimizations can be used to reduce overall expenditures on hardware of an IBM PC/XT setup or network. However, many of them are the only alternatives to users who have no more device addresses available. For example, DOS 1.0 and 1.1 provide for only one serial device address, AUX or COM1, and one Centronics parallel port address, LPT1 or PRN. Depending on the environment, these ports can be used up rather quickly. For example, a PC configuration including a modem and dot matrix printer is not uncommon for a significant number of the installed PCs. If the PC is running DOS 1.1, all the reserved device names, COM1 and LPT1, are then taken up. If the user also desires a letter-quality printer, it cannot be connected and addressed as a separate device. The user must disconnect the dot matrix printer and then connect the letter-quality printer. DOS 2.0 adds COM2, LPT2, and LTP3 for more addressing flexibility and expansion. However, with the use of a modem and a mouse (serial), all serial-addressable ports are used. Should a serially interfaced plotter or a different high-speed modem be desired, they cannot be operated without disconnecting one of the other devices. Both economical and physical address reasons dictate the need for a means of sharing a port among multiple devices.

Switches: Several devices exist to solve the address and cost problems. These units are switches, units that connect multiple devices together by the mere flick of a finger. These devices include computers, printers, and modems, among others. A single computer connected to a switch can access both a dot matrix and letter-quality printer with a single DOS device address. A similar switch could allow a computer to share both a modem and printer in the same fashion. Two computers can share the same printer or multiple printers. Many possibilities exist for switches, as they are available in both serial and parallel versions. Some of them are activated manually, whereas others accept control characters for software control.

Parallel Switches: One such unit is the Intra Computer Printer Switch, shown in Figure 6-28. This switch allows the IBM PC to be physically connected

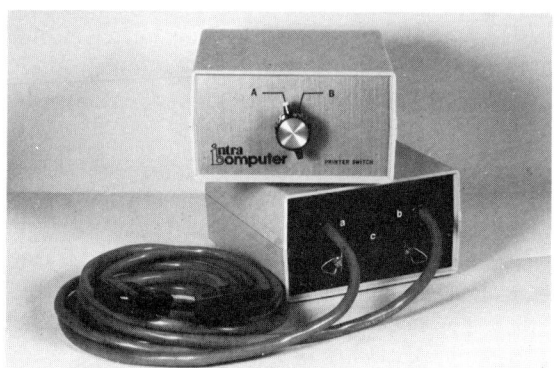

Figure 6-28 IntraComputer Parallel Printer Switch

to two devices simultaneously using a parallel interface. An Amphenol connector on the box back plane is to be connected to the IBM PC. This requires a conversion between the DB25 connector on the computer board and the Centronics socket connector on the box. Black Box Catalog's PCPA cable can be used for this purpose. Extending from the back of the printer switch are two cables with Amphenol plugs for connection to the devices to be shared. Once connected, the two peripherals may be referred to as device A or B, corresponding to the cables attached. The switch on the front panel switches between the two devices. The two devices may be connected to the PC, which is termed the C device. These switches will often be termed ABC switches because of the foregoing relation. ABCDE switches are also available to allow the PC access to four devices. These parallel ABC switches allow for extensions to the DOS physical address limitations. In addition, a single LPT port can be used for multiple devices, resulting in cost savings for hardware computer boards.

Serial ABC Switches: The parallel ABC switches described above satisfy the parallel interface requirements. Units supporting serial interfaces are also available. RS-232 switches were actually the predecessors of the Centronics switches. The generic name "ABC switch" is used because of the Centronics addition, but early boxes were called *EIA switches,* as they switched EIA RS-232 devices. Black Box Catalog offers a variety of ABC switches, both parallel and serial. In addition to both an ABC and an ABCDE switch, they offer an X Switch. Their serial ABC switches function in the same manner as the aforementioned parallel switches. They share a single PC port among two or four devices with serial interfaces. Also, four PCs can share a single modem or printer. However, their X Switch allows two computers to share two devices. This switch is important if two PCs are to share both a dot matrix printer and a letter-quality printer. Alternatively, they could share different modems or a printer and a modem. As with ABC switches, many combinations exist for such units.

Chap. 6   Connecting Printers to the IBM

One factor to consider is the number of leads that are supported through the switch. Some serial switches may switch all 25 leads of the RS-232 standard. Others may not pass all leads, supporting only the leads used in most asynchronous environments. In this case hardware flow control must be considered, as pins 11 and 19 are not necessary leads that are supported. This may not be as big a problem as it seems if the null-modem cable with flow-control leads is properly placed. Consult Chapter 9 for proper placement of cables. If the unit is to be used in a synchronous configuration, more leads must be specified when the unit is ordered, as pins 15, 17, and 24 must be supported for timing. The only other factor with which a user should be concerned is the gender of the connectors on the boxes, as they may dictate the purchase of more cables. This is of concern only when users desire to use cables already in their possession.

Code-Activated Switch: Another useful switch is similar in concept to the switches above except that it is code-activated. Instead of having to throw a switch manually to select a particular device, a code is transmitted to perform the same function. For example, a "Control T 1" would select the port connected to a printer, while a "Control T 2" could select the modem also connected to the switch. This is extremely important, as the switch does not have to be located near the PC user for a manual throwing of the switch. In some regards these units may be considered to provide a local area network function, as they allow sharing of devices. A number of vendors offer such units, including Black Box Catalog and Advanced Systems Concepts, Inc. ASCI offers a unit known as the ASCI switch (see Figure 6-29). Model APOS-11 connects one peripheral or computer to four. Two modes are supported. The automatic mode allows software selection of the ports. The manual override mode allows the ports to be turned on or off selectively via switches on the front panel. The pins that are switched are 2 to 6, 8, 17, 19, and 20, in addition to supporting the ground leads, 1 and 7. A Centronics parallel version is available that switches 25 leads.

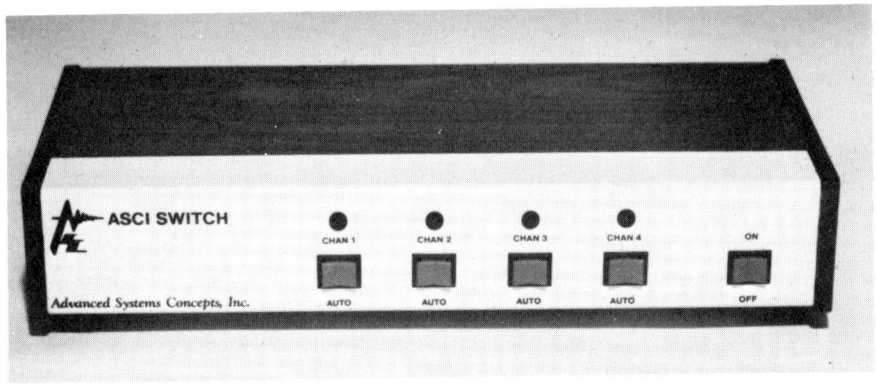

Figure 6-29   Advanced Systems Concept's Code-Activated Switch

Printer Options: The preceding sections covered the physical connections of the peripherals, usually printers, to the PC. The use of serial interfaces, Centronics parallel ports, breakout boxes, and other tools has been described in great detail. The final aspect of interfacing peripherals to the IBM PC is the option settings. No matter how perfectly the cables are configured, or how well the configuration is optimized, if the options are not set properly, the user can expect nothing but grief. The user needs to be familiar with the main options to understand the proper settings. The following sections describe each option with the various possible settings, followed by a discussion of each as it relates to interfacing equipment.

Speed: The port speed of both devices should be consistent to prevent data from being garbled. If the maximum rate of operation for a printer is 300 bps, the device sending data to the printer must also be set at 300 bps. If both devices can transmit and receive at 9600, set them both at 9600 bps. The speed of transmission through an RS-232 port becomes extremely important when a printer is involved, due to the aspects of buffering and flow control. Refer to the flow-control option for further clarification. This option is nonexistent in a parallel interface, as all bits are transferred at once.

Flow Control: Flow control, discussed in this chapter and in Chapter 3, involves the regulation of data transferred between two devices. Improper setting of this option could cause data to be lost, garbled, or not transmitted at all. Data flow must be regulated between devices, specifically the PC and a printer or plotter. Even though both devices' transmission speeds are set the same, the speed of operation differs. The printer, because it is partially mechanical, may have a printing speed substantially less than the transmission speed, while the PC has the capability of transmitting at a much higher speed. Because of this, either the data must be buffered for delayed printing or flow control must occur to regulate when a printer is capable of receiving more data. For example, if the transmission speed is 4800 bps and each character has 10 bits, 480 cps are being transmitted by the computer (4800 divided by 10). However, the printer may be capable of printing only 100 cps. In these cases, flow control may be used to ensure that no loss of data occurs. Choices for flow control usually involve either XON/XOFF, ETX/ACK, ENQ/ACK, or hardware via one of the RS-232 pins. As discussed earlier, XON/XOFF is a software flow-control method in which characters are transmitted to indicate the status of the printer's condition. ETX/ACK and ENQ/ACK are similar in concept to XON/XOFF. The connection of pins such as pins 4, 11, 19, and 20 to a required input signal at the computer is termed *hardware flow control*. Flow control, used in conjunction with a buffer in the PC or printer, makes for a very efficient operation at maximum transmission speeds. With or without a buffer, flow control offers a means of overcoming the relatively slow operational speed of a printer. The important aspect is that both ports are configured for the same flow-control method, software and/or hardware. With the IBM PC, unlike some other computers, software flow control is totally up to the software in the PC itself. Although other computers incorporate this into the I/O board itself, the PC does not. This places the user at a disadvantage because you never know what to expect. The reason for this is that the system printer for the PC is parallel, with its own hardware flow control. It is only when a printer with a serial interface is being used that this potential problem arises. The author usually constructs a cable that supports hardware flow control, but also connects pins 2 and 3 between the printer and PC to support software flow control.

Parity: Any of the parity types discussed in Chapter 2 are acceptable. Simply be consistent at both ends to prevent the garbling of data.

Character Length: Another factor causing garbled data is the variation in character lengths. For example, there is 7- and 8-bit ASCII. Regardless of the code, if parity is involved, determine if the character-length option includes the parity bit, and option accordingly at both ends. Be consistent.

Number of Stop Bits: Ensure that the same stop bit length is selected at both ends. Check this option if garbled data appear sporadically. Chapter 2 describes the function of the stop bits. The selections are generally 1, 1.5, or 2. Choose the same number for both ends of the configuration.

Mode: Generally, three modes of operation are available: simplex, half-duplex, full-duplex. Selection should be consistent, as this option could determine which RS-232 signals are generated or monitored by a port. For example, if a printer is optioned for simplex mode (receive-only), pin 4 may not be generated. In a null-modem cable, this pin may be crossed to pin 8 at the computer end. If the computer requires pin 8 to be on before it will transmit, data transmission will never occur. Choose the mode that fits the environment, and option both ends accordingly.

Echoplex: This option refers to the displaying of characters. Echoplex is closely related to the half- and full-duplex modes, and the terms are often used interchangeably by vendors to describe options. Some terminals have the option of either displaying characters locally as they are typed or leaving this up to the far end. The PC may be optioned not to display the characters until they are "echoed" back from the far end, even though they are typed on the keyboard. If the far end is to echo the characters back to the originating device, this is termed *echoplexing*. By its very nature of operation, echoplexing implies that data will be both transmitted and received simultaneously (full-duplex). This option becomes important when communication software or terminal emulation software is run on the PC. For example, if the PC is connected to a remote computer that is optioned for echoplexing, a character typed at the keyboard is not displayed until the remote computer transmits it back. If you think of this in RS-232 terms, the characters that leave on pin 2, transmit data, are not displayed until they are received on pin 3, received data. This may be used as a form of error detection. If the character displayed is not the same as the one typed, chances are that a parity error has occurred. The PC operator can then backspace and retype the character.

The device that is to echo the characters should be optioned for echoplexing. As indicated, echoplexing is often confused with the duplexes. If a character such as A is typed, and appears on the terminal as AA, the far end is echoplexing while the PC software is set up for local displaying of the characters as they are typed. Sometimes this is the half-duplex option. Half-duplex in this environment means that the PC is generating the typed character locally. This, in conjunction with the far-end echoplexing, produces the double vision. To alleviate the problem, change the PC software to full-duplex or the remote device to no echoplexing. If, on the other hand, after an A is typed, nothing appears, the PC software is probably optioned for full-duplex while the far end is not set up to echoplex. Change to half-duplex locally or enable echoplexing at the far end to resolve the problem. Because they may not always be used interchangeably, the duplexes and echoplexing, as used in your devices, should be thoroughly understood for proper optioning.

Line Feeds: This option generally offers three choices: 0, 1, or 2. Coordination between the two devices is in order to allow proper spacing on a terminal or printer. Generally, the devices may be optioned to perform a line feed upon the occurrence of a carriage return. If the PC transmits a carriage return to a printer, the device will perform line feeds according to this option. An option of 0 in this circumstance will produce overwriting on the same line, as no vertical spacing takes place. If 1 is selected, single spacing will occur. Double spacing can be accomplished by selecting 2. Care should be taken in that the computer may already transmit a line feed together with a carriage return. In summary, if unwanted spacing occurs, this option should be checked.

Transmission Mode: Three choices are generally available for this option: asynchronous, synchronous, or isochronous. *Asynchronous* implies that start and stop bits are required for timing purposes. In an asynchronous environment, be sure to check the number of stop-bit options. *Synchronous* transmission involves the use of clocks to transmit the data. Option one of the devices in a synchronous environment to provide the timing and check that the proper leads are present in the cables. The third choice is *isochronous,* which is a combination of the other two. Data in an asynchronous format are transmitted synchronously. Ensure that both ends have the same option.

Polarity: Polarity has to do with whether a signal is positive or negative. The importance of polarity is generally realized in the area of hardware flow control. For example, if pin 19 is used for the busy signal, a option may exist for the signal on pin 19 to be either positive or negative when the buffer of the device has room available for more data. A determination should be made as to the transmitting devices's requirements. If the transmitting device requires a positive voltage on the

Chap. 6   Connecting Printers to the IBM   133

busy signal to enable transmission, as the PC does, option the printer (or receiving device) to generate a positive, or true, signal. Some devices require the reverse or a negative signal for this; however, a positive indication is used with the IBM. Option accordingly.

Interfaces: This generally exists because some printers offer one or more variations as a standard feature. For example, it is possible that both a parallel and a serial interface may be available on the machine. It is more likely, however, that only one of them comes as a standard feature. The addition of the other is possible, but this disables the factory-installed interface. An example is the Epson FX-80 printer. A Centronics parallel interface comes with the printer. Should an RS-232 interface be desired, the option must be purchased separately. Practical Peripherals, Inc. offers a serial board which plugs onto the motherboard of the Epson printer. Once installed, the parallel interface is disabled. Thus no option has to be set to disable the parallel interface, as must be done on some printers. Another interface often comes standard if a serial interface is included on the printer. This interface, known as *current loop*, is declining in popularity. Once prevalent because of limited electronic component requirements, current loop has taken a back seat to RS-232. However, this interface is generally offered as an option, as it uses the same DB25 connector as the RS-232 interface. The IBM Asynchronous Communication Adapter offers support for either RS-232 or current loop, both using the DB25 connector for attachment to a printer. Whether the current loop, RS-232, or Centronics parallel interface is to be used, ensure that the option setting in the printer matches the option on the PC port to which it is connected.

On-Line/Off-Line: This is a rather straightforward option, as it determines the condition of the printer upon power-up. If the switches are set for on-line, the printer is immediately ready to receive data once power is applied. The converse places the printer in an off-line mode and must be manually placed in on-line mode before data reception can occur.

Lines/Characters Per Inch: The standard typewriter permits six lines per inch. Many printers allow this number to be increased to eight. If standard $8\frac{1}{2}$- by 11-inch paper is used, 88 lines are possible rather than the standard 66. This satisfies the vertical expansion, but what about the horizontal spacing or pitch? A feature prominent in dot matrix printers is shrinking or compression of the print. The standard dimensions are 10 cpi. Dot matrix printers allow a switch to be set that permanently squeezes more than 10 cpi. Typical options are 10, 12, and 17.1 cpi. Either of these may be selected, but there is an alternative to the hardware switch selection. Software control codes are supported for altering the pitch temporarily. These codes are used to shrink the print size, to change printer fonts to italics, and to enable double striking, among other options. Consult Appendix E for a list by printer of control codes and their functions. With this feature in mind, it is generally desirable to set the hardware switch to the standard 10 cpi and use the control sequences within the application programs executing on the PC to alter the default. Most applications offer a printer setup feature. Use the control sequences in this portion of the application if shrinkage of the number of characters or lines per inch is desired.

Wraparound: If your printer is limited to 80-column printing and lines of 132-column length are being output to the printer, disaster may occur if this option is not correctly set. Enabling of the wraparound feature would cause the remaining 52 characters to print on the next line. Disabling it would cause the printer either to print these last 52 characters in the eightieth-column position or to overwrite the first 52 characters of the same line. Some printers may merely disregard any characters over 80. Spreadsheets can be prime offenders of this if wraparound is not enabled. Another means of avoiding this is to shrink the print, as discussed earlier. Shrinking the print to 17.1 cpi allows 132 colmns to be squeezed into the 8 inches of an 80-column format. This is calculated by multiplying 8 inches times 17.1 characters per inch, yielding approximately 136 columns. Should this length be exceeded, wraparound would still be a worthwhile feature.

Page Length: Page or form length is an option useful for informing the printer as to the length of the paper being used. This setting is generally available to the user without removal of the printer cover in the form of a thumbwheel or switch on the front panel of the printer. Selection of a length allows the printer to know the location of the boundaries of the paper. Once selected, generally the top of the form has to be positioned for a complete setting. Align the paper and then set the top of form by either pushing a button on the front panel or by powering the printer off, then back on. Either of these actions generally establishes the top of the form, from which the printer bases its page length. It will use this option setting when form feeds are issued.

SUGGESTED READINGS

1. *IBM Technical Reference,* Publ. 6025005, pp. 1-91 to 1-130, and 1-223 to 1-250.
2. Black Box Catalog, January 1984 catalog.
3. *RS-232 Made Easy,* by Martin D. Seyer, Prentice-Hall, Inc., Englewood Cliffs, NJ, 1984.
4. *PC Magazine,* "A Plentitude of Printers, Part I," pp. 284–320, Vol. 2, No. 5, October 1983.
5. *PC Magazine,* "A Plentitude of Printers, Part II," pp. 621–630, Vol. 2, No. 6, November 1983.
6. *PC Magazine,* "Putting It on Paper with the PC," pp. 257–272, Vol. 2, No. 5, October 1983.
7. *Mini-Micro Systems,* "Impact Matrix Printers Reach for Daisy Quality," pp. 145–160, Vol. XVI, No. 1, January 1983.

8. *Printronix MVP 150B User's Reference Guide,* Doc. 110856 (B), 1983.
9. *Toshiba P1350 High Quality Printer Owner's Manual,* Publ. 72R115770 A.
10. *Okidata Pacemark 2410 Operator's Manual,* Publ. 59206301.
11. *Epson FX-80 Printer User's Manual,* Publ. 8294014.
12. *IBM Disk Operating System,* Publ. 6024061, pp. 6-13 and 6-109 to 6-116.
13. *Data Communications,* "The Indispensible Breakout Box," pp. 121–124, Vol. 12, No. 9, September 1983.

CHAPTER

7

miscellaneous

IBM peripherals

and

their connections

Connections to the PC up to this point involved either serial or parallel interfaces. Printers could be connected through either serial or parallel interfaces, with many ways of obtaining these types of ports. Modems could be added either as plug-in boards or as stand-alone units through an RS-232 port. A number of other peripherals for the IBM PC/XT exist but do not fall into the printer or modem category. They may or may not be connected in a standard fashion. This chapter describes other items that augment a PC installation. In particular, these peripherals will include power protection units, game paddles, plotters, and monitors. Alternative data entry methods, including different keyboards, bar code and magnetic stripe readers, and the use of a mouse are also covered.

AC Noise and Spike Suppressors: Before acquiring a PC, most users probably did not pay much attention to a small factor known as electricity. However, once the PC was plugged in, the user may have experienced a flickering of the monitor. If in the home, this may occur as your spouse prepares leftovers in the microwave oven. At the office the nuisance correlates directly with the kicking on of the air conditioner of heater. Should this begin to interfere with your successful operation of the PC, equipment to alleviate the problems should be considered. The interference from various sources involves electrical noise, voltage dips, spikes from lightning, or power surges. Depending on their severity, noise and interference factors could destroy the precious data that the user has been working with on the PC. Generally, the interference is through the ac power outlet and the phone line, or the RS-232 connector, which could involve the other two.

The various protectors for these nuisances generally have a common goal. That is to rid the user of the concern for loss of data due to power-related problems. If the ac power source is a problem, surge protectors are available to cure the problem. Also known as noise suppressors, these units are extremely valuable in industrial environments. Furthermore, lightning storms are the major cause of these power-line disturbances affecting your PC. The areas of high risk in the United States are Florida, Louisiana, Colorado, and parts of Texas. These problems are not limited to buisness environments. They may occur in the home. Simple hand tools, small appliances, fluorescent lights, and microwave ovens may all produce annoying and perhaps costly interference. Some of the noises in the home are not totally suppressible. As a matter of fact, the author was raised in a family of eight children; the best noise suppressors in such environments are headphones. Beyond these types of noises, the suppressors serve as filtering devices for strange variations in the power source. The goal is to maintain a constant level of power throughput to the PC. These units are plugged into the ac outlet with the PC and other peripherals are plugged into the noise suppressor. With these devices plugged in-line, the glitches of lightning-related spikes, dirty power, and electrical noise are kept from extending to the PC.

As with most PC-related products, the user has an array of devices from which to select. What appears to be an easy decision perhaps deserves more careful insight. Some units may offer spike protection but allow high-frequency noise to pass through. Some units may not be able to handle repeated voltage spikes, protecting your PC only from the initial spike. The reason for this is that the unit may require time to settle before it can accept the next hit. Single- and multiple-outlet suppressors are available. Depending on the PC with peripheral configuration, multiple suppressors may be required. The peripherals used with the PC may generate some interference, so a two-way protection unit may be desired.

Depending on the environment, all or a portion of these factors may be applicable. Units are available from Electronic Specialists, Inc. for commercial environments, including the home, office, and small businesses. Their ISO-1 and ISO-2 offer multiple isolated channels. Each of the channels includes multiple outlets for use with all the PC's peripherals. Industrial-grade isolators are offered for the factory, shop, or classroom setups. Models ISO-3 and ISO-11 are used for those environments that potentially have greater suppression requirements.

Phone-Line Suppressors: In addition to the ac-related problems, occasionally phone-line pollution can cause the same effects as those mentioned above. This is usually the outcome of a storm-induced high-voltage spike, radio transmitter interference, or even the phone company equipment in their central office. If this is to be avoided, Electronic Specialists has a Kleen Line series for modem and data protection. Model PDS-11/SFK plugs into the ac outlet with the modem plugging into the PDS. The modem's phone line connections plugs into the box through a modular jack. Then the modular jack protruding from the PDS is connected to the RJ-11 jack in the wall. RJ-11 is a jack with four leads of the type found in homes throughout the country. Another version is available for the RJ-45 series jacks used in some office environments. Should filtering of an RS-232 interface be needed, the Black Box Catalog offers a surge protector designed to protect equipment using serial interfaces from surges or power changes that could cause power failure interference.

Back-Up Power Supplies: Power inconsistencies are nuisances for PC owners because of their potential altering of the data in the computer's memory or the affect on disk-drive use. But what about environments where total power outages are common? Certain applications involving the PC are of such a sensitive nature that data simply cannot be lost. In the case of potential brownouts or total blackouts, products should be used to provide auxiliary power to the PC and perhaps its peripherals. Generally, backup power units consist of a battery and inverters that convert dc voltage to the 120 V ac required by the PC. These power supplies are generally of two types. One is a standby unit that recharges as the normal ac power is on. This unit is switched into use automatically when needed with only a few

Chap. 7   Miscellaneous IBM Peripherals and Their Connections   139

milliseconds of delay. The other is an uninterruptible power supply that is switched in at all times with no delays should the ac be lost. Only a few factors must be considered during acquisition. The length of time the unit will provide power is usually the primary concern. Other factors include the battery life and the delay when switching in the reserve power supply. Topaz Electronics Division offers the Source 2 series, which provides up to 60 minutes of power after an ac failure.

Alternative Keytops: The aforementioned units were used to restrict the input of unwanted data into the PC. What about data that are to be entered into the PC? Are there alternatives to the IBM keyboard? Some PC owners were users of other personal computers or terminals that offered a more friendly feeling in the keyboard. For example, the Enter key is of nonstandard size and slightly out of place. Depending on the speed of the typists, the Shift key was like hitting a moving target. Should the user be unable to adjust to the new keyboard feel, the Hooleon Company offers a solution. They have the TOUCHDOWN series of keytops to enlarge the Backspace, Return/Enter, Shift, Tab, O/Ins, Ctrl, and Alt keys to the normal expected size. These enhance the existing IBM PC/XT keyboard. Should emulation software be running on the IBM as discussed in Chapter 2, there is no need for the user to suffer from keyboard-mania as Hooleon also offers terminal-specific keytops. If the PC is emulating a 5251 display station, a 3270 series terminal, or a 5291 mainframe terminal, TOUCHDOWN allows the user to adapt quickly to the PC keyboard. This is an inexpensive method of adjusting the keyboard. These sets cost about $20 and are easily installed; they are merely pressed down over the existing keys.

Keyboards: Should the PC keyboard totally disorient the user, Key Tronic Corporation offers a plug-compatible keyboard, Model KB5150, with familiar key legends rather than mere symbols. The Shift and Return keys are in the familiar typewriter locations. There is never a question of whether or not the lock keys are on. The Shift Lock and Numeric Lock keys have LED indicator lights for status. There is even a deluxe version offering functions keys across the top of the keyboard with additional cursor positioning keys. These keyboards plug into the standard port on the back of the PC reserved for the keyboard.

Mouse: The keyboard of the PC offers a common input mechanism familiar to most users. However, the evolution of application programs is bringing about alternative means for quicker input of data. The most recent addition for keyboard alternatives is the introduction of the mouse. The mouse is an adjunct unit connected to the PC in one of two ways. The concept is a simple one, allowing speedy cursor positioning and selection. Typically used with menu-driven applications, the mouse's operation is that of a ball being rolled around for cursor movement. Once properly positioned, a button is depressed on the mouse for actual selection of the item. Some units require the use of a separate pad for mouse movement, whereas others need merely a coarse surface. The full benefit of these devices has not yet been

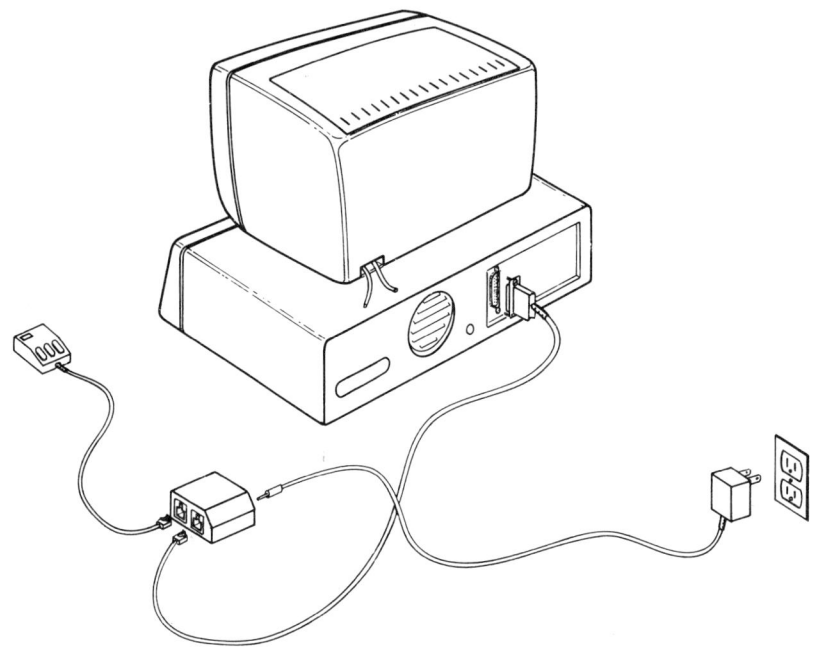

Figure 7-1 Mouse Systems PC Mouse

realized, but they are becoming increasingly popular with spreadsheets and word processing systems.

There are two methods of connecting the mouse to the PC/XT. One is with an RS-232 cable for connection to a serial port provided by the ACA or a multi-function board. For example, Mouse Systems offers the PC Mouse, shown in Figure 7-1. The PC Mouse connects to the PC through an RS-232 port. The unit comes with the actual mouse, an interface box with two modular telephone jacks, a power supply adapter, and a DB25 to modular cord. The mouse and cord are plugged into the interface adapter with modular jacks. The other end of the cord is a DB25 female socket for connection to the male ACA or equivalent port. The power supply adapter is then plugged into the wall outlet and the interface box. The PC Mouse uses a pad for movement, with three buttons on the top of the mouse for selection of different functions. The mouse is addressed as either COM1 or COM2 from a software perspective. A software disk is available with patches for certain software packages and other learning aids. Because an RS-232 port is used, the optimization techniques discussed in Chapter 6 may be applied. The mouse may share the same ports as modem, printers, or plotters. Consult Chapter 6 for techniques available for typical connections.

The other method of connecting a mouse to the PC is through a special board. Generally, the mouse is directly connected to this port and is addressed as an LPT device. One such animal is the Microsoft Mouse. Microsoft's mouse is available and is fully supported with their software packages, Multiplan and Word.

Chap. 7   Miscellaneous IBM Peripherals and Their Connections   141

Bar Code Readers: Another method for rapid entry of data into the PC or XT is a bar code reader. Bar code readers are common in supermarkets as a means of rapidly entering a product's price into a computerized cash register. Each product has a product number on the label. In addition to the number, a representation of the number is encoded in the form of thin vertical bars. The bar code is read as it passes across some sort of scanner. Once the bar code is read, the cash register does a file look-up and pulls appropriate information about the product, including product name and price.

The same concept is being used in libraries to track and check out books. Each book has a bar code that can be read for various reasons. The checkout is the same as the grocery market principle. However, in some libraries the return of books causes a problem, as their proper shelf location must be identified for replacement. The same read action allows a look-up function to find the correct location. These examples are only two of the many uses of bar code readers with computers. Because of the varied uses, different bar codes are used. The Universal Product Code is generally found in supermarkets. Other codes, such as Codabar and Code 39, are also in common use. In all cases the alternative to keying in each item manually is the use of the bar code reader.

This capability is now possible with the PC, as TPS Electronics offers the PC-300 Bar Code Reader. This reader supports an array of codes, including the three just covered. Refer to Figure 7-2 for a picture of the reader. The nice feature of this bar code reader is that it does not require the use of one of the limited addresses supported in DOS. Neither serial nor parallel ports are required for

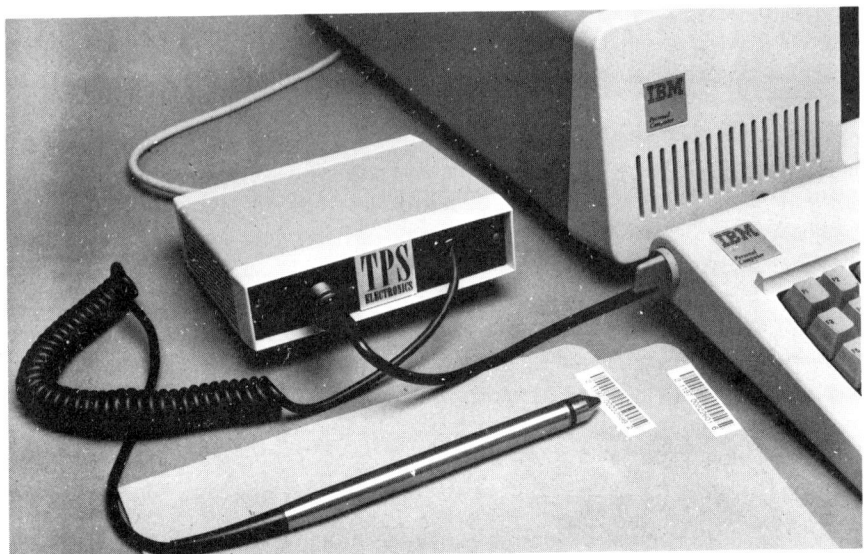

Figure 7-2   TPS Electronics PC-300 Bar Code Reader (Courtesy of TPS Electronics)

connection of the reader, making the COM# and LPT# ports available for other connections and not using up a precious slot in the computer. The PC-300 plugs directly in-line between the keyboard and the PC. The PC keyboard plugs into the TPS unit with a cord and in then plugged into the keyboard port on the back plane of the PC. A hand-held wand provides the scanning functions using an infrared optical system. Information may be rapidly read and consequently input into the PC as if the data had been entered on the keyboard. A carriage return is output after each bar code reading, signifying the end of input to the PC. No special power is needed, as it uses the same power as the PC keyboard. This addition to the PC allows for applications, including point-of-sale automation, inventory control, security identification, and many others yet to be developed.

Magnetic Card Readers: Another means of rapid entry of data is a magnetic card reader. This reader is found frequently when a consumer desires to make a purchase with a credit card. The card is run through a reader which is on-line to a database for credit verification. Another frequent use of card readers is in card entry systems. Building entry can be controlled by requiring tenants to carry cards that are read by readers to determine access. TPS Electronics PC-500 is a magnetic card reader available for connection to the IBM PC. This unit is microprocessor-controlled, yet requires no additional software for its use. As with the bar code reader the PC-500 plugs directly in-line between the IBM keyboard and the PC. It requires no special power arrangements or boards in the PC slots. The magnetic stripe reader supports all of the popular encoding standards, including Track 2, ABA, ANSI X 4.16, and ISO 3554, with other tracks available. The unit is operated by running the card through the reader, causing it to input the encoded sequence followed by a carriage return. Patches could actually be written for IBM's DOS to check for a valid card input through the reader. This could be a useful to control access to databases on a hard-disk system. Many other possiblities exist for this form of input.

Game Paddles: The final alternative to keyboard input is associated with the lighter side of the PC. The game paddle offers a form of input usable in business applications but best suited for game playing. IBM offers the Game Control Adapter for IBM-plug-compatible peripherals. Other boards, such as STB's SuperRIO multifunction boards, offer, in addition to the two serial ports, parallel port, clock, and memory, a game paddle adapter that fits either Apple or IBM game paddles. These adapters allow the use of four paddles or two joysticks. The paddles and joysticks incorporate a variable resistor that changes value as the control knob or lever is moved. The circuitry on the board then converts this movement into pulses for the software to interpret and determine the appropriate action to be reflected in the game. The game adapter connector is a 15-pin D-shell connector. Recall that these connectors resemble the letter "D" and are so named.

Monitors: One piece of gear that is often taken for granted is the user's vision of the PC's power, the monitor. Both monochrome and color monitors are available for the PC. IBM offers both types in addition to the boards that connect them to the PC. IBM provides separate boards, depending on the monitor desired, whereas other vendors offer single boards that support both monochrome and color displays. Monitor boards also offer features other than mere display capabilities, as the next sections will show. Should a monochrome monitor be desired, IBM's Monochrome Adapter provides both a Centronics parallel port and a monochrome display nine-pin interface connector. Should adaptations be necessary for non-IBM monitors, pins 1 and 2 are ground, 3 to 5 are not used, 6 is intensity, 7 is video, 8 is horizontal, and 9 is vertical signal. The screen size is 80 columns by 25 lines. Two cables are used to connect the monochrome display to the PC. One is for power, with the other plugging directly into the adapter board.

Other sources of monochrome adapter boards are available. Amdek offers its Multiple-Adapter Interface (MAI), which yields, among other features, a monochrome port. California Computer System offers the SuperVision board, giving a port for the IBM Monochrome Display, a parallel printer port, and a full-screen editor program. A nice feature found on the CCS board is the ability to display 132 columns by 44 lines of text. Terminal emulator software vendors have capitalized on this feature with their VT100 emulation software packages. One feature of a VT100 terminal not always implemented on the PC is its ability to display 132 columns of text. Persoft uses the CCS SuperVision board to fully emulate the 132-column capability available on a VT100. This is useful in programming environments but also when spreadsheets are used. As an example, Multiplan 1.06 and 1.1 both work in the 132-column mode offered by the SuperVision board. Some word processing systems and database management systems also use this feature, including Wordstar 3.3 by MicroPro International and dBASE II 2.4 from Ashton-Tate. As businesses recognize that such boards exist, demands for 132-column support will increase.

RGB Monitors: Monochrome monitors are the less expensive of the two alternatives to displaying text generated by the PC. However, color is becoming extremely popular, despite its relatively high price. The color monitors available for the PC have small but important differences between them. One of the chief differences is the clarity or resolution. The IBM Color Display is what is known as an RGB monitor, for red, green, and blue colors. This is in contrast to composite color monitors. The difference is in the form of the signals used to display information. Two signals are required by any color monitor. They are the color and synchronization signals. The purpose of the color signal should be obvious, with the synchronization signal being used to keep the color image in place. All these signals arrive mixed, requiring the monitor to separate them. During separation some of the clarity or ability to reproduce a clear, sharp image is lost. RGB has separate red, green, and blue signals. The synchronization signal is either received separately or included and separated from only one of the other color signals. The reduction in the amount of decoding allows for a better picture.

Monitors offer either 8 or 16 different colors. What determines this? The three colors, red, green, and blue, combine to form eight different colors. If a single intensity is supported by the monitor, this is the limit. If two intensities are offered, the number of colors supported doubles to 16.

The actual resolution of the monitor is ultimately determined by the number of bits of information available to display an image within a given area. Known as *dot pitch,* the smaller and closer these dots are, the higher the resolution. For example, the IBM Color Display offers 0.43-mm dot pitch. Princeton Graphics Systems offers the HX-12 color monitor with 0.31-mm dot pitch, resulting in better resolution. This monitor has a nonglare feature and may also be used with Apple computer systems that support RGB monitors.

Color/Graphics Adapter: The use of an RGB monitor requires a color board. IBM offers the Color/Graphics Adapter supporting RGB, an RF modulator for TV connection, a composite-video port, and a light-pen connector. The pins for the different ports on the board are listed in Figure 7-3. Many other vendors offer color display support, yet offer additional features on the same board. For example, Amdek offers the MAI board, yielding both color graphics and monochrome support, a parallel connector, a light-pen port, and additonal user memory. Furthermore, an erasable PROM allows easy modification of character sets for special applications or languages. Universal research offers the MultiDisplay Adaptor Card, which combines the functions of the IBM Monochrome Adapter and those of the Color/Graphics Adapter. One thing to keep in mind when acquiring a monitor and adapter board is that board manufacturers maintain a list of supported monitors. Ensure prior to purchase that the board and monitor are known to be compatible.

RGB		Light pen	
Pin	Function	Pin	Function
1	Ground	1	light pen input
2	Ground	2	not used
3	Red	3	light pen switch
4	Green	4	chassis ground
5	Blue	5	+5 volts
6	Intensity	6	+12 volts
7	Not used		
8	Horizontal		
9	Vertical		

RF modulator		Composite signal port	
Pin	Function	Pin	Function
1	+12 volts	1	Peak-to-peak amplitude
2	Not used	2	Chassis ground
3	Composite video		
4	Logic ground		

Figure 7-3 Color Graphics Adapter ports with pin assignments

Chap. 7 Miscellaneous IBM Peripherals and Their Connections 145

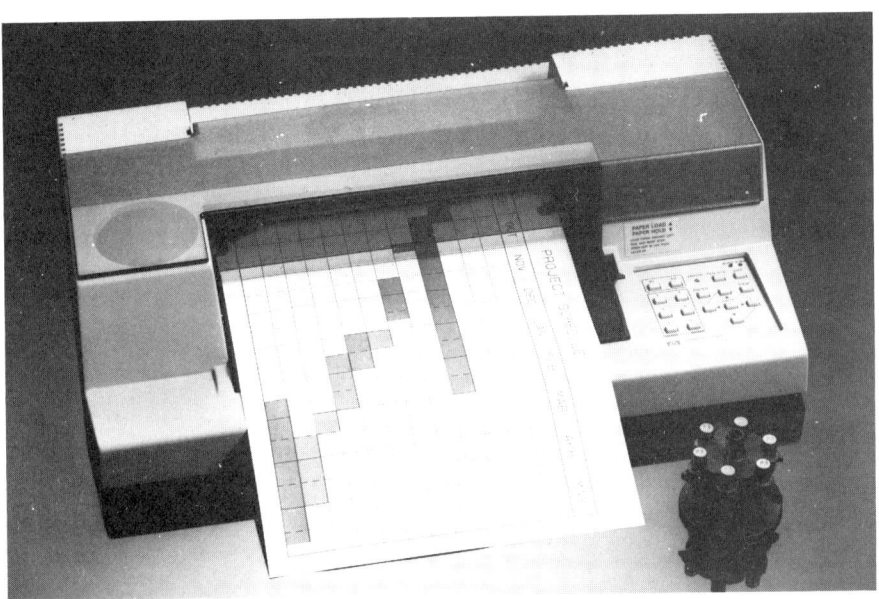

Figure 7-4 Hewlett-Packard 7475A Graphics Plotter (Courtesy of Hewlett-Packard Company)

Plotters: A hard-copy device not covered in Chapter 6 is the plotter. A plotter is a special hard-copy device for producing high-quality graphic representations. The most popular plotter systems offer multicolor printing capabilities. These units connect to the PC through either a serial or a parallel interface. The same procedures for installation and optimization outlined in Chapter 6 should be followed. Some of the major factors to consider when selecting a plotter are its ability to print a multiple-size forms, special papers such as overhead transparencies, and the variety of color pins that may be used. The standard paper size of $8\frac{1}{2}$ by 11 inches should be supported, but sizes up to 11 by 17 inches allow for more flexible output. Special commands are available for producing output under the PC's control. However, a manual drawing capability exists through directional keys on the plotter.

The Hewlett-Packard 7475A Graphics Plotter is such a unit. The HP 7475A, pictured in Figure 7-4, offers an RS-232 serial interface for connection to the PC at speeds up to 9600-bps operation. Few option settings are required to set up the plotter, including speed, parity, and paper size. The paper is loaded from the front of the plotter. The unit offers a removable pen wheel for easy loading and changing of pens. The user can quickly get an appreciation for the HP's capability, as there is a built-in demonstration program that draws bar charts, pies, and prints headings. When connecting the plotter to the PC, the HP should be optioned for 9600 bps, no parity, 7 data bits, and 1 stop bit. XON/XOFF and ENQ/ACK are supported in addition to hardware flow control on pin 20. A null-modem cable is used between the HP and the PC, with pin 20 from the plotter connected to pins 5, 6, and 8 on the ACA or equivalent for hardware flow control. The plotter requires a male connector, while the PC needs a female connector. A sample five-line program is provided for testing the installation. The use of a plotter such as the HP 7475A offers a colorful alternative for effective display of information produced on the PC.

SUGGESTED READINGS

Electrical Power Related Peripherals
1. *Interference Control and Electronic Products Catalog,* Electronic Specialists, Inc.
2. *Popular Computing,* "What Happens When the Lights Go Off?" pp. 97–102, Vol. 1, No. 10, August 1982.

Input Mechanisms and Display Monitor Connections
1. *PC Mouse User Manual,* Mouse Systems, August 23, 1983.
2. PC-300 Bar Code Reader product description, TPS Electronics, August 1983.
3. PC-500 Magnetic Stripe Reader product description, TPS Electronics, October 1983.
4. *IBM Technical Reference,* Publ. 6025005, pp. 1-211 to 1-216, and 1-223 to 1-158.
5. *Supervision User Manual,* California Computer Systems, Publ. 42000137 -01.

Plotters
1. *RS-232 Made Easy,* by Martin D. Seyer, Prentice-Hall, Inc., Englewood Cliffs, N.J., 1984.
2. *HP-7475A Graphics Plotter Operation and Interconnection Manual,* pp. 2-21 to 2-23 and 3-24.
3. *HP-7475A Graphics Plotter Interfacing and Programming Manual,* pp. 10-1 to 10-44.

CHAPTER

8

installing other operating systems on the PC/XT

DOS: The Disk Operating System is a very popular operating system for the IBM PC, and many computers using it have been sold. Furthermore, it is becoming increasingly more powerful as each release becomes available. Considering the short time that the IBM PC has been in existence, many business and pleasure applications have been developed. But what about the operating systems in widespread use prior to the introduction of the PC? What about all the Z80/(Zilog)-based 8-bit systems that were the forerunners of the PC? The bulk of them use a common operating system known as CP/M (Control Program/Microprocessor). Furthermore, many Apple II, IIe, and IIc computers have been sold using their own version of DOS. UNIX is currently thought by many to be the operating system of the future. Thousands of programs have been written for each of these system programs, and a PC owner would benefit from being able to execute some of these. The major software vendors convert their packages to run under each of these operating systems to solve the problem. But what about the thousands of programs that have not been converted to run on the PC? What about the data files created on an Apple computer? Can they be used on the PC? The following sections discuss several ways of providing different operating systems on the PC to share programs and data files.

CP/M: The most widely used operating system for 8-bit computers is CP/M. Thousands of operating systems are in existence for this operating system. Written by Digital Research, Inc., this operating system supported some of the early versions of applications currently available on the IBM PC. For example, Wordstar from MicroPro International was originally written for the CP/M operating system. An easy way to get this powerful operating system on the PC is to install a board that provides it. Some of them offer serial or parallel ports, a clock, a RAM disk, and print spoolers. One of the key factors to consider is whether the board acquisition also gives you the operating system or whether it must be purchased separately. California Computer Systems offers a Z/Plus plug-in board which includes a Z80 microprocessor together with 64K of RAM. This gives you CP/M capability in addition to the standard DOS on the Intel 8088 chip of the PC. A serial port and CP/M-80 Version 2.2 are included with an option for an additonal 128K of memory, bringing the total RAM size to 192K. The RS-232 port is compatible with the IBM asynchronous communications port of the ACA and is used for modem or printer connection, as discussed earlier. This port may be configured as either COM1 or COM2 but does not support a current loop. A serial teletype (TTY) interface is emulated by the CP/M Basic I/O System console routines. These routines support special video routines offered on a Lear Siegler ADM-31 terminal. The standard input device normally found in CP/M is the IBM PC keyboard. The output device may be the IBM 80 CPS Matrix Printer connected via the parallel interface. The

CP/M-80 Physical device	IBM PC Physical device
CRT:	Input = keyboard
CRT:	Output = keyboard
PTR:	Input = keyboard
PTP:	Output = video display
LTP:	Parallel printer port
TTY:	Video display
UC1:	Serial port
UR1:	Serial port
UR2:	Serial port
UP1:	Serial port
UP2:	Serial port
UL1:	Input = current RDR setting
BAT:	Output = current LST setting

Figure 8-1 Cross references between the IBM PC and CP/M-80 for the physical devices

physical devices of the IBM PC correspond to the physical devices of the CP/M-80 operating system listed in Figure 8-1. The board requires one PC slot to add the versatility of both 8- and 16-operating-system capability in the same machine. Documentation for the CP/M operating system is included with the board.

UNIX: What about the operating system receiving the majority of attention these days, UNIX? People who have used this operating system admit that DOS 2.0 closely resembles it, with its features of piping, redirection of I/O, and the file system. The praise for UNIX stems largely from its built-in programmer tools, editors, and document preparation utilities. Its filing system offers trees, roots, and branches for a hierarchical file structure. This feature is also present in DOS 2.0 and is receiving good reviews. Another feature of UNIX is the C programming language. This is a high-level language with features found only in low-level assemblers. These are a few of the many reasons for UNIX's growth in popularity. IBM has announced the availability of UNIX on the PC and XT. The offering is known as PC/IX and features the following: hierarchical file system, shell, foreground and background processes, full-screen editor, and C programming language, among other items. UNIX can be coresident with PC-DOS on fixed disk partitions.

If the user cannot wait or does not desire IBM's approach, Sritek offers a 68000 Processor Expansion Product for the PC. This offering gives the PC user UNIX running on a Motorola microprocessor with additional memory on a single board. This board uses the standard serial and parallel ports of the PC's other boards. It is a single plug-in board offering easy hardware installation. Bringing up XENIX, a version of UNIX by Microsoft, requires more time or an experienced programmer or a combination of both. This is due to the extreme complexity and size of the UNIX-like operating systems. Nonetheless, once installed, the PC user has a flexible configuration for an array of applications.

There is yet another means of using UNIX on or from a PC/XT. AT&T, the developers of UNIX, offer PC users the best of both worlds. Through a product called PC interface, PC users can run MSDOS locally on the PC and have total access to all the features of a UNIX system. PC interface, designed to link PCs to AT&T's UNIX-based computer products, including the 3B5 and 3B2 systems, provides all the necessary software to make this possible. This includes appropriate device drivers and file transfer software.

PCs may be connected to the UNIX system in one of two fashions. A standard RS-232 connection is possible in addition to a local area network based on the Ethernet standard. The software includes appropriate device drivers for MSDOS to provide a myriad of benefits to the PC user. The UNIX system (assume a 3B2 system) appears to the PC as another disk drive. For example, drive C under MSDOS would equate to the file system on the 3B2 computer. Once set up, standard MSDOS commands are used to access files on the 3B. PC interface has built-in file transfer capabilities which are transparent to the PC operator. For example, to get a file from UNIX to drive A on the PC, a standard copy command is used. The file transfer software then performs the copy over the connection, either RS-232 or Ethernet. This ability offers economic benefits when a business owns many PCs. With the mass storage capacities of the 3B, PCs may be used instead of XTs. Perhaps even single floppy PCs may be used instead of dual-drive systems. Furthermore, archiving may be done centrally on the 3B system instead of at each PC, thus reducing overall storage media costs. The benefits of the PC interface parallel those of local area networks because of this file serving capability. Many PCs now have access to the same databases of information if stored centrally on the UNIX system. Now only a single copy of an application program may be required by storing it on the UNIX computer. If an Ethernet network is used, the file systems of multiple UNIX systems could be made available to each PC operator. Each of the UNIX systems would merely be identified by a different drive name, such as C, D, E, or F. Regardless of the configuration used, the benefit is that the PC operator treats all file systems as if they were locally housed in the PC.

The use of UNIX file systems provides many economic advantages. But equally important is the PC interface feature, allowing the PC access to UNIX. The PC may log into UNIX as a standard asynchronous ASCII device would, deriving full use of the UNIX operating system with all its unique features, including the C programming language. These two operations, MSDOS enhancements and terminal access to UNIX, need not be mutually exclusive. They can occur simultaneously, allowing the user to use one operation without disturbing the other. For example, a PC database file being utilized from the UNIX file system may be acted on by a standard UNIX function, such as the sort command. This command is issued from the same PC using the database file as if it were a local file. From this use of the PC interface, the PC operator has the best of both worlds, mainframe feature/functionality in addition to the powerful PC's capabilities.

AppleDOS: The final operating system to be reviewed in this section is that of the Apple II/IIe/IIc computer system. Because Apple's operating system is

Chap. 8   Installing Other Operating Systems on the PC/XT   151

also known as DOS, we will use the term AppleDOS to distinguish it. This operating system is used on every Apple computer system sold with disk drives. Because of the large number of installations, a vast number of applications have been developed. Many of the forerunners of today's PC packages were developed to run under AppleDOS. How does a PC owner use programs or files written on an Apple? Why would a user have this need? Suppose that an Apple is used for word processing purposes to write a book. After the book is completed the author purchases an IBM PC for future writing. A second book is then written which requires material from the first book. How does the new PC owner take advantage of perhaps hundreds of pages of text without having to retype them? If files are kept of vendors and their products using an Apple database management system such as VisiFile from VisiCorp and dBASE II from Ashton-Tate is to be used on the PC, can these files be converted? Prior to discussing these concerns, several issues and differences between the two computers must be understood.

PCDOS and AppleDOS differences: The disks of an Apple II/IIe/IIc system are not formatted in the same manner as the disks on a PC. The number of tracks, sectors, and characters on the disks are not equal. IBM does not use half-track, whereas some of the Apple programs do. This does not allow the user merely to insert the Apple disks into the IBM drives to read the files. The operational aspects are different. The keyboards are used differently to provide cursor positioning and function keys, among other items. The BASIC programming languages are substantially different, limiting the sharing of programs. Also, the operating systems handle all I/O operations differently. Because of these differences, alternative means of sharing files and programs will be discussed, including printing files, files transfers, and special boards.

File transfers to the PC: To overcome the problem of incompatible formats of the disks, one alternative is to perform a file transfer from the Apple to the IBM PC. All files to be transferred should be text files. If the Apple files are not text files, they should be converted to text files by means of the procedures provided in the AppleDOS documentation. Refer to the section in the AppleDOS manual on controlling the Apple via a text file. This outlines the procedure for accomplishing the conversion. If the file to be transferred is an Apple BASIC file, the following program may be used to convert it into text format.

```
1 REM: FILE IN LINES 5, 6, 9; "FILE" SHOULD BE THE NAME OF YOUR FILE
2 REM: LINE 8 CONTAINS THE RANGE OF LINES TO BE MOVED TO THE TEXT FILE
3 REM: SO SUBSTITUTE IN LINE 8 AS APPROPRIATE
4 D$ = CHR$(4)
5 PRINT D$; "OPEN FILE"
6 PRINT D$; "WRITE FILE"
7 POKE 33,30
```

```
 8 LIST 12,10000
 9 PRINT D$; "CLOSE FILE"
10 TEXT
11 END
```

Once the text file is ready, the software discussed in Chapters 2 to 4 of this book may be used to transfer the file from the Apple to the IBM. Most terminal emulators or communication software packages offer the ability to transmit and receive a text file. For example, VisiTerm from Visicorp is a package that is available on the Apple. Also, Crosstalk from Microstuf is one of the packages for the IBM, so we will use them as examples. Communication software on both machines need not be the same but only offer file transfer capabilities. The telephone link between the two computers should be established in the normal fashion. If the two computers are close enough, a null-modem cable could be used in place of the modems. Refer to Figure 8-2 for possible connections. Nonetheless, VisiTerm on the Apple should be set up to transfer file 1 while the IBM is set up to receive or log this file onto disk. Once the file is transferred and saved onto the IBM disk, the link can be disconnected.

Another difference between the two file structures is that the Apple II/IIe/IIc computer delineates the lines of text with only a carriage return. The PC uses both a carriage return and a line feed. This becomes evident once the files are transferred to the IBM and displayed on the screen. This can be viewed by using the TYPE command followed by the filename. All text will appear in the same line because no line feeds are present. Once transferred, the line feed must be added to each line of text. The following program, may be used to add a line feed to each line once the file is on the PC disk.

```
 10 CR$=CHR$(13)
 20 LF$=CHR$(10)
 30 INPUT "PLEASE TYPE NAME OF FILE TO CONVERT FOLLOWED BY A RETURN: ",F1$
 40 OPEN F1$ FOR INPUT AS #1
 50 INPUT "NOW ENTER FILE NAME YOU WANT THIS SAVE UNDER: ";F2$
 60 OPEN F2$ FOR OUTPUT AS #2
 70 L$ = INPUT$(1,1)
 80 IF L$<>CR$ THEN PRINT #2, L$; ELSE PRINT #2, CR$ + LF$;
 90 IF EOF(1) THEN CLOSE
100 END
110 GOTO 70
```

This program looks at every single character of the text file, one at a time. If a carriage return is found, it is replaced with a carriage return and line feed. Any other characters are merely written back to the output file. The exceptions to this requirement are serial boards for the Apple that output a line feed if a carriage return is passed through them. In this case the program to add a line feed will not need to be run. Once again the TYPE command can be used to determine if this

Chap. 8   Installing Other Operating Systems on the PC/XT   153

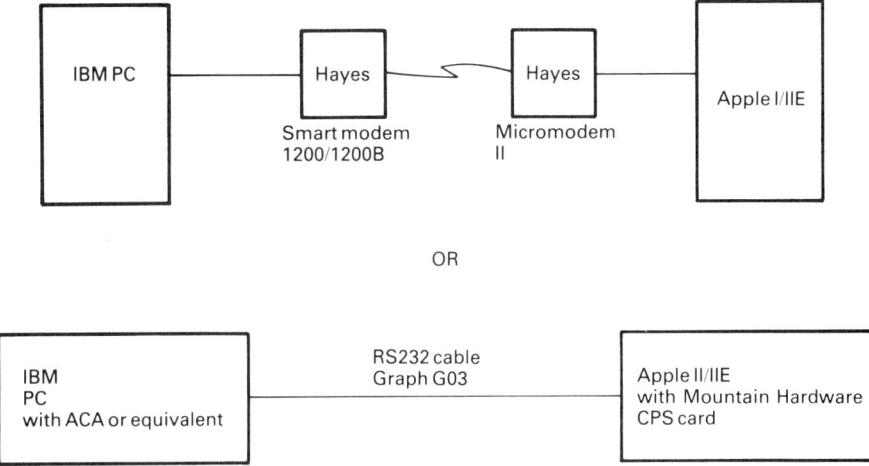

Figure 8-2 PC to APPLE connections

program needs to be executed. Once finished, word processing packages on the IBM should be able to read the text files once confined to the Apple.

Print Files: Another method of transferring a file between the Apple and the IBM will be demonstrated using databases. Assume that data from a VisiFile data base are to be used in a dBASE II application. Once again data must be transferred between the two machines. However, this method will require that only the IBM PC be running communication software. At the Apple end a print sequence will be used. VisiFile offers that ability to print reports from a database. The first step in this process is to build a report format. Follow the instructions provided in the VisiFile manual to accomplish this. The only consideration is to place all the desired fields onto the same line of the report. This is easily done in the Report section of VisiFile's Print routines. Up to 132 characters may be placed in a single report line, establishing a limit on database size. As the user prepares this, note that the tab position in VisiFile is increased by the field length plus two. This will be important when the dBASE program is to be used. Once the report form is prepared, establish the link between the two machines. A serial port is required on the Apple and the associated port must be set up in the VisiFile configuration file. Connect this port to the IBM's serial port if the machines are close enough to one another. If they are separated by a distance, establish a communication link. The port on the Apple should be checked to determine if it is DCE or DTE, with the appropriate cable used before connecting to the PC or a modem. Load and run the communication software, such as Crosstalk, on the IBM, logging to a file the data received. Just about any communication software with file transfer capabilities may be used, with one exception. Some software can receive only 80 characters of data per line. A carriage return is automatically inserted after the eightieth character is received. Ensure that your communication software or terminal emulation software does not do this automatically, allowing for reception of 132 columns of data before a carriage return. Once the link between the two machines is established, print the report on the Apple. Crosstalk should receive the file as it would be output on a printer. Upon completion, TYPE the file on the PC and edit out the unnecessary lines of information using the DOS EDLIN commands found in the DOS manual. These lines will generally contain the headings of the report. If necessary, run the program to add line feeds to the text.

Now the dBASE II database must be created. Using the Create command of dBASE II, build a database. A length of two characters must be added to the field lengths when creating the database. Recall that the tab function of VisiFile automatically added these two spaces between fields. Once the database is created, the first record should be added. This is necessary for the next operation, which is the Append command. Under dBASE II the command sequence APPEND FROM FILE. NAME SDF should be entered. Using the current file that contains the single record just entered, the VisiFile records transferred from the Apple will be added to the dBASE database. The user should then check the records and edit them where appropriate.

APPLE–IBM Connection: Another software alternative to the need for file transfer is Alpha Software Corporation's Apple–IBM Connection product. This software package includes disks that run on both the Apple II/IIe and the IBM PC/XT. Utilities for converting Apple BASIC programs to text format and for adding and deleting line feeds are included in addition to file transfer programs. The Apple and IBM may be connected with modems or a null-modem cable. Any combination of personal computers is possible. This allows PC-to-PC, PC-to-Apple, and Apple-to-Apple communication in addition to the Apple-to-PC file transfers. Earlier versions of the software imposed specific hardware restrictions. Current versions operate in the Apple with either a Hayes Micromodem II or external modems. The boards that are supported on the Apple by the Connection include the Mountain Hardware CPS card, the California Computer Systems Model 7710 card, or an Apple Super Serial card. These provide an RS-232 port for external modems or for a null-modem cable connection. Any board providing an IBM ACA-compatible RS-232 port may be used in the PC. Figure 8-2 depicts the possible connections. It is a menu-driven package allowing easy transfer of files between the two systems. We discussed the physical hookup of these two machines in earlier chapters.

QUADLINK: A popular solution allowing not only the sharing of files but also the actual execution on the IBM of programs written for the Apple is offered by Quadram Corporation. This program execution capability is extremely important to some users, as over 16,000 programs exist for the Apple II series of computers. The Quadlink is a plug-in expansion card for the PC. This hardware and software solution includes all the necessary cables, disks, and documentation to turn the IBM PC/XT into an Apple II-compatible computer. The plug-in board offering this capability, displayed in Figure 8-3, incorporates a 6502 8-bit computer, 64K of

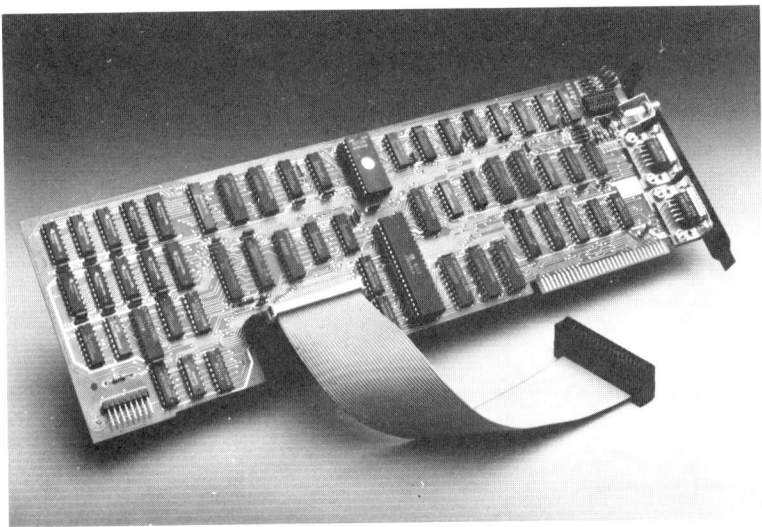

Figure 8-3 Quadram's QUADLINK board

memory, and three screen display modes. Apple joysticks may be plugged directly into the board for Apple game software that the user may want to run. The sound effects of the games are produced through the IBM's internal speaker. The documentation includes setup procedures as well as Apple-specific instructional material. This kit differs from the previous file-sharing techniques in that programs may actually be executed as if the IBM were an Apple computer. Furthermore, a copy program is provided for transferring files between the IBM PC and the Apple II/IIe. This allows complete information exchange between the two computers. If an Apple is used in the home while an IBM is used in the office, the incompatibility problem is solved. If peripherals such as printers and modems are already connected to the PC, the Quadlink package will use them for its I/O. If none currently exist, consult earlier chapters for selection and installation procedures.

How easy is it to turn the IBM into an IBM/Apple? The installation of the Quadlink is fairly straightforward. It involves removing the existing boards from the IBM's motherboard slots. The Quadlink is laced between existing devices of the PC. For example, the disk controller plugs into the Quadlink, which in turn plugs back into the drives. The speaker and video connections function in the same manner. Once the optional game paddles are connected, the hardware installation is complete.

The two disks provided are booted to load the Apple-compatible mode capability. Once executed, the user has access to both Apple and PC modes through a single keystroke. Control/Alt/A accesses the Apple-compatible mode, while control/Alt/I places the user in the standard IBM mode. The user familiar with the standard Apple cursor-positioning keys will find that they are fully supported with the Quadlink. In addition to these standard keystrokes, function key 10 is a freeze command. Function key 2 is also used to toggle between color and black-and-white display modes. The Apple command PR#1 sends data to the IBM LPT1 device. PR#2 will access the device attached to the COM1 port. PR#6 is the Apple DOS command to reboot the system and behaves the same way within the Quadlink setup. Currently only the 40-column mode of Apple is supported. However, 80-column capability is under development by Quadram and will be available free to all purchasers of the Quadlink. XT owners should be aware that Quadlink will run under IBM DOS 2.0 but may not access the hard disk. So unless additional floppy disks are installed on the IBM XT, it will be limited to single-drive operation in the Apple mode. For a user who switches from the Apple II/IIe to IBM, the Quadlink system is a welcome solution to ease the pains of conversion.

IBM's Newest PC Additions: IBM shocked many people with its late 1983 announcement for the PC/XT computers. This announcement included enhancements permitting the PC to function in mainframe environments. The XT-370 Workstation offers the capability of executing the operating system and application programs normally found on the 370 series of IBM mainframe computers. The 3270-PC offers processing power to a terminal series otherwise totally dependent on the mainframe for services. Another offering is the 3278/79 Terminal Adapter, which turns existing PCs into terminals behind 3274 Cluster Controllers. Each of these requires connections to non-PC equipment but also supports the standard PC peripherals. Consult the Appendixes B and C for the standard gear.

XT/370: Probably the most interesting of the three additions is the XT/370 Workstation. With the XT/370 IBM has created a totally new market for application software. At the same time, the PC-plug-compatible vendors were brought to the edges of their seats. The 370 mainframe series is used by large companies offering a variety of services to many users. Hundreds of terminals are supported by a single 370. Because of the number of terminals, many applications have been developed to run on the 370. The XT/370 offers a means of executing these application programs on a distributed basis. The XT can now run programs normally limited to the Virtual Machine/Conversational Monitor System (VM/CMS) operating system. The operating system of the XT is VM/PC. This operating system runs on the plug-in processor boards that are included with the "microframe" system. Three boards are required. One of them is the processor board, which holds multiple microprocessors, including two Motorola 68000 chips in addition to the Intel 808X chips, giving the system approximately half the processing power of an IBM 4321 mainframe. A RAM board contains 768,000 bytes of main memory. The other board provides a coaxial cable attachment enabling the processor to act as a 3277 Model 2 terminal to be connected to a 3274 controller. The standard XT processor and memory remain inactive until I/O is required by VM/PC. At this time the XT interfaces to peripherals exactly as discussed in earlier chapters. Peripherals on the mainframe are also available to the XT/370 and access through the VM/PC operating system. Also included automatically is the ability to convert files. The 370 main-

Chap. 8   Installing Other Operating Systems on the PC/XT   **157**

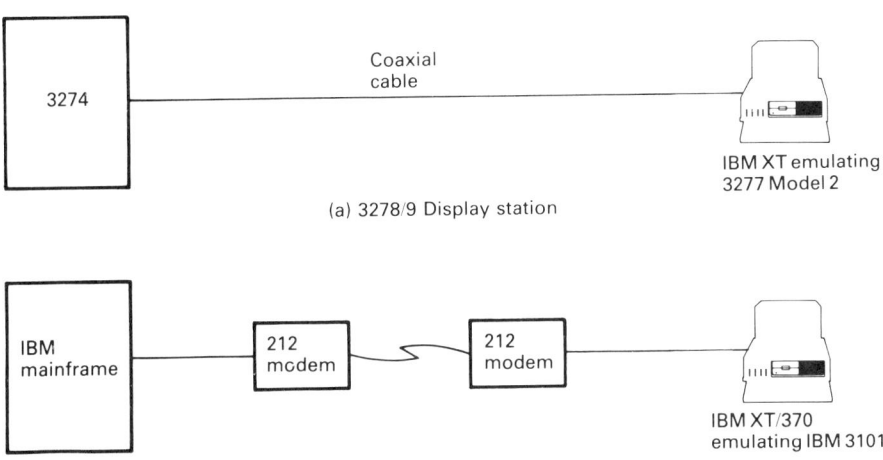

Figure 8-4   IBM XT/370 connections
a) 3278/9 Display Station
b) IBM 3101 asynchronous terminal emulation

frame requires a character code known as EBCDIC, which is an acronym for Extended Binary-Coded Decimal Interchange Code. This 8-bit code differs from the XT internal character format, which is ASCII. The ability to translate the data between these character sets is built in. This facilitates accurate file transfers between mainframe and microframe.

This arrangement allows the XT to take on three personalities, as the user chooses. The most obvious is the VM/PC, providing the mainframe CMS functions. The XT/370 can also become a terminal behind a cluster controller, for communication to a mainframe as a synchronous terminal. Furthermore, the unit can emulate an IBM 3101 asynchronous ASCII terminal. Figure 8-4 depicts the latter two possibilities. The flexibility offered by the XT/370 makes it difficult for plug-compatible vendors to keep their equipment truly compatible. They must contend with the increased processing power as well as the communication capabilities, both of which are of great interest to large data processing business environments. The cost will range between $9000 and $12,000 for the XT/370 workstation, depending on the capacity of the hard-disk medium.

3270 PC: Another offering is of interest to data processing and telecommunication managers who are responsible for acquiring 3270 synchronous terminals. IBM now offers a 3270 PC. From the product name it is clear that the unit encompasses both the 3270 terminal and PC capabilities. This allows on-line communication with mainframes such as the IBM 370, 3080, and 4300 series mainframes, as shown in Figure 8-4(a). A coaxial connection to a 3274 controller permits this on-line communication. In addition, the 3270 PC has the same capabilities as the stand-alone PC, including local processing and file storage. The peripherals of the PC are connected as usual but are also supported in the BSC and SDLC communication environments. Included are seven windows, to allow access to multiple applications concurrently. Four of the windows are used for the mainframe connection. This enables the user to be logged on to as many as four different applications. Two of the windows can be used for electronic mail or a data display area. The remaining window is for the standard PC operations. The cost of the 3270 PC begins at $4300, depending on the memory included, which can be up to 640K.

3278/79 Terminal Adapter: Also available is this adapter, which converts an existing PC/XT into a 3270 terminal. The adapter also offers coaxial cable for connection to the 3274 controller.

SUGGESTED READINGS

1. *Z/Plus Card Reference Manual,* Publ. 860088220–1, Revision A, pp. 1–20, July 1983.
2. *IBM Disk Operating System,* Publ. 6024061.
3. *PC World,* "The Apple IBM Connection," pp. 196–200, Vol. 1, No. 3, April 1983.
4. *Apple DOS Manual,* Publ. A2L0036, pp. 74–77, 1981.
5. *Data Communications,* "New Products," pp. 273–276, Vol. 12, No. 11, November 1983.
6. *PC Magazine,* "The Mainframe Marketplace: XT/370 and 3270 PC," pp. 146–150, Vol. 3, No. 1, January 1984.
7. *PC Magazine,* "The XT/370: A Technical Overview," pp. 151–154, Vol. 3, No. 1, January 1984.
8. *Quadlink User's Guide,* Quadram Corp. July 1983.

CHAPTER 9

optimization techniques for various PC/XT installations

All of the previous explanations have provided the user with useful technical insights for understanding and implementing various connections to the IBM. Whether the peripherals to be connected are modems, printers, plotters, or any of the many different devices available, the reader should now have a functional knowledge of the intricacies of serial and parallel connections. The actual selection and subsequent installation of configurations offers much opportunity for optimizations. A significant reduction in hardware and software investment can be achieved if the user successfully plans for the installation prior to actual purchases. The following section offers various configurations to aid the user in simplifying and optimizing a PC/XT environment. Both asynchronous and synchronous alternatives are provided, including device-sharing techniques. The following list will assist the reader to understand the various configurations.

F = female (socket) RS-232 connector
M = male (pin/plug) RS-232 connector
Gxx = cable configuration from Appendix B to connect devices with pin assignments listed in Appendix A
ACA = IBM's Asynchronous Communication Adapter
PC = Personal Computer or XT
XT = XT only

Each configuration includes a short description of the environment, cable requirements, optioning, and software setup considerations. The following alternatives are provided to aid the user:

1. A printer and a plotter sharing a single RS-232 port in the IBM PC/XT (Figure 9-1).
2. Two PCs sharing a modem and a printer (Figure 9-2).
3. One PC port connected to both a letter-quality and a dot matrix printer, both using serial ports (Figure 9-3).
4. Two computers sharing a single modem (Figure 9-4).
5. Two printers with parallel ports connected to a single IBM PC port (Figure 9-5).
6. A PC with a single RS-232 port accessing both a modem and a parallel printer (Figure 9-6).
7. A PC and printer connected using a short-haul modem because of the long distance between them (Figure 9-7).
8. Two PCs connected together for file transfers (Figure 9-8).

9. A single PC sharing two printers that use the same hardware flow-control lead (Figure 9-9).
10. Use of a code-activated switch to give a single PC RS-232 port access to multiple devices (Figure 9-10).
11. A single PC emulating a 3780 station but serving multiple PCs (Figure 9-11).
12. A PC emulating a 5251 Remote Work Station connected to a host (Figure 9-12).
13. A PC emulating a 3270 Binary Synchronous Cluster and a 3278 Display Station (Figure 9-13).
14. Multiple PCs connected together through a local area network (Figure 9-14).
15. Multiple PCs connected to a UNIX computer system (Figure 9-15).

Although many variations exist for optimizing computer installations, those described below should aid the user for most environments.

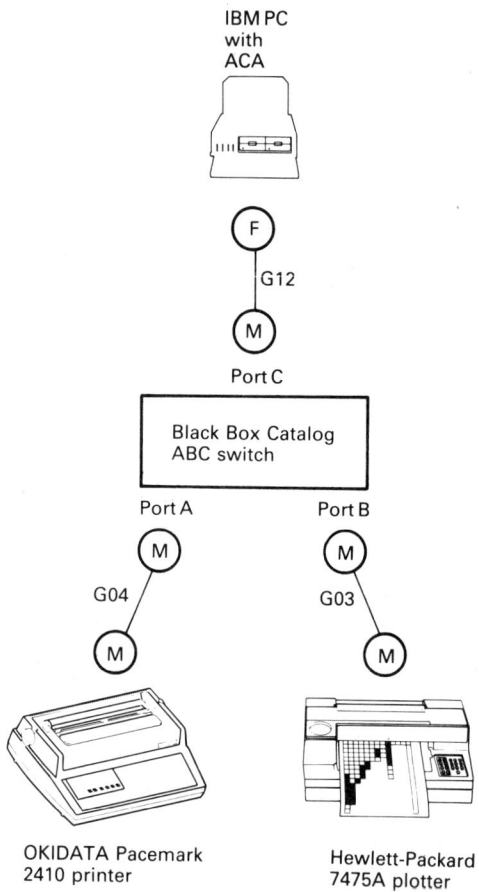

Figure 9-1 A printer and a plotter sharing a single RS-232 port in the IBM PC/XT. Figure 9-1 outlines the connection of an Okidata Pacemark 2410 printer and a Hewlett-Packard 7475A Graphics Plotter to an ACA or equivalent port. A Black Box Catalog ABC serial switch is used to provide this optimization. The following items should be considered in this configuration.
1. ACA is set up with the command, "MODE COM1:96,N,8,2,P" followed by a re-direction of I/O with the command, "MODE LPT1: = COM1"
2. Okidata printer is optioned with default factory settings of 9600 bps, no parity, 8 bits per character, 1 stop bit, and hardware control on pin 11.
3. HP-7475A is set up at 9600 bps, no parity, and hardware flow control on pin 20.
4. No timing leads, pins 15, 17, or 24, are needed in any of the cables.
5. The switch in the A position connects the PC to the Okidata; position B connects the HP-7475A to the PC.

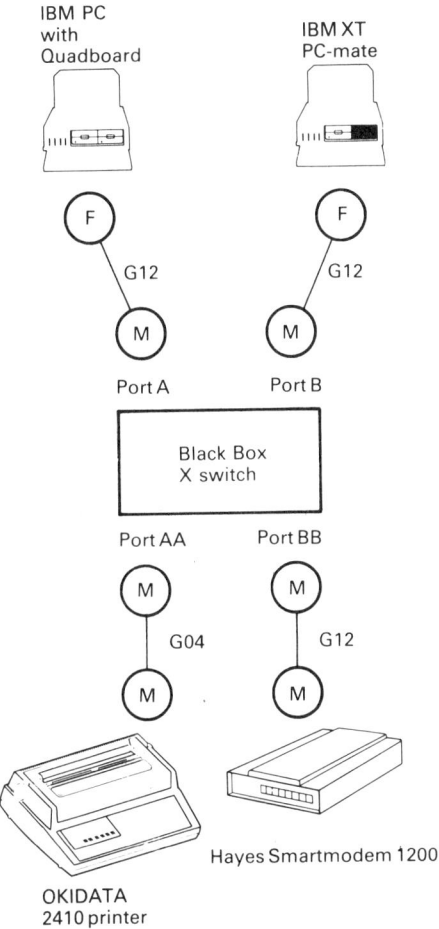

Figure 9-2 Two PCs sharing a modem and a printer. Figure 9-2 displays a configuration allowing a modem and printer to be used alternatively, between a PC with a Quadram Quadboard and an XT with a Tecmar PC-Mate. Assume that both serial ports are optioned as COM2. The following items should be considered when installing.

1. The switch offers the following connections
—the PC to the Okidata printer and the XT to the Hayes modem or
—the PC to the Hayes modem and the XT to the Okidata printer
2. The user of the Okidata printer sets up the COM2 port to match the option settings. If the default options are used the commands, "MODE COM2: 9600,N,8,1,P" and "MODE LPT1: = COM2", can be used.
3. The user of the Hayes modem should use a communication software package as discussed in Chapter 3 of this text. Packages such as Smartcom II, Crosstalk XVI, or PC-Talk III are but a few of such programs as listed in Appendix H.
4. No timing leads, pins 15, 17, or 24, are needed in any of the cables.

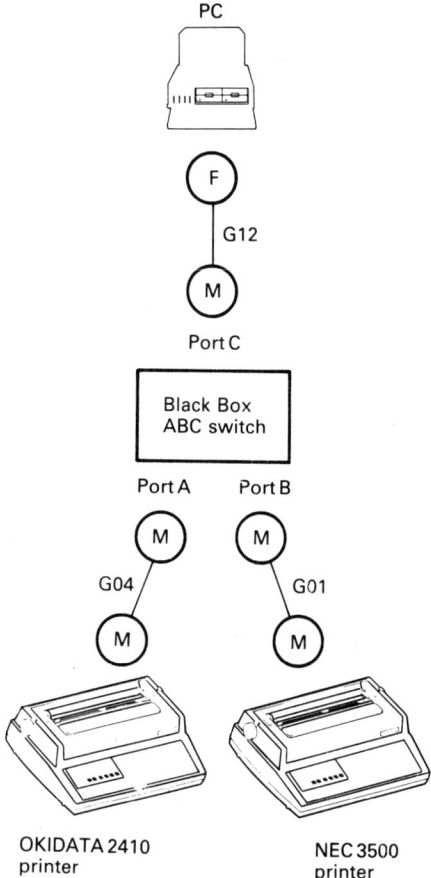

Figure 9-3 One PC port connected to both a letter quality and a dot matrix printer, both using serial ports. Often both a high speed dot matrix and a slower speed letter quality printer are needed in the same environment. If only a single RS-232 port is available, Figure 9-3 provides an easy solution. In this installation both an Okidata Pacemark 2410 and an NEC 3500 Spinwriter printer are accessible by the PC through a serial port. A Black Box ABC switch is used to accommodate this need. The following considerations should be taken into account.

1. The ACA is set up to match the printer options, dependent on which is accessed, dictated by the position of the ABC switch. It is advisable to option both printers exactly the same.
2. The switch in position A connects the PC to the Okidata; while position B connects the PC to the NEC.
3. No timing leads, pins 15, 17, and 24, are needed in any of the cables.

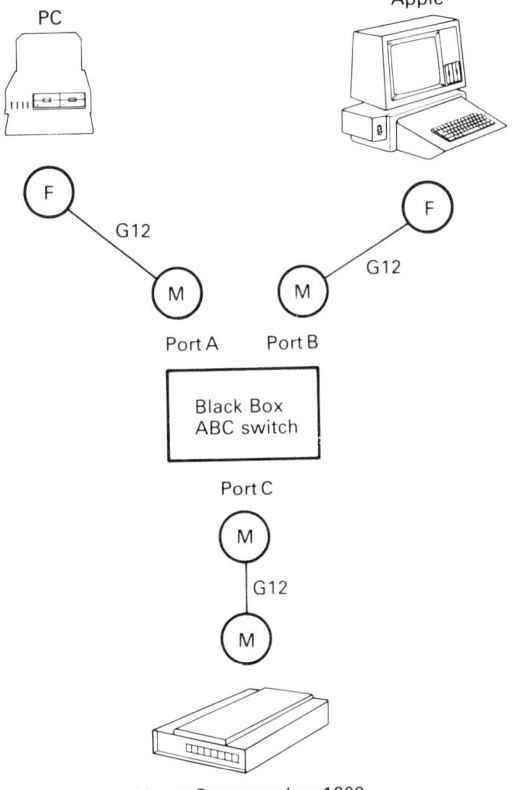

Figure 9-4 Two computers sharing a single standalone modem. Figure 9-4 depicts a PC with an AST SixPakPlus and an Apple IIe with a Super Serial Card sharing a single modem. This is done using an ABC switch.
1. Switch position A gives the PC access to the modem.
2. Switch position B gives the Apple control of the modem.
3. The PC could use Smartcom II, Crosstalk XVI, SmarTerm/PC, or other software to access the remote computer using the Hayes.
4. The Apple IIe user could issue a PR#1/IN#1 command if the Super Serial Card or equivalent is in slot 1, to gain access to the Hayes commands. Alternately, communication software such as VisiTerm, Crosstalk, or Data Capture could be used offering communication control.
5. The cables in this figure assume that the Super Serial Card is optioned with the shunt plug in the modem position, allowing the card to emulate data terminal equipment.

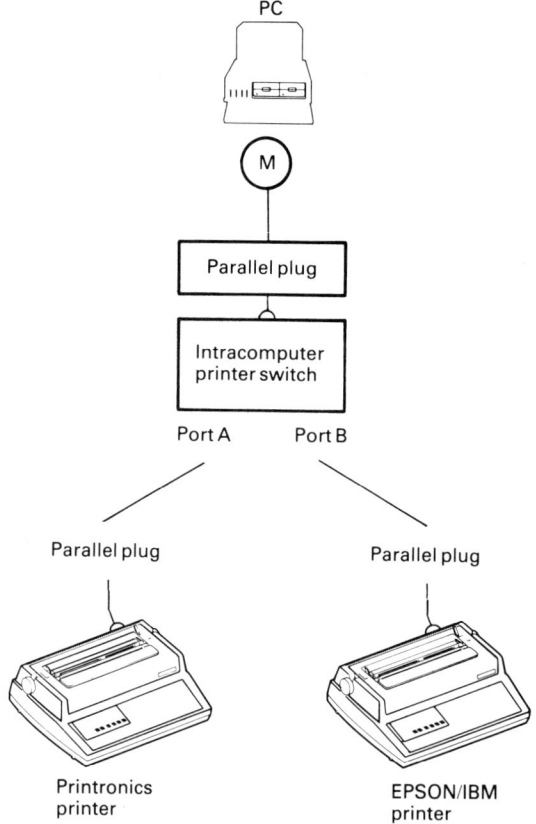

Figure 9-5 Two printers with parallel ports connected to a single IBM PC port. A PC with one of the many boards providing a parallel port, such as IBM's Monochrome Adapter board, California Computer System's Supervision board, or Tecmar's PC-Mate will offer a parallel port. This port, through a switch such as IntraComputer's Printer Switch, can access multiple printers. In this installation both a Printronix MVP 150B and an Epson/IBM printer are using the same port.

1. The cable between the PC and the IntraComputer switch is a cable described in Chapter 6, such as Black Box's PCPA or equivalent.
2. Ports A & B come standard with cables for parallel printer attachment. This saves the user cable charges.
3. Position A of the switch connects the PC to the Printronix.
4. Position B of the switch connects the PC to the Epson/IBM printer.

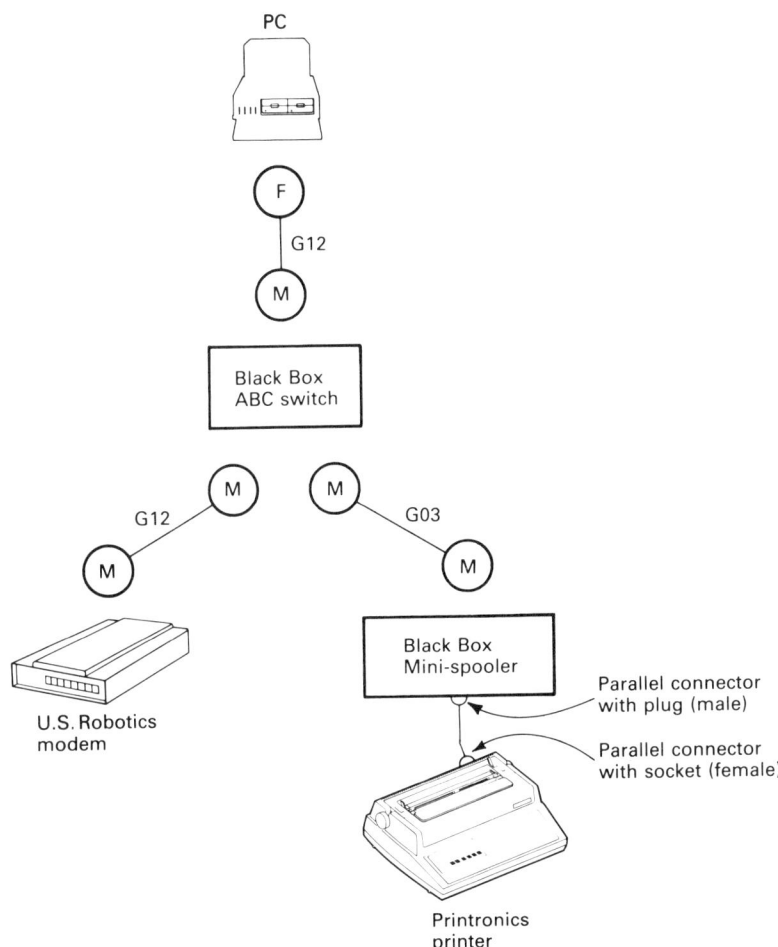

Figure 9-6 PC using a single RS-232 port to access both a modem and a parallel printer. A Quadram Quadboard's serial port is connected to an ABC switch to share both a serially interfaced U.S. Robotics Password modem, and the parallel port of a Printronix MVP 150B printer. A Black Box Mini-Spooler is used to provide a standalone buffer as well as serial to parallel conversion. The opposite conversion is also possible for those installations requiring it.

1. With the switch in position A, the Password modem is accessed. A communication software program, such as Crosstalk, Inner Loop's Video Display Terminal Emulator, Mark of the Unicorn's PC/InterComm, among others provides the communication capability.
2. Position B of the switch connects the serial port on the board to the input side of the spooler. The port on the PC should be set up to match the spooler with the appropriate command, such as "MODE COM1:9600,E,7,1" followed by the I/O redirection command "MODE LPT1: = COM1".
3. Hardware flow control from the Mini-Spooler is provided on pin 20 of the RS-232 cable. No timing leads, pins 15, 17, and 24, are required.
4. The spooler converts the serially received data to parallel data format for output to the printer. Inherent flow control in the Centronics interface controls the data exchange between the buffer and the printer.

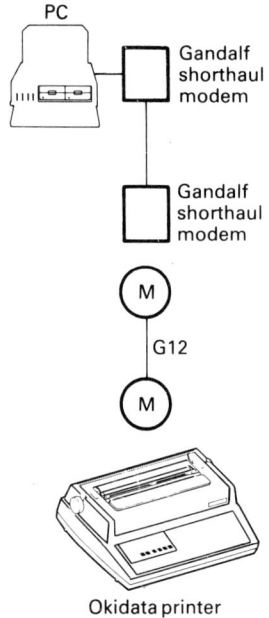

Okidata printer

Figure 9-7 A PC and printer connected using a short-haul modem due to a distance greater than 50 feet separating them. A Gandalf MDLS 122 short-haul modem is used to connect an Okidata Pacemark 2410 printer to a serial port in the PC.

1. The MDLS short-haul modem, because it has a female port (DB25S), plugs directly into the ACA or equivalent.
2. The Okidata printer at the far end, with its female port, causes a mismatch in the gender of the ports. That is why the cable is used instead of plugging the short-haul modem directly into the printer port.
3. The wire between the two modems can be standard housewire, as long as two pair (four wires) are available.
4. The ACA port is set up with the commands; "MODE COM1:96,N,8,1,P" and "MODE LPT1:=COM1".
5. Software flow control is recommended.

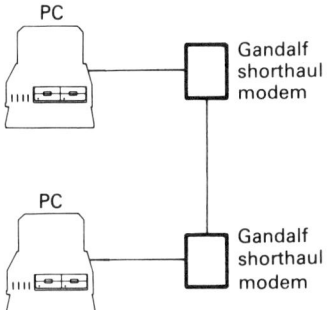

Figure 9-8 Two PCs are permanently connected together for file transfers. Two PCs, perhaps on different floors of a building, need to be permanently connected for uploading and downloading files.
1. Gandalf MDLS 122 short-haul modems plug directly into each PC.
2. Communication software such as Crosstalk XVI may be used for error free file transfers. If the remote access feature is ordered from Microstuf, one of the PCs wouldn't need human intervention.

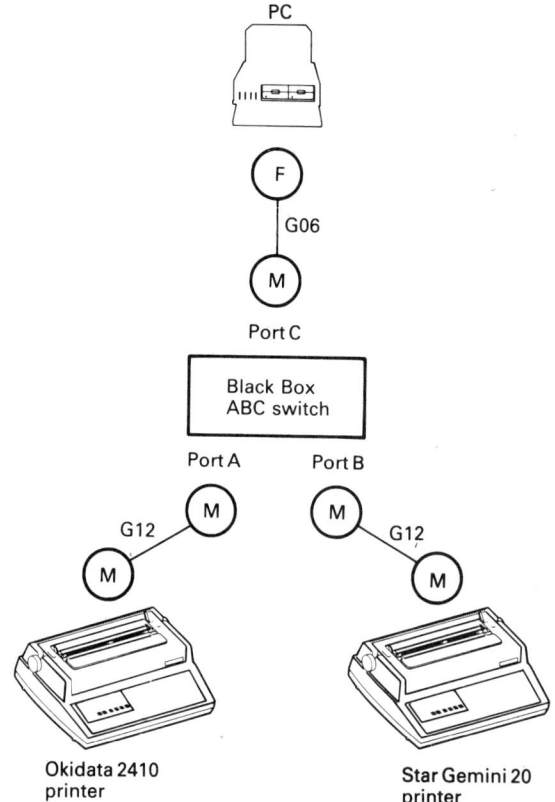

Figure 9-9 A single PC sharing two printers that use the same hardware flow control lead. Note the placement of the non-straight through cable to minimize the cost of special cables. Insure that the ABC switch includes pin 11 so hardware flow control is possible.
1. Switch position A connects the Okidata to the PC.
2. Switch position B connects the Star Gemini 10 to the PC.
3. Insure that the polarity option in the Star printer is set so that pin 11 is high/on when the printer is ready to receive. This lead on both printers is used for hardware flow control.
4. The PC port is set up with the MS-DOS commands; "MODE COM1:96,N,8,1,P" and "MODE LPT1:=COM1". Insure that both printers have the same character and speed related options.

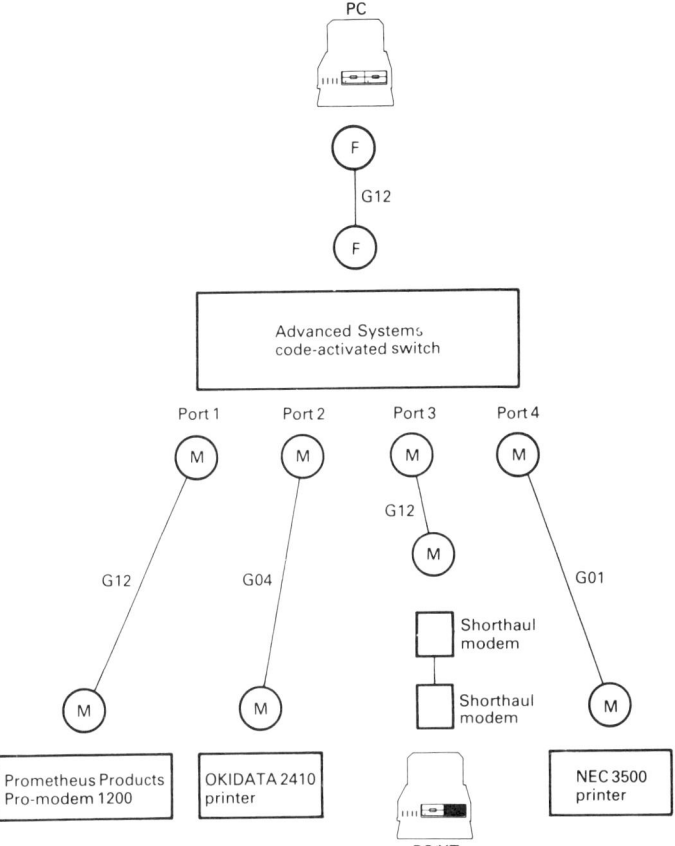

Figure 9-10 Use of a code-activated switch to give a single PC RS-232 port access to multiple devices. By using an Advanced Systems Inc. switch, the PC can be physically connected to devices such as a Prometheus Products' Pro-Modem 1200, Okidata Pacemark 2410, another PC, and a letter quality printer such as an NEC 3500 printer. A control code sequence is issued to select a given device. The ports, 1–4, are addressed by issuing a Control T followed by a 0,1,2, or 3. Note that the address is one less than you would expect. Should the user desire to permanently connect to a device, regardless of any other connection, a switch may be thrown giving this capability.

1. Switch B on the ASCI switch tells the box that pin 2 should be monitored for the control sequence. Off would cause a search on pin 3. For this configuration, set it on.
2. The default, Control T, will be used. This is the equivalent of a DC4 or decimal '20'. The speeds must match between the PC and the switch so it can detect the control sequences. Set the switch speed to 9600 for this configuration and then set the PC port speed to match for the actual port selection. Once selected the PC port can be reset to match whatever device it is connected to.
3. The short-haul modem between the ASCI switch and the XT can't be plugged directly into the switch because of gender problems.
4. Control T 0 accesses the Prometheus model. Use a communication software package for the communication.
5. Control T 1 accesses the Okidata printer. Use the MODE command to set up the PC port.
6. Control T 2 accesses the other XT. Communication software such as PC-Talk III can be used for transferring files. Software flow control is assumed.
7. Control T 3 accesses the NEC Spinwriter printer. Use the MODE command to set up the PC port.

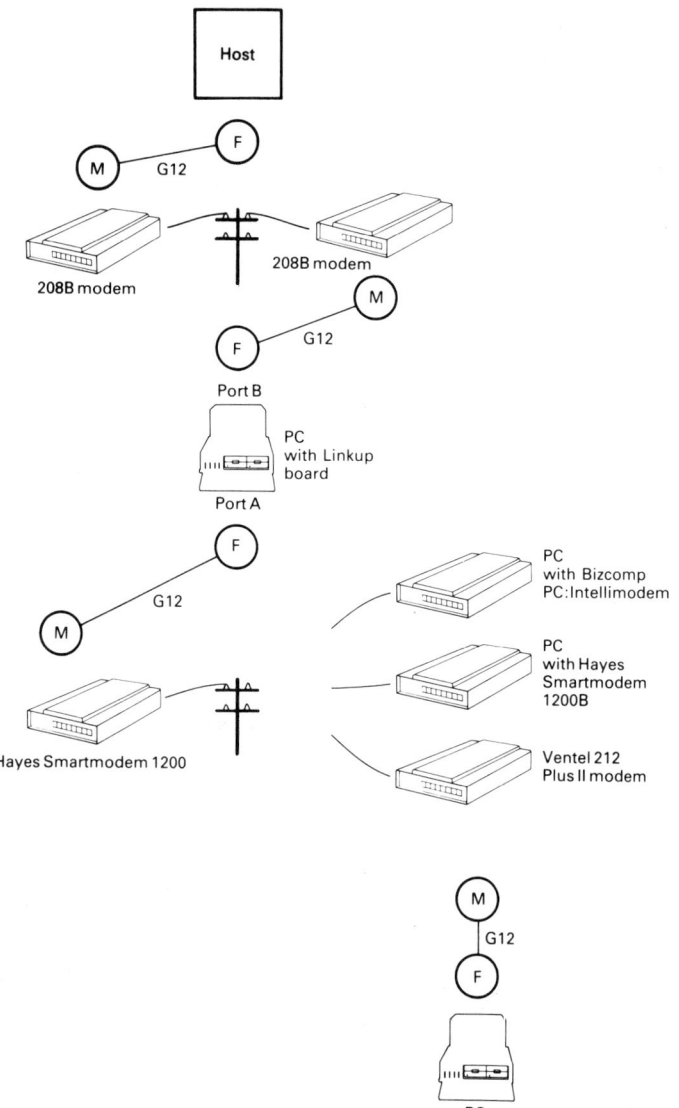

Figure 9-11 A single PC emulating a 3780 workstation to upload and download files, but serving multiple PC requirements. If multiple PCs need access to the same synchronous port of a mainframe for file exchange, Figure 9-11 offers an alternative to manually carry disks to a central site. Using Information Technologies' Linkup system in the PC, both asynchronous and synchronous communications are possible. If a 212 modem is on Channel A of the Linkup, remote PCs can call in and upload files. The central PC can then transfer files into the host over the 3780 private line. Downloading to the central PC is also possible. The PC can then distribute its received files, as appropriate, to the outlying PCs. This reduces the number of synchronous connections to the host. The line between the central PC and the host could also be dial up using an AT&T 208B modem or equivalent. Another possible configuration is a board-level asynchronous 212 modem, such as Bizcomp's IntelliModem and an AST Research 3780 board, or BARR Systems' BARR/HASP system, instead of the Linkup board.

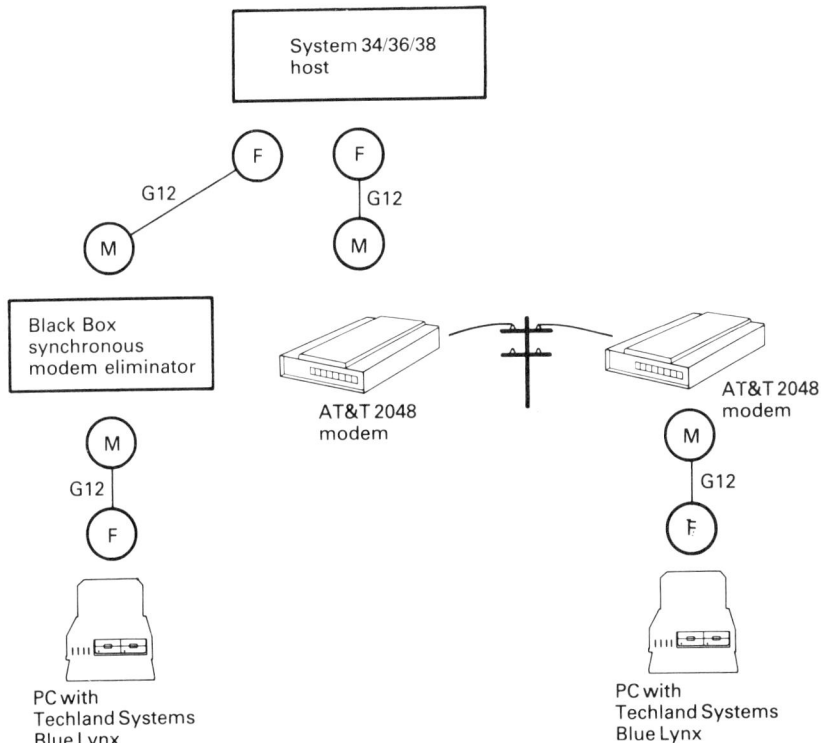

Figure 9-12 A PC emulating a 5251 Remote Work Station connected to a host. If communication is required between a System 34, 36, or 38 minicomputer and a PC, Techland Systems' Blue Lynx system can be installed in a PC. This allows either dial-up or private line access to these minicomputers. One of the synchronous modems between the two systems should be optioned to provide the timing, with the other set up for slave timing. Alternatively, a synchronous modem eliminator can be used if the systems are close together.

1. The cables between the modem and the data terminal equipment should provide timing leads, 15 and 17.
2. The Black Box Synchronous Modem Eliminator provides the standard null modem in addition to providing the necessary timing.

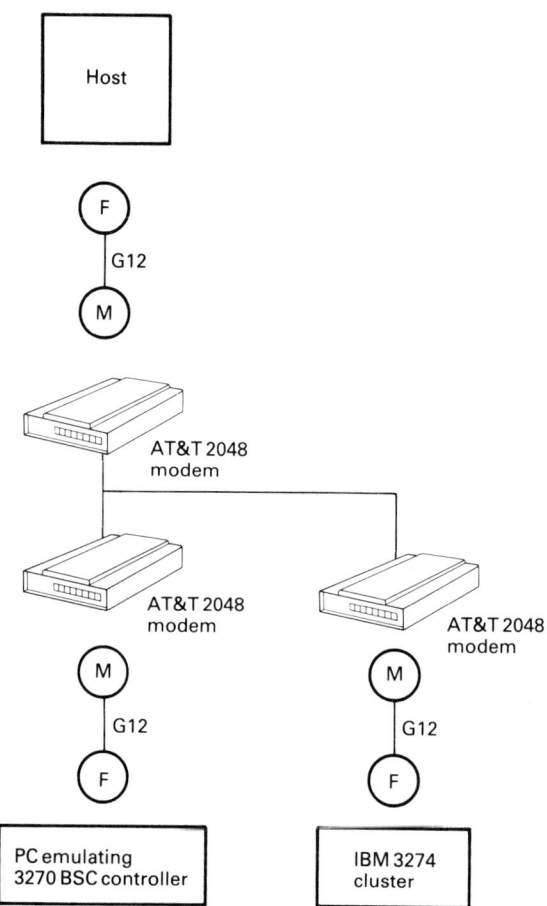

Figure 9-13 A PC emulating a 3270 Binary Synchronous Cluster and 3278 Display Station. A Phone 1 Adapter can be installed along with software to provide this emulation. As in Figure 9-12, a synchronous modem eliminator may be used if the distances allow for it.
1. The cables should provide for timing leads, 15 and 17.
2. If a synchronous modem eliminator is used, such as Black Box's SME, it provides both timing and a null modem cable function.

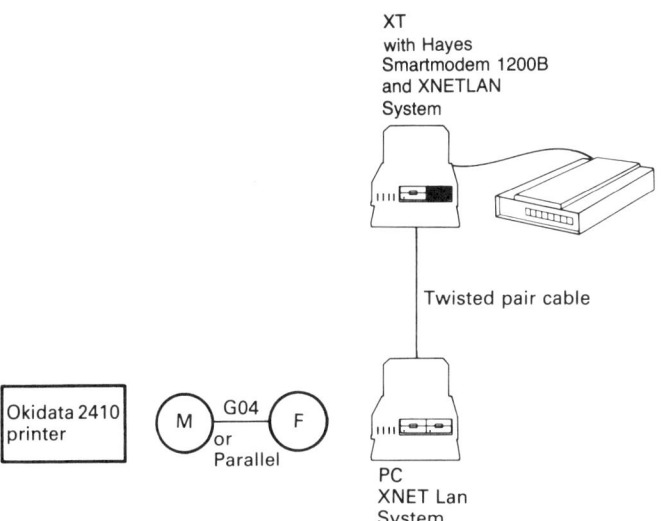

Figure 9-14 Multiple PCs in a local area network. Should multiple PCs be in the same general proximity, resource sharing is possible through the installation of a local area network. XCOMP's X-NET is such a network that allows many PCs and XTs to be connected together. A printer on the PC in this network can be accessed by both the XT and the PC. The files on the XT can be set up to be available to anyone on the network. The 10 megabytes could be divided into private partitions for each user. A board-level modem in the XT could be set up as only available to the XT. The modem could be accessible by either the XT or the PC. These are only a few of the possibilities offered by a LAN. Restrictions and capabilities are controlled by the network administrator.
1. This configuration is possible with an X-NET Starter Kit. Additional PC/XTs may be added.
2. Both the XT and the PC must have terminator plugs on the LAN board as they are the endpoints in the network. These plugs are provided.
3. The XT could be set up as physical address 01 and mnemonic address 'XT'.
4. The PC could be set up as physical address 02 and mnemonic address 'PC'.
5. The Okidata could be identified from the XT's perspective as 'PRINTER'. This is done through macros provided with the X-NET software. A single command on the XT issues the appropriate command to set up the printer.
6. The PC user could access the XT hard disk system through a similar procedure as in step 5.

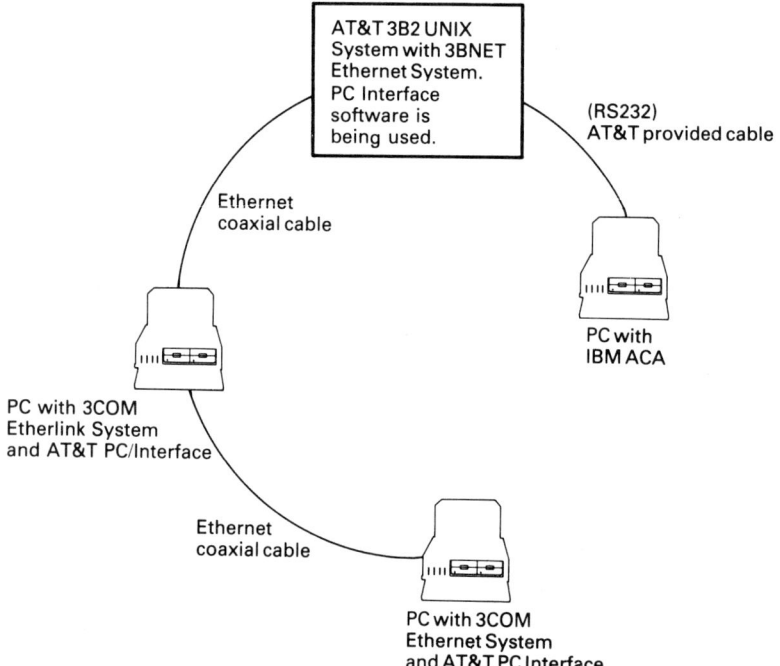

Figure 9-15 Multiple PCs connected to an AT&T 3B2 UNIX system. PC INTERFACE software is required on all PCs as well as the 3B2 system. A 3BNET board is used to provide an Ethernet compatible interface on the 3B2. A 3COM Etherlink system is used on each PC for Ethernet compatibility. Should a PC desire access to the 3B2 using an Asynchronous ASCII interface (TTX), the 3B2 and PC should be equipped for RS-232 ports.
1. The 3B2 can function as a file server.
2. The PC operators treat the 3B2 as if it were a hard disk drive and access it as such, with standard MS-DOS commands.
3. All PCs now have access to the full UNIX operating system.
4. All PCs may utilize peripherals, such as modems and printers, associated with the 3B2 system.
5. PCs maintain full MS-DOS capabilities.
6. A PC user may run a program under UNIX as well as a local MS-DOS program simultaneously, alternating between the two systems as appropriate.

APPENDICES

APPENDIX

RS-232 circuit summary with CCITT equivalents

Figure A-1 is a summary of the RS-232 interface pin assignments. For ease of reference, each signal is grouped into one of the categories of ground, data, control, or timing. For explanations of each, refer to the text. Both the EIA and CCITT nomenclatures are given for cross-reference between the U.S. and international versions of the standard.

Pin	Interchange Circuit	CCITT Equivalent	Description	Gnd	Data From DCE	Data To DCE	Control From DCE	Control To DCE	Timing From DCE	Timing To DCE
1	AA	101	Protective ground	X						
7	AB	102	Signal ground/common return	X						
2	BA	103	Transmitted data			X				
3	BB	104	Received data		X					
4	CA	105	Request to send					X		
5	CB	106	Clear to send				X			
6	CC	107	Data set ready				X			
20	CD	108.2	Data terminal ready					X		
22	CE	125	Ring indicator				X			
8	CF	109	Received line signal detector				X			
21	CG	110	Signal quality detector				X			
23	CH	111	Data signal rate selector (DTE)					X		
23	CI	112	Data signal rate selector (DCE)				X			
24	DA	113	Transmitter signal element timing (DTE)							X
15	DB	114	Transmitter signal element timing (DCE)						X	
17	DD	115	Receiver signal element timing (DCE)						X	
14	SBA	118	Secondary transmitted data			X				
16	SBB	119	Secondary received data		X					
19	SCA	120	Secondary request to send					X		
13	SCB	121	Secondary clear to send				X			
12	SCF	122	Secondary received line signal detector				X			

Figure A-1 RS-232 Circuit Summary with CCITT Equivalents

APPENDIX

B

RS-232 pin assignments for PC boards, terminals, and peripherals

Included in this appendix are computers, printers, and terminals (CRTs). Charts displaying RS-232-C pin assignments, together with their functions and directions, are available for the ports offered on the various devices. In addition, pertinent facts relating to items such as flow control are included. These items are extremely important when connecting combinations of computers, modems, and peripherals.

From these lists, a determination can be made for the construction of an RS-232 cable for connecting equipment. Once the devices have been selected, note the corresponding pin configuration. Use this pin configuration in conjunction with Appendix C to build the appropriate cable.

Every attempt was made to include as many different devices and accurate pin configurations as possible. However, should a device not be included, merely match its RS-232 configuration with one that is listed. Note the corresponding pin configuration and use this for a reference in Appendix C.

Company: Addmaster Corp.
Product: 170/180 Printers
Port: RS232   Pin Configuration: P02

Pin	Function	Direction
1	Chassis ground	N/A*
3	Received data	To printer
4	Request to send	From printer
5	Clear to send	To printer
7	Signal ground	N/A

Company: Alphacom Inc.
Product: 20/40/84 Printers
Port: RS-232   Pin Configuration: P03

Pin	Function	Direction
2	Transmitted data	From printer
3	Received data	To printer
4	Request to send	From printer
5	Clear to send	To printer
6	Data set ready	To printer
7	Ground	N/A
20	Data terminal ready	From printer

Note: Pin 20 should be used for flow control.

App. B RS-232 Pin Assignments for PC Boards, Terminals, and Peripherals

Company: Amperex Electronic Corp.
Product: GP300 Printer
Port: RS-232   Pin Configuration: P03

Pin	Function	Direction
1	Protective ground	N/A
2	Transmitted data	From GP300
3	Received data	To GP300
4	Request to send	From GP300
5	Clear to send	To GP300
6	Data set ready	To GP300
7	Signal ground	N/A
8	Data carrier detect	To GP300
20	Data terminal ready	From GP300

Notes: (a) Pin 20 may be used for a busy indicator. (b) The GP300 also supports XON/XOFF and ACK/NAK sequences.

Company: Anacom General Corp.
Product: 150/160 Printers
Port: Serial   Pin Configuration: P04

Pin	Function	Direction
1	Chassis ground	N/A
3	Received data	To printer
4	Request to send	From printer
7	Signal ground	N/A
11	Printer busy	From printer
20	Data terminal ready	From printer
22	External power	To printer

Note: Pin 11 may be used for flow control.

Company: Anadex Inc.
Product: DP8000 and DP9000 Series Printers
Port: EIA (optioned for full-duplex)   Pin Configuration: P01

Pin	Function	Direction
1	Protective ground	N/A
2	Transmitted data	From DP8000
3	Received data	To DP8000
4	Request to send	From DP8000
5	Clear to send	To DP8000
6	Data set ready	To DP8000
7	Signal ground	N/A
8	Data carrier detect	To DP8000
19	Secondary request to send	From DP8000
20	Data terminal ready	From DP8000

Notes: (a) Pins 4 and 5 are internally jumpered, as are pins 6 and 8. (b) Pin 19 can be used for flow control. (c) A simplex mode of operation is possible using only pins 3, 7, and 19.

Company: Anderson Jacobson, Inc.
Product: AJ 520 CRT
Port: Primary Communications Port   Pin Configuration: T01

Pin	Function	Direction
1	Protective ground	N/A
2	Transmitted data	From AJ 520
3	Received data	To AJ 520
4	Request to send	From AJ 520
5	Clear to send	To AJ 520
6	Data set ready	To AJ 520
7	Signal ground	N/A
8	Carrier detect	To AJ 520
9	Same as pin 18	
10	Same as pin 25	
11	Same as pin 19	
12	Secondary carrier detect	To AJ 520
15	Transmit clock	To AJ 520
17	Receive clock	To AJ 520
18	Modem remote test	N/A
19	Secondary request to send	From AJ 520
20	Data terminal ready	From AJ 520
22	Ring indicator	To AJ 520
25	Modem local test	N/A

Company: Anderson Jacobson, Inc.
Product: AJ 650 Ink Jet Printer
Port: RS-232-C   Pin Configuration: P05

Pin	Function	Direction
1	Protective ground	N/A
2	Transmitted data	From AJ 650
3	Received serial data	To AJ 650
4	Request to send	From AJ 650
5	Clear to send	To AJ 650
6	Data set ready	To AJ 650
7	Signal return	N/A
8	Data carrier detect	To AJ 650
11	Busy	From AJ 650
13	Alternate transmitted data	From AJ 650
14	Alternate busy	From AJ 650
15	Alternate data terminal ready	From AJ 650
20	Data terminal ready	From AJ 650

Notes: (a) Has software XON/XOFF transmit capability. (b) Pin 8 must be high for the printer to receive data. (c) Pin 11 can be used for hardware flow control.

Company: Anderson Jacobson, Inc.
Product: AJ 862 Printer Terminal
Port: EIA   Pin Configuration: P01

Pin	Function	Direction
1	Protective ground	N/A
2	Transmitted data	From AJ 862
3	Received data	To AJ 862
4	Request to send	From AJ 862
5	Clear to send	To AJ 862
7	Signal ground	N/A
8	Carrier detect	To AJ 862
11	Supervisory trans. data	From AJ 862
12	Supervisory rec. data	To AJ 862
14	Supervisory trans. data	From AJ 862
16	Supervisory rec. data	To AJ 862
19	Supervisory trans. data	From AJ 862
20	Data terminal ready	From AJ 862
25	Analog loopback/long func.	Special

Note: Pins 11, 12, 14, 16, and 19 are used in 202 mode only.

Company: Anderson Jacobson, Inc.
Product: AJ 880 Printer Terminal
Port: EIA Interface   Pin Configuration: P03

Pin	Function	Direction
1	Protective ground	N/A
2	Transmitted data	From AJ 880
3	Received data	To AJ 880
4	Request to send	From AJ 880
5	Clear to send	To AJ 880
6	Data set ready	To AJ 880
7	Signal ground	N/A
8	Carrier detect	To AJ 880
11	Secondary request to send	From AJ 880
12	Secondary carrier detect or speed indicator	To AJ 880
19	Secondary request to send	From AJ 880
20	Data terminal ready	From AJ 880
23	Speed select	From AJ 880

Note: Pin 20 (DTR) is dropped when any of these conditions is present: power is off, AJ 880 is in local, or a paper fault occurs.

Company: Ann Arbor Terminals, Inc.
Product: Ambassador Terminals
Port: Computer and Printer   Pin Configuration: T04

Pin	Function	Direction
2	Transmitted data	From Ambassador
3	Received data	To Ambassador
4	Request to send	From Ambassador
5	Clear to send	To Ambassador
7	Signal ground	N/A
20	Data terminal ready	From Ambassador

Note: The bottom port is generally for the computer, while the top port is for the printer.

App. B RS-232 Pin Assignments for PC Boards, Terminals, and Peripherals

Company: Apple Computer Inc.
Product: Apple III
Port: Port C   Pin Configuration: C01

Pin	Function	Direction
1	Protective ground	N/A
2	Transmitted data	From Apple III
3	Received data	To Apple III
4	Request to send	From Apple III
5	Clear to send	To Apple III
6	Data set ready	To Apple III
7	Signal ground	N/A
8	Data carrier detect	To Apple III
20	Data terminal ready	From Apple III

Notes: (a) If pin 6 is on, the Apple III assumes that the remote device is on and operational. (This could be used for hardware flow control.) (b) If pin 8 is on, the Apple III assumes that the remote device is ready to transmit data.

Company: Apple Computer Inc.
Product: Apple Communication Interface Card
Port: Serial   Pin Configuration: C05

Pin	Function	Direction
2	Transmitted data	From Comm. Card
3	Received data	To Comm. Card
4	Request to send	From Comm. Card
5	Clear to send	To Comm. Card
7	Signal ground	N/A

Notes: (a) Pins 6 and 20 are internally connected. (b) Pins 4 and 8 are internally connected.

Company: Apple Computer Inc.
Product: Super Serial Card
Port: Modem Position   Pin Configuration: C01

Pin	Function	Direction
1	Frame ground	N/A
2	Transmitted data	From SSC
3	Received data	To SSC
4	Request to send	From SSC
5	Clear to send	To SSC
6	Data set ready	To SSC
7	Signal ground	N/A
8	Data carrier detect	To SSC
19	Secondary clear to send	To SSC
20	Data terminal ready	From SSC

Note: The super serial card in this mode emulates data terminal equipment.

Company: Apple Computer Inc.
Product: Super Serial Card
Port: Terminal Position   Pin Configuration: C02

Pin	Function	Direction
1	Frame ground	N/A
2	Received data	To SSC
3	Transmitted data	From SSC
4	Request to send	To SSC
5	Clear to send	From SSC
6	Data set ready	From SSC
7	Signal ground	N/A
8	Data carrier detect	From SSC
20	Data terminal ready	To SSC

Note: This connection can be tricky if you fail to realize that in this mode the super serial card is emulating data communication equipment. It is internally jumpered to provide a null-modem cable function.

App. B RS-232 Pin Assignments for PC Boards, Terminals, and Peripherals **189**

Company: Applied Digital Data Systems Inc.
Product: Regent 40 and 60
Port: EIA   Pin Configuration: T01

Pin	Function	Direction
1	Protective ground	N/A
2	Transmitted data	From Regent
3	Received data	To Regent
4	Request to send	From Regent
5	Clear to send	To Regent
6	Data set ready	To Regent
7	Signal ground	N/A
8	Rec. line signal detector	To Regent
11	Secondary request to send	From Regent
12	Secondary RLSD	To Regent
20	Data terminal ready	From Regent

Company: Applied Digital Data Systems Inc.
Product: Viewpoint CRT
Port: EIA   Pin Configuration: T04

Pin	Function	Direction
1	Protective ground	N/A
2	Transmitted data	From Viewpoint
3	Received data	To Viewpoint
4	Request to send	From Viewpoint
5	Clear to send	To Viewpoint
7	Signal ground	N/A
11	Secondary break indicator	From Viewpoint
20	Data terminal ready	From Viewpoint

Note: Supports up to 19,200 bps operation.

Company: AST Research Inc.
Product: CC-232 Communication Board
Port: A and B   Pin Configuration: C01

Pin	Function	Direction
2	Transmit data	From CC-232
3	Receive data	To CC-232
4	Request to send	From CC-232
5	Clear to send	To CC-232
6	Data set ready	To CC-232
7	Signal ground	N/A
8	Data carrier detect	To CC-232
15	Transmit timing	To CC-232
17	Receive timing	To CC-232
20	Data terminal ready	From CC-232
24	Transmit timing	From CC-232

Company: AST Research Inc.
Product: CC-332 Communication Board
Port: DTE   Pin Configuration: C01

Pin	Function	Direction
2	Transmit data	From CC-332
3	Receive data	To CC-332
4	Request to send	From CC-332
5	Clear to send	To CC-332
6	Data set ready	To CC-332
7	Signal ground	N/A
8	Data carrier detect	To CC-332
15	Transmit timing	To CC-332
17	Receive timing	To CC-332
20	Data terminal ready	From CC-332

Company: Axiom Corp.
Product: EX-800 Printers
Port: HS Option   Pin Configuration: P06

Pin	Function	Direction
1	Protective ground	N/A
3	Received data	To printer
7	Circuit ground	N/A
20	Buffer overrun	From printer

Note: Without the HS option, the printers merely use the ground leads and pin 3 for input of data.

App. B RS-232 Pin Assignments for PC Boards, Terminals, and Peripherals

Company: Axiom Corp.
Product: IMP Printers
Port: HS Option   Pin Configuration: P05

Pin	Function	Direction
1	Chassis ground	N/A
2	Transmitted data	From printer
3	Received data	To printer
4	Request to send	From printer
6	Data set ready	To printer
7	Signal ground	N/A
8	Carrier detect	To printer
11	Busy	From printer
20	Off-line	From printer

Notes: (a) Two configurations are possible with the HS option: Configuration 1 is compatible with the standard Axiom; configuration 2 is compatible with the TI-810 printer. (b) Pins 6 and 8 must be on for the printer to receive data. (c) Pin 11 should be used for flow control.

Company: Axiom Corp.
Product: IMP Printers
Port: RS-232   Pin Configuration: P06

Pin	Function	Direction
1	Chassis ground	N/A
3	RS-232 input	To printer
7	Signal ground	N/A
20	Busy	From printer

Note: Option must be set to provide RS-232 as opposed to TTL levels on pin 20 before it may be used for busy signal.

Company: BARR Systems, Inc.
Product: BARR/HASP
Port: RS232   Pin Configuration: C01

Pin	Function	Direction
2	Transmit data	From BARR/HASP
3	Receive data	To BARR/HASP
4	Request to send	From BARR/HASP
5	Clear to send	To BARR/HASP
6	Data set ready	To BARR/HASP
7	Signal ground	N/A
15	Transmit timing	To BARR/HASP
17	Receive timing	To BARR/HASP
20	Data terminal ready	From BARR/HASP

Company: Beehive International
Product: DM 10/20/30, Basic (DM 5), Standard (DM 5A), Plus (DM 5B)
Port: Main   Pin Configuration: T01

Pin	Function	Direction
1	Protective ground	N/A
2	Transmitted data	From terminal
3	Received data	To terminal
4	Request to send	From terminal
5	Clear to send	To terminal
6	Data set ready	To terminal
7	Signal ground	N/A
20	Data terminal ready	From terminal

Note: If pin 5 is low, data transmission is prohibited. This can be used in flow control.

Company: Bell System
Product: DATASPEED 40 Printer
Port: RS-232   Pin Configuration: P05

Pin	Function	Direction
1	Protective ground	N/A
2	Transmitted data	From 40
3	Received data	To 40
4	Request to send	From 40
5	Clear to send	To 40
6	Data set ready	To 40
7	Signal ground	N/A
8	Data carrier detect	To 40
11	Supervisory transmitted data	From 40
12	Supervisory received data	To 40
20	Data terminal ready	From 40
22	Ring indicator	To 40
23	Alarm	N/A

App. B   RS-232 Pin Assignments for PC Boards, Terminals, and Peripherals

Company: Bell System
Product: DATASPEED 40/2 Terminal
Port: COMM   Pin Configuration: T01

Pin	Function	Direction
1	Protective ground	N/A
2	Transmitted data	From 40/2
3	Received data	To 40/2
4	Request to send	From 40/2
5	Clear to send	To 40/2
6	Data set ready	To 40/2
7	Signal ground	N/A
8	Rec. line signal detector	To 40/2
11	Secondary request to send	From 40/2
19	Secondary request to send	From 40/2
20	Data terminal ready	From 40/2
22	Ring indicator	To 40/2

Note: If this port is optioned for full-duplex, pins 4, 11, and 19 are not present.

Company: Bell System
Product: DATASPEED 4420 Terminal
Port: Modem   Pin Configuration: T01

Pin	Function	Direction
1	Frame ground	N/A
2	Transmitted data	From 4420
3	Received data	To 4420
4	Request to send	From 4420
5	Clear to send	To 4420
6	Data set ready	To 4420
7	Signal ground	N/A
8	Rec. line signal detector	To 4420
11	Secondary request to send	From 4420
12	Secondary RLSD	To 4420
15	Transmission timing	To 4420
17	Receiver timing	To 4420
19	Secondary request to send	From 4420
20	Data terminal ready	From 4420
22	Ring indicator	To 4420

Note: Pins 15 and 17 are used with isochronous operation.

Company: Bell System
Product: Model 43 Teleprinter
Port: EIA   Pin Configuration: P03

Pin	Function	Direction
1	Protective ground	N/A
2	Transmitted data	From 43
3	Received data	To 43
4	Request to send	From 43
5	Clear to send	To 43
6	Data set ready	To 43
7	Signal ground	N/A
8	Carrier detect/RLSD	To 43
20	Data terminal ready	From 43
22	Ring indicator	To 43

Note: Pin 20 is affected by the paper supply.

Company: Bell System
Product: TP-1000 Teleprinter
Port: EIA   Pin Configuration: P01

Pin	Function	Direction
1	Protective ground	N/A
2	Transmitted data	From TP-1000
3	Received data	To TP-1000
4	Request to send	From TP-1000
5	Clear to send	To TP-1000
6	Data set ready	To TP-1000
7	Signal ground	N/A
8	Data carrier detect	To TP-1000
19	Secondary request to send	From TP-1000
20	Data terminal ready	From TP-1000
22	Ring indicator	To TP-1000

Note: Pin 19 can be used for flow control.

App. B RS-232 Pin Assignments for PC Boards, Terminals, and Peripherals

Company: Black Box Catalog
Product: Mini-Print Spooler
Port: Serial Input (Socket)   Pin Configuration: P03

Pin	Function	Direction
1	Protective ground	N/A
2	Transmit data	From Spooler
3	Receive data	To Spooler
4	Request to send	From Spooler
6	Data set ready	To Spooler
7	Signal ground	N/A
20	Data terminal ready	From Spooler

Note: Pin 20 is used for hardware flow control. XON/XOFF and ETX/ACK software flow control are also supported

Company: Black Box Catalog
Product: Mini-Print Spooler
Port: Serial Output   Pin Configuration: C09

Pin	Function	Direction
1	Protective ground	N/A
2	Transmit data	To Spooler
3	Receive data	From Spooler
5	Clear to send	From Spooler
6	Data set ready	From Spooler
7	Signal ground	N/A
20	Data terminal ready	To Spooler

Note: Pin 20 is used for hardware flow control and must be on for the Spooler to transmit data on pin 3. Software flow-control methods XON/XOFF and ETX/ACK are supported.

Company: California Computer Systems
Product: Z/Plus Computer Board
Port: Serial   Pin Configuration: C01

Pin	Function	Direction
2	Transmit data	From Z/Plus
3	Receive data	To Z/Plus
4	Request to send	From Z/Plus
5	Clear to send	To Z/Plus
6	Data set ready	To Z/Plus
7	Signal ground	N/A
8	Data carrier detect	To Z/Plus
20	Data terminal ready	From Z/Plus
22	Ring indicator	To Z/Plus

Company: Cardinal Scale Manufacturing Co.
Product: 2170 Printer
Port: Serial   Pin Configuration: P03

Pin	Function	Direction
1	Chassis ground	N/A
2	Transmitted data	From 2170
3	Received data	To 2170
4	Request to send	From 2170
5	Clear to send	To 2170
6	Data set ready	To 2170
7	Signal ground	N/A
8	Data carrier detect	To 2170
9	VCC	N/A
19	Signal ground	N/A
20	Data terminal ready	From 2170

Notes: (a) The printer can apply back pressure on pin 20. This is used for flow control. (b) Clear to send must be high. Manufacturer also recommends jumpering pins 8 to 9 and 7 to 19.

App. B   RS-232 Pin Assignments for PC Boards, Terminals, and Peripherals   197

Company: Casio Inc.
Product: FX 9000P
Port: RS-232   Pin Configuration: P03

Pin	Function	Direction
1	Protective ground	N/A
2	Transmitted data	From Casio
3	Received data	To Casio
4	Request to send	From Casio
5	Clear to send	To Casio
6	Data set ready	To Casio
7	Signal ground	N/A
8	Data carrier detect	To Casio
20	Data terminal ready	From Casio
22	Ring indicator	To Casio

Notes: (a) A cable is connected to J3 to allow the 25-pin connector. (b) Either pin 4 or pin 20 can be used to indicate a busy signal.

Company: Centronics Data Computer Corporation
Product: 150 and 350 Series, 704-9, Adaptable Serial Interface
Port: Serial   Pin Configuration: P05

Pin	Function	Direction
1	Protective ground	N/A
2	Transmitted data	From printers
3	Received data	To printers
4	Request to send	From printers
5	Clear to send	To printers
6	Data set ready	To printers
7	Signal ground	N/A
8	Data carrier detect	To printers
11	Secondary request to send	From printers
20	Data terminal ready	From printers

Note: Pin 11 can be used for flow control.

Company: Centronics Data Computer Corporation
Product: 737-3 Printer
Port: RS-232   Pin Configuration: P07

Pin	Function	Direction
1	Protective ground	N/A
2	Transmitted data	From 737
3	Received data	To 737
6	Data set ready	To 737
7	Signal ground	N/A
8	Data carrier detect	To 737
11	Reverse channel	From 737
20	Data terminal ready	From 737

Notes: (a) Pins 6 and 8 must be on to allow data reception. (b) Pin 11 should be used for flow control.

Company: Centronics Data Computer Corporation
Product: 761 Teleprinter
Port: RS-232   Pin Configuration: P05

Pin	Function	Direction
1	Protective ground	N/A
2	Transmitted data	From 761
3	Received data	To 761
4	Request to send	From 761
5	Clear to send	To 761
6	Data set ready	To 761
7	Signal ground	N/A
8	Data carrier detect	To 761
11	Transmit reverse channel	From 761
14	Transmit reverse channel	From 761
12	Receive reverse channel	To 761
16	Receive reverse channel	To 761
20	Data terminal ready	From 761
22	Ring indicator	To 761

Notes: (a) Pin 8 must be on for the printer to receive data. (b) Pin 11 or 14 may be used for flow control.

App. B   RS-232 Pin Assignments for PC Boards, Terminals, and Peripherals   **199**

Company: C. Itoh Electronics Inc.
Product: Comet I/II, Starwriter I/II, Prowriter I/II, and F10 Series Printers
Port: Serial   Pin Configuration: P06

Pin	Function	Direction
1	Frame ground	N/A
3	Received data	To printers
7	Signal ground	N/A
20	Data terminal ready	From printers

Note: Pin 20 can be used for the hardware XON/XOFF function. Software XON/XOFF is available on Prowriters and F10s only. In the latter case, pins 2, 4, 5, 6, and 8 are used normally.

Company: Columbia Data Products, Inc.
Product: 1600 (MPC) Computer
Port: Console/Serial   Pin Configuration: C01

Pin	Function	Direction
1	Ground	N/A
2	Transmitted data	From MPC
3	Received data	To MPC
4	Request to send	From MPC
5	Clear to send	To MPC
6	Data set ready	To MPC
7	Ground	N/A
8	Data carrier detect	To MPC
20	Data terminal ready	From MPC
22	Ring indicator	To MPC

Company: Comrex International Inc.
Product: Comriter Printer
Port: RS-232-C   Pin Configuration: P05

Pin	Function	Direction
1	Frame ground	N/A
2	Transmitted data	From Comriter
3	Received data	To Comriter
4	Request to send	From Comriter
5	Clear to send	To Comriter
6	Data set ready	To Comriter
7	Signal ground	N/A
8	Rec. line signal detector	To Comriter
11	Reverse channel	From Comriter
20	Data terminal ready	From Comriter

Notes: (a) Pins 5, 6, and 8 must be on before data can be transmitted. (b) Pin 4 is high when printer has power. (c) Pin 11 or pin 20 may be used for printer status. (d) The Comriter also supports XON/XOFF control characters.

Company: Data General Corporation
Product: Dasher D100/200 and G300 Display Terminals
Port: EIA   Pin Configuration: T01

Pin	Function	Direction
2	Transmitted data	From terminals
3	Received data	To terminals
4	Request to send	From terminals
5	Clear to send	To terminals
6	Data set ready	To terminals
7	Signal ground	N/A
8	Data carrier detect	To terminals
20	Data terminal ready	From terminals

Note: If pin 5 is off, the terminal cannot transmit data.

Company: Data General Corporation
Product: Dasher TP1 Terminal Printer
Port: EIA   Pin Configuration: P08

Pin	Function	Direction
2	Transmitted data	From TP1
3	Received data	To TP1
7	Signal ground	N/A
20	Data terminal ready	From TP1

Note: Pin 20 controls the printer busy status and can be used for flow control.

App. B   RS-232 Pin Assignments for PC Boards, Terminals, and Peripherals

Company: Data General Corporation
Product: Dasher TP2 Printer
Port: Serial   Pin Configuration: P08

Pin	Function	Direction
2	Transmitted data	From TP2
3	Received data	To TP2
4	Request to send	From TP2
5	Clear to send	To TP2
6	Data set ready	To TP2
7	Signal ground	N/A
20	Data terminal ready	From TP2

Note: Pin 4 is held tight as long as data can be received. Should the buffer begin to fill up, this lead will go low. This can be used for hardware flow control; however, software XON/XOFF can be used.

Company: Data Impact Printer, Inc.
Product: DIP-85 Printer
Port: RS-232   Pin Configuration: P08

Pin	Function	Direction
1	Chassis ground	N/A
2	Transmitted data	From DIP-85
3	Received data	To DIP-85
5	Clear to send	From DIP-85
7	Signal ground	N/A
20	Data terminal ready	From DIP-85

Notes: (a) Pins 5 and 20 may be used for busy indicator. (b) The DIP-85 supports XON/XOFF characters.

Company: Dataproducts Corp.
Product: M-100 Printer
Port: Serial   Pin Configuration: P01

Pin	Function	Direction
1	Protective ground	N/A
2	Transmitted data	From printer
3	Received data	To printer
4	Request to send	From printer
5	Clear to send	To printer
6	Data set ready	To printer
7	Signal ground	N/A
8	Rec. line signal detector	To printer
11	Busy	From printer
19	Busy	From printer
20	Data terminal ready	From printer
22	Ring indicator	To printer

Notes: (a) Either pin 11 or pin 19 may be used for flow control. (b) Pins 4, 5, 6, and 20 must be on before the printer can transmit data. (c) Pin 20 and, optionally, pins 6 and 8 must be on for the printer to receive data.

Company: DATASOUTH Computer Corp.
Product: DS 180 Printer
Port: RS-232   Pin Configuration: P07

Pin	Function	Direction
1	Chassis ground	N/A
2	Serial data out	From DS 180
3	Serial data in	To DS 180
7	Signal ground	N/A
8	Carrier detect	To DS 180
11	Data terminal ready	From DS 180
20	Data terminal ready	From DS 180

Notes: (a) Either pin 11 or pin 20 may be used for busy indicator. (b) The DS 180 does support XON/XOFF protocol.

Company: Datavue Corporation
Product: 100, 200, 300 Series Displaymaster CRTs
Port: Communications Port   Pin Configuration: T01

Pin	Function	Direction
1	Chassis ground	N/A
2	Transmitted data	From CRT
3	Received data	To CRT
4	Request to send	From CRT
5	Clear to send	To CRT
6	Data set ready	To CRT
7	Signal and logic ground	N/A
20	Data terminal ready	From CRT

Note: Optionally, pins 15 and 17 can be transmit and receive clocks, respectively, for synchronous operation.

Company: Diablo Systems, Inc.
Product: Model 1610/1620 Printers
Port: EIA   Pin Configuration: P03

Pin	Function	Direction
1	Protective ground	N/A
2	Transmitted data	From printers
3	Received data	To printers
4	Request to send	From printers
5	Clear to send	To printers
6	Data set ready	To printers
7	Signal ground	N/A
8	Rec. line signal detector	To printers
20	Data terminal ready	From printers
23	Data signal rate selector	N/C

Notes: (a) Pin 23 is included for possible future use. (b) These printers support the ETX/ACK protocol and should be used when operating at 1200 bps to prevent overflow.

Company: Diablo Systems, Inc.
Product: KSR 1640/1650
Port: EIA   Pin Configuration: P03

Pin	Function	Direction
1	Protective ground	N/A
2	Transmitted data	From printers
3	Received data	To printers
4	Request to send	From printers
5	Clear to send	To printers
6	Data set ready	To printers
7	Signal ground	N/A
8	Rec. line signal detector	To printers
20	Data terminal ready	From printers

Notes: (a) Pin 4 is always high. (b) Pin 6 must be high to receive data. (c) Pin 5 must be high to transmit data. (d) Pin 20 can provide flow control.

Company: Diablo Systems, Inc.
Product: Model 620
Port: Serial   Pin Configuration: P03

Pin	Function	Direction
2	Transmitted data	From 620
3	Received data	To 620
4	Request to send	From 620
6	Data set ready	To 620
7	Signal ground	N/A
20	Data terminal ready	From 620

Notes: (a) Pin 4 is always high. (b) Pin 6 must be on to before data can be received. (c) Flow control is switch-selectable. (d) Pin 20 is used for the hardware XON/XOFF function.

App. B RS-232 Pin Assignments for PC Boards, Terminals, and Peripherals

Company: Diablo Systems, Inc.
Product: RO 630
Port: EIA   Pin Configuration: P05

Pin	Function	Direction
1	Protective ground	N/A
2	Transmitted data	From 630
3	Received data	To 630
4	Request to send	From 630
5	Clear to send	To 630
6	Data set ready	To 630
7	Signal ground	N/A
8	Rec. line signal detector	To 630
11	Printer ready	From 630
20	Data terminal ready	From 630

Notes: (a) Pin 4 is always high. (b) Pin 6 must be on before 630 can receive data. (c) Pin 20 can be used for hardware flow control instead of pin 11.

Company: Digital Equipment Corp.
Product: LA Series Printers
Port: EIA   Pin Configuration: P01

Pin	Function	Direction
1	Frame ground	N/A
2	Transmitted data	From printer
3	Received data	To printer
4	Request to send	From printer
5	Clear to send	To printer
6	Data set ready	To printer
7	Signal ground	N/A
8	Data carrier detect	To printer
11	Secondary request to send	From printer
12	Speed indicator/SDCD	To printer
19	Secondary request to send	From printer
20	Data terminal ready	From printer
22	Ring indicator	To printer
23	Speed select	From printer

Note: Either pin 11 or pin 19 may be used for hardware flow control, although software XON/XOFF capability exists.

Company: Digital Equipment Corp.
Product: Rainbow PC-100
Port: Communication   Pin Configuration: C01

Pin	Function	Direction
1	Protective ground	N/A
2	Transmitted data	From PC-100
3	Received data	To PC-100
4	Request to send	From PC-100
5	Clear to send	To PC-100
6	Data set ready	To PC-100
7	Signal ground	N/A
8	Carrier detect	To PC-100
15	Transmit clock	To PC-100
17	Receive clock	To PC-100
19	Secondary request to send	From PC-100
20	Data terminal ready	From PC-100
22	Ring indicator	To PC-100
23	Speed select	From PC-100

Company: Digital Equipment Corp.
Product: VT-100 Series Terminals
Port: Communication   Pin Configuration: T01

Pin	Function	Direction
1	Protective ground	N/A
2	Transmitted data	From VT-100
3	Received data	To VT-100
4	Request to send	From VT-100
5	Clear to send	To VT-100
6	Data set ready	To VT-100
7	Signal ground	N/A
8	Carrier detect	To VT-100
11	Secondary request to send	From VT-100
12	Secondary carrier detect	To VT-100
15	Transmit clock	To VT-100
17	Receive clock	To VT-100
19	Secondary request to send	From VT-100
20	Data terminal ready	From VT-100
22	Ring indicator	To VT-100
23	Secondary request to send	From VT-100

Notes: (a) Pins 5, 6, 8, 15, 17, and 22 are ignored at all times by the basic VT-100 terminals. (b) Pins 11, 19, and 23 may also be used for a speed select signal from the VT-100. (c) Pin 4 is asserted at all times when the VT-100 is on.

App. B RS-232 Pin Assignments for PC Boards, Terminals, and Peripherals

Company: Epson America, Inc.
Product: MX-70/80/100 Series
Port: RS-232-C   Pin Configuration: P07

Pin	Function	Direction
1	Protective ground	N/A
2	Transmitted data	From MX
3	Received data	To MX
6	Data set ready	To MX
7	Signal ground	N/A
8	Data carrier detect	To MX
11	Reverse channel	From MX
20	Data terminal ready	From MX

Notes: (a) Pin 6 must be on for the printer to receive data. (b) Pin 8 is the same signal as pin 6. (c) Pin 11 can be used for flow control.

Company: Extel Corporation
Product: B318 Series
Port: RS-232   Pin Configuration: P10

Pin	Function	Direction
1	Protective ground	N/A
2	Transmitted data	From Extel
3	Received data	To Extel
4	Request to send	From Extel
5	Clear to send	To Extel
6	Data set ready	To Extel
7	Signal ground	N/A
8	Data carrier detect	To Extel
20	Data terminal ready	From Extel

Note: Loss of pin 6 restricts data transmission.

Company: Facit, Inc.
Product: 4500 Series Printer
Port: RS-232   Pin Configuration: P03

Pin	Function	Direction
1	Protective ground	N/A
2	Transmitted data	From printer
3	Received data	To printer
4	Request to send	From printer
5	Clear to send	To printer
6	Data set ready	To printer
7	Signal ground	N/A
8	Rec. line signal detector	To printer
15	Transmit timing	To printer
17	Receive timing	To printer
20	Data terminal ready	From printer

Notes: (a) Pin 20 may be optioned for flow control. (b) The printers support XON/XOFF characters.

Company: Florida Data Corp.
Product: OSP100 Series Printer
Port: Serial   Pin Configuration: P05

Pin	Function	Direction
1	Frame ground	N/A
2	Transmitted data	From printer
3	Received data	To printer
4	Request to send	From printer
5	Clear to send	To printer
6	Data set ready	To printer
7	Signal ground	N/A
11	Ready	From printer
20	Data terminal ready	From printer

Notes: (a) XON/XOFF and ETX/ACK protocols are supported. (b) Pin 11 or pin 20 may be used for hardware flow control. (c) Pin 6 must be on for data reception to occur. (d) Pin 5 must be on for data transmission to occur.

App. B   RS-232 Pin Assignments for PC Boards, Terminals, and Peripherals

Company: Fujitsu America, Inc.
Product: SP830 Character Printer
Port: Serial   Pin Configuration: P03

Pin	Function	Direction
1	Protective ground	N/A
2	Transmitted data	From SP830
3	Received data	To SP830
4	Request to send	From SP830
5	Clear to send	To SP830
6	Data set ready	To SP830
7	Signal ground	N/A
8	Data carrier detect	To SP830
20	Data terminal ready	From SP830

Note: Either pin 20 or pin 11 may be used for hardware flow control, although software XON/XOFF capability can be used.

Company: General Electric Company
Product: GE 2120 Printer
Port: EIA   Pin Configuration: P03

Pin	Function	Direction
1	Protective ground	N/A
2	Transmitted data	From 2120
3	Received data	To 2120
4	Request to send	From 2120
5	Clear to send	To 2120
6	Data set ready	To 2120
7	Signal ground	N/A
8	Rec. line signal detector	To 2120
11	Secondary request to send	From 2120
12	Secondary RLSD (202)	To 2120
12	Speed indicator (212)	To 2120
19	Secondary request to send	From 2120
20	Data terminal ready	From 2120
22	Ring indicator	To 2120
23	Speed selector (212)	From 2120

Notes: (a) The function of pin 12 depends on the environment of either a 202 or 212 modem configuration. (b) XON/XOFF is supported; pin 20 is also optionable for hardware flow control.

Company: General Electric Company
Product: 2030 Printer
Port: EIA   Pin Configuration: P03

Pin	Function	Direction
1	Protective ground	N/A
2	Transmitted data	From 2030
3	Received data	To 2030
4	Request to send	From 2030
5	Clear to send	To 2030
6	Data set ready	To 2030
7	Signal ground	N/A
8	Rec. line signal detector	To 2030
20	Data terminal ready	From 2030
22	Ring indicator	To 2030

Notes: XON/XOFF is supported; pin 20 is also optionable for hardware flow control.

Company: General Electric Company
Product: TermiNet 300 Printer
Port: Modem   Pin Configuration: P03

Pin	Function	Direction
1	Protective ground	N/A
2	Transmitted data	From 300
3	Received data	To 300
5	Clear to send	To 300
6	Data set ready	To 300
7	Signal ground	N/A
8	Rec. line signal detector	To 300
20	Data terminal ready	From 300
22	Ring indicator	To 300

Company: Gulton Industries, Inc.
Product: AP-20 Printer
Port: Serial (TAC314-A)   Pin Configuration: P11

Pin	Function	Direction
1	Protective ground	N/A
3	Received data	To printer
6	Data set ready	To printer
7	Signal ground	N/A
20	Data terminal ready	From printer

Note: Pin 20 should be used for hardware flow control.

App. B RS-232 Pin Assignments for PC Boards, Terminals, and Peripherals 211

Company: Hazeltine Corporation
Product: 1400, 1500, Esprit I and II, and Executive Series CRTs
Port: EIA   Pin Configuration: T01

Pin	Function	Direction
1	Protective ground	N/A
2	Transmitted data	From CRT
3	Received data	To CRT
4	Request to send	From CRT
5	Clear to send	To CRT
6	Data set ready	To CRT
7	Signal ground	N/A
8	Data carrier detect	To CRT
20	Data terminal ready	From CRT

Note: Certain models of the Esprit and Executive series offer a bidirectional auxiliary port.

Company: Heath Company
Product: H-25 Printer
Port: Serial   Pin Configuration: P12

Pin	Function	Direction
1	Protective ground	N/A
2	Serial output	From printer
3	Serial input	To printer
4	Busy	From printer
7	Signal common	N/A

Notes: (a) Pin 4 is used for flow control. (b) The cable supplied with the printer connects pins 1–7, 11, and 20 straight through.

Company: Hewlett-Packard
Product: HP125 Computer
Port: 2   Pin Configuration: C01

Pin	Function	Direction
1	Shield	N/A
2	Transmitted data	From HP125
3	Received data	To HP125
4	Request to send	From HP125
5	Clear to send	To HP125
6	Data mode	To HP125
7	Signal ground	N/A
8	Receive ready	To HP125
20	Data terminal ready	From HP125

Company: Hewlett-Packard
Product: HP7475A Graphics Plotter
Port: RS-232   Pin Configuration: P03

Pin	Function	Direction
1	Protective ground	N/A
2	Transmit data	From HP
3	Receive data	To HP
4	Request to send	From HP
5	Clear to send	To HP
6	Data set ready	To HP
7	Signal ground	N/A
8	Data carrier detect	To HP
14	Secondary transmit data	From HP
16	Secondary receive data	To HP
17	Receive timing	To HP
20	Data terminal ready	From HP
23	Data signal rate selector	From HP

Note: Pin 20 may be used for hardware flow control. Software flow-control techniques used include XON/XOFF and ENQ/ACK.

Company: HI-G Co., Inc.
Product: 9/80 and 9/132 Printers
Port: RS-232   Pin Configuration: P04

Pin	Function	Direction
1	Frame ground	N/A
2	Transmitted data	From printer
3	Received data	To printer
4	Request to send	From printer
7	Signal ground	N/A
11	Auxiliary busy	From printer
20	Data terminal ready	From printer

Note: Pin 11 should be used for flow control.

Company: IBM
Product: 3101 Display Terminal
Port: Communication Interface   Pin Configuration: T01

Pin	Function	Direction
1	Frame ground	N/A
2	Transmitted data	From 3101
3	Received data	To 3101
4	Request to send	From 3101
5	Clear to send	To 3101
6	Data set ready	To 3101
7	Signal ground	N/A
8	Data carrier detect	To 3101
11	Supervisory transmitted data	From 3101
12	Supervisory received data	To 3101
20	Data terminal ready	From 3101

Company: IBM
Product: IBM PC/XT
Port: Asynchronous Communications Adapter
Pin Configuration: C01

Pin	Function	Direction
2	Transmitted data	From PC
3	Received data	To PC
4	Request to send	From PC
5	Clear to send	To PC
6	Data set ready	To PC
7	Signal ground	N/A
8	Carrier detect	To PC
20	Data terminal ready	From PC
22	Ring indicator	To PC

Company: IBM Corporation
Product: Asynchronous Communications Adapter
Port: RS-232   Pin Configuration: C01

Pin	Function	Direction
2	Transmit data	From ACA
3	Receive data	To ACA
4	Request to send	From ACA
5	Clear to send	To ACA
6	Data set ready	To ACA
7	Signal ground	N/A
8	Data carrier detect	To ACA
20	Data terminal ready	From ACA
22	Ring indicator	To ACA

Company: IBM Corporation
Product: BSC Adapter
Port: RS-232   Pin Configuration: C01

Pin	Function	Direction
2	Transmit data	From BSC Adapter
3	Receive data	To BSC Adapter
4	Request to send	From BSC Adapter
5	Clear to send	To BSC Adapter
6	Data set ready	To BSC Adapter
7	Signal ground	N/A
8	Receive line signal detector	To BSC Adapter
11	Select standby	From BSC Adapter
15	Transmit timing	To BSC Adapter
17	Receive timing	To BSC Adapter
18	Test (IBM modems only)	From BSC Adapter
20	Data terminal ready	From BSC Adapter
22	Ring indicator	To BSC Adapter
23	Data signal rate selector	From BSC Adapter
25	Test indicate (IBM modems only)	To BSC Adapter

Company: IBM Corporation
Product: SDLC Adapter
Port: RS232   Pin Configuration: C01

Pin	Function	Direction
2	Transmit data	From SDLC Adapter
3	Receive data	To SDLC Adapter
4	Request to send	From SDLC Adapter
5	Clear to send	To SDLC Adapter
6	Data set ready	To SDLC Adapter
7	Signal ground	N/A
8	Receive line signal detector	To SDLC Adapter
11	Select standby	From SDLC Adapter
15	Transmit timing	To SDLC Adapter
17	Receive timing	To SDLC Adapter
18	Test (IBM modems only)	From SDLC Adapter
20	Data terminal ready	From SDLC Adapter
22	Ring indicator	To SDLC Adapter
23	Data signal rate selector	From SDLC Adapter
25	Test indicate (IBM modems only)	To SDLC Adapter

Company: Information Technologies Inc.
Product: Linkup Communications Suppport System
Port: 1 and 2   Pin Configuration: C01

Pin	Function	Direction
1	Protective ground	N/A
2	Transmit data	From Linkup
3	Receive data	To Linkup
4	Request to send	From Linkup
5	Clear to send	To Linkup
6	Data set ready	To Linkup
7	Signal ground	N/A
8	Data carrier detect	To Linkup
15	Transmit timing	To Linkup
17	Receive timing	To Linkup
20	Data terminal ready	From Linkup

Company: Infoscribe, Inc.
Product: 500 Printer
Port: Serial Interface   Pin Configuration: P04

Pin	Function	Direction
2	Received data	To 500
3	Received data	To 500
4	Request to send	From 500
7	Signal ground	N/A
10	Chassis ground	N/A
11	Busy	From 500

Notes: (a) Either pin 2 or pin 3 is used for incoming data, but not both. (b) Pin 11 is used for flow control.

Company: Integral Data Systems, Inc.
Product: Prism, 560, 460, 440, and 445 Printers
Port: Serial   Pin Configuration: P08

Pin	Function	Direction
1	Protective ground	N/A
2	Transmitted data	From printer
3	Received data	To printer
7	Signal ground	N/A
20	Data terminal ready	From printer
25	Fault (EIA level)	From printer

Notes: (a) 440 and 445 do not use XON/XOFF; the other printers do support it. (b) Pin 20 on all printers may be used for hardware flow control of the buffer status. (c) The fault signal (pin 25) is forced low when a paper-out or error condition is detected; otherwise it is high.

App. B RS-232 Pin Assignments for PC Boards, Terminals, and Peripherals **217**

Company: Integrex, Inc.
Product: CX80 Printer
Port: RS-232   Pin Configuration: P07

Pin	Function	Direction
1	Protective ground	N/A
2	Transmitted data	From CX80
3	Received data	To CX80
6	Data set ready	To CX80
7	Signal ground	N/A
8	Data carrier detect	To CX80
11	Reverse channel	From CX80
20	Data terminal ready	From CX80

Notes: (a) Pins 6 and 8 must be high for the CX80 to receive data. (b) Pin 11 may be used for flow control. (c) The buffered version of this printer supports XON/XOFF and allows for pins 4 and 5 to be functional but removes pin 8 from the interface.

Company: Juki Industries of America, Inc.
Product: 6100 Printer
Port: RS-232   Pin Configuration: P03

Pin	Function	Direction
1	Protective ground	N/A
2	Transmitted data	From 6100
3	Received data	To 6100
4	Request to send	From 6100
5	Clear to send	To 6100
6	Data set ready	To 6100
7	Signal ground	N/A
11	Secondary transmitted data	From 6100
20	Data terminal ready	From 6100

Notes: (a) XON/XOFF and ETX/ACK are supported. (b) Pin 20 may be used for hardware flow control.

Company: Lear Siegler, Inc.
Product: 310 Ballistic Printer
Port: Serial   Pin Configuration: P01

Pin	Function	Direction
1	Chassis ground	N/A
2	Transmitted data	From 310
3	Received data	To 310
4	Request to send	From 310
5	Clear to send	To 310
6	Data set ready	To 310
7	Signal ground	N/A
8	Carrier detect	To 310
14	Busy	From 310
15	External transmit clock	To 310
17	External receive clock	To 310
19	Busy	From 310
20	Data terminal ready	From 310

Note: This connection is via a cable from the J5 interface.

Company: Lear Siegler, Inc.
Product: ADM-5 and ADM-3A
Port: Modem   Pin Configuration: T04

Pin	Function	Direction
1	Protective ground	N/A
2	Transmitted data	From ADM
3	Received data	To ADM
4	Request to send	From ADM
5	Clear to send	To ADM
7	Signal ground	N/A
8	Carrier detect	To ADM
11	Secondary channel control	From ADM
12	Secondary received data	To ADM
20	Data terminal ready	From ADM

App. B   RS-232 Pin Assignments for PC Boards, Terminals, and Peripherals

Company: Lear Siegler, Inc.
Product: ADM-31, ADM-32, and ADM-42
Port: Modem   Pin Configuration: T01

Pin	Function	Direction
1	Equipment ground	N/A
2	Transmitted data	From ADM
3	Received data	To ADM
4	Request to send	From ADM
5	Clear to send	To ADM
6	Data set ready	To ADM
7	Signal ground	N/A
8	Data carrier detect	To ADM
19	Secondary request to send	From ADM
20	Data terminal ready	From ADM

Company: Malibu Electronics Corp.
Product: Dual-Mode 200 Printer
Port: Serial   Pin Configuration: P03

Pin	Function	Direction
1	Chassis ground	N/A
2	Transmitted data	From 200
3	Received data	To 200
4	Request to send	From 200
5	Clear to send	To 200
7	Signal ground	N/A
20	Data terminal ready	From 200

Note: Pin 20 may be used for flow control, even though XON/XOFF is supported.

Company: Mannesmann Tally Corp.
Product: MT-180 and MT-160 Printers
Port: RS-232-C   Pin Configuration: P07

Pin	Function	Direction
1	Chassis ground	N/A
2	Transmitted data	From printer
3	Received data	To printer
7	Signal ground	N/A
11	Busy	From printer
19	Busy	From printer
20	Data terminal ready	From printer

Notes: (a) Pins 11 and 19 may be used for hardware flow control. (b) The printers support both the XON/XOFF and ETX/ACK protocols.

Company: Mannesmann Tally Corp.
Product: MT-1605, MT-1705, and MT-1805 Printers
Port: RS-232   Pin Configuration: P07

Pin	Function	Direction
1	Chassis ground	N/A
2	Transmitted data	From printer
3	Received data	To printer
5	Clear to send	To printer
6	Data set ready	To printer
7	Signal ground	N/A
11	Busy	From printer
19	Busy	From printer
20	Data terminal ready	From printer

Notes: (a) Pins 11 and 19 may be used for hardware flow control. (b) The printers support XON/XOFF characters.

Company: Mannesmann Tally Corp.
Product: MT-1612 Printer Terminal
Port: RS-232-C   Pin Configuration: P01

Pin	Function	Direction
1	Protective ground	N/A
2	Transmitted data	From 1612
3	Received data	To 1612
4	Request to send	From 1612
5	Clear to send	To 1612
5	Data set ready	To 1612
7	Signal ground	N/A
8	Rec. line signal detector	To 1612
11	Secondary request to send	From 1612
12	Secondary RLSD	To 1612
19	Secondary request to send	From 1612
20	Data terminal ready	From 1612
22	Ring indicator	To 1612

Notes: (a) Pins 11 and 19 may be used for flow control. (b) Terminal supports XON/XOFF protocol.

App. B RS-232 Pin Assignments for PC Boards, Terminals, and Peripherals

Company: Mannesmann Tally Corp.
Product: Tally 2000 Printer
Port: TTY Serial   Pin Configuration: P05

Pin	Function	Direction
1	Chassis ground	N/A
3	Received data	To 2000
4	Request to send	From 2000
6	Data set ready	To 2000
7	Signal ground	N/A
8	Data carrier detect	To 2000
11	Supervisory transmitted data	From 2000
20	Data terminal ready	From 2000
22	Ring indicator	To 2000

Notes: (a) Pin 4 is held off, maintaining the printer in the receive mode. (b) Pin 11 should be used for flow control.

Company: Mannesmann Tally Corp.
Product: T-3000 Printer
Port: ACA Interface   Pin Configuration: P05

Pin	Function	Direction
1	Chassis ground	N/A
2	Transmitted data	From T-3000
3	Received data	To T-3000
4	Request to send	From T-3000
5	Clear to send	To T-3000
6	Data set ready	To T-3000
7	Signal ground	N/A
11	Reverse channel	From T-3000
20	Data terminal ready	From T-3000

Notes: (a) Pin 11 should be used for hardware flow control. (b) This printer also supports the XON/XOFF and ENQ/ACK protocols.

Company: Megatek Corporation
Product: Whizzard 7200 Terminal
Port: Serial   Pin Configuration: T04

Pin	Function	Direction
1	Protective ground	N/A
2	Transmitted data	From 7200
3	Received data	To 7200
4	Request to send	From 7200
5	Clear to send	To 7200
7	Signal ground	N/A
8	Data carrier detect	To 7200
20	Data terminal ready	From 7200

Note: Pin 5 must be received to enable the transmission of data.

Company: Microtek, Inc.
Product: MT-80S Printer
Port: Serial   Pin Configuration: P08

Pin	Function	Direction
1	Chassis ground	N/A
2	Received data	To printer
5	Clear to send	From printer
7	DC common	N/A
20	Data terminal ready	From printer

Note: Pin 5 or pin 20 may be used for flow control.

Company: Mountain Computer Inc.
Product: CPS Multifunction Card
Port: Serial   Pin Configuration: C01

Pin	Function	Direction
1	Protective ground	N/A
2	Transmitted data	From CPS
3	Received data	To CPS
4	Request to send	From CPS
5	Clear to send	To CPS
6	Data set ready	To CPS
7	Signal ground	N/A
8	Data carrier detect	To CPS
20	Data terminal ready	From CPS

Notes: (a) Pin 5 must be high before incoming data will be accepted. (b) Pin 8 must be high before transmitting or receiving data. (c) Pin 6 must be high before transmitting or receiving data.

App. B RS-232 Pin Assignments for PC Boards, Terminals, and Peripherals 223

Company: NEC Information Systems, Inc.
Product: 3500R Printer
Port: Serial   Pin Configuration: P13

Pin	Function	Direction
2	Transmitted data	From printer
3	Received data	To printer
4	Request to send	From printer
6	Data set ready	To printer
7	Signal ground	N/A
19	Reverse channel	From printer
20	Data terminal ready	From printer

Notes: (a) Pin 6 must be on for the printer to operate. (b) Pin 19 can be used for flow control, but polarity must be checked.

Company: NEC Information Systems, Inc.
Product: 3500 Series (except 3500R) and 7700 Series Printers
Port: Serial   Pin Configuration: P01

Pin	Function	Direction
2	Transmitted data	From printer
3	Received data	To printer
4	Request to send	From printer
5	Clear to send	To printer
6	Data set ready	To printer
7	Signal ground	N/A
8	Carrier detect	To printer
11	Reset	To printer
18	Keyboard inhibit	To printer
19	Reverse channel	From printer
20	Data terminal ready	From printer
21	Print inhibit	To printer
22	Buzzer	To printer
23	Paper out/ribbon end	From printer
25	Interrupt/break	From printer

Notes: (a) Pins 5, 6, and 8 must be on before the printers will operate. (b) Pin 19 can be used for flow control, but the correct polarity must be chosen.

Company: NEC Information Systems, Inc.
Product: Advanced Personal Computer
Port: Serial   Pin Configuration: C01

Pin	Function	Direction
1	Signal ground	N/A
2	Transmitted data	From APC
3	Received data	To APC
4	Request to send	From APC
5	Clear to send	To APC
6	Data set ready	To APC
7	Signal ground	N/A
15	Transmit clock	To APC
17	Receive clock	To APC
20	Data terminal ready	From APC
24	Transmit clock	From APC

Company: North Star Computers, Inc.
Product: Advantage Computer
Port: Serial   Pin Configuration: C01

Pin	Function	Direction
1	Chassis ground	N/A
2	Transmitted data	From Advantage
3	Received data	To Advantage
4	Request to send	From Advantage
5	Clear to send	To Advantage
6	Data set ready	To Advantage
7	Signal ground	N/A
8	Carrier detect	To Advantage
17	Receive clock	To Advantage
20	Data terminal ready	From Advantage
24	Transmit clock	From Advantage

App. B   RS-232 Pin Assignments for PC Boards, Terminals, and Peripherals

Company: North Star Computers, Inc.
Product: Horizon Computer System
Port: Serial   Pin Configuration: C01

Pin	Function	Direction
1	Chassis ground	N/A
2	Transmitted data	From Horizon
3	Received data	To Horizon
4	Request to send	From Horizon
5	Clear to send	To Horizon
6	Data set ready	To Horizon
7	Signal ground	N/A
8	Carrier detect	To Horizon
15	Transmit clock	To Horizon
17	Receive clock	To Horizon
20	Data terminal ready	From Horizon
24	Transmit clock	From Horizon

Company: Okidata Corporation
Product: Microline 82/83 and 82A/83A Printers
Port: High-speed RS-232-C   Pin Configuration: P05

Pin	Function	Direction
1	Protective ground	N/A
2	Transmitted data	From printer
3	Received data	To printer
4	Request to send	From printer
5	Clear to send	To printer
6	Data set ready	To printer
7	Signal ground	N/A
8	Carrier detect	To printer
11	Supervisory transmitted data	From printer
20	Data terminal ready	From printer

Notes: (a) Pin 11 can be used for flow control and to check polarity. (b) Pin 20 can be used for paper-out indicator. (c) Pins 5, 6, and 8 should be on to allow data reception.

Company: Okidata Corporation
Product: Pacemark 2410 Printer
Port: RS-232   Pin Configuration: P05

Pin	Function	Direction
1	Protective ground	N/A
2	Transmit data	From Pacemark
3	Receive data	To Pacemark
4	Request to send	From Pacemark
5	Clear to send	To Pacemark
6	Data send ready	To Pacemark
7	Signal ground	N/A
8	Data carrier detect	To Pacemark
11	Supervisory send data	From Pacemark
20	Data terminal ready	From Pacemark

Note: Either pin 11 or 20 may be used for hardware flow control according to the printer option setup. A multitude of software flow-control methods are supported, including XON/XOFF and STX/ETX.

Company: Olivetti OPE
Product: TH 240 Printer
Port: Serial   Pin Configuration: P03

Pin	Function	Direction
1	Protective ground	N/A
2	Transmitted data	From printer
3	Received data	To printer
4	Request to send	From printer
6	Data set ready	To printer
7	Signal ground	N/A
8	Rec. line signal detector	To printer
11	Reverse channel	From printer
14	Secondary transmitted data	From printer
19	Secondary request to send	From printer
20	Data terminal ready	From printer

Notes: (a) Pin 2, 11, or 14 may be used for flow control. (b) Pin 20 goes off when anomaly conditions occur.

Company: Olympia USA Inc.
Product: ES101 KRO Printer
Port: Serial   Pin Configuration: P03

Pin	Function	Direction
1	Protective ground	N/A
2	Transmitted data	From 101
3	Received data	To 101
4	Request to send	From 101
20	Data terminal ready	From 101

Notes: (a) Request to send can be optioned to occur on pin 4, 5, 6, 8, or 20. (b) Pin 20 can be used for flow control, in which case it cannot be used for request to send because a conflict will occur.

Company: Olympia USA Inc.
Product: ESW 102/103 Printers
Port: RS-232-C   Pin Configuration: P12

Pin	Function	Direction
2	Transmitted data	From printer
3	Received data	To printer
4	Request to send	From printer
5	Clear to send	To printer
7	Signal ground	N/A

Notes: (a) Pin 4 is used for flow control when XON/XOFF is not selected. (b) Note that there is no pin 20.

Company: Perkin-Elmer Corporation
Product: 550 and 1251 CRTs
Port: Serial   Pin Configuration: T01

Pin	Function	Direction
1	Protective ground	N/A
2	Transmitted data	From CRT
3	Received data	To CRT
4	Request to send	From CRT
5	Clear to send	To CRT
6	Data set ready	To CRT
7	Signal ground	N/A
8	Carrier detect	To CRT
20	Data terminal ready	From CRT

Company: Practical Peripherals, Inc.
Product: Microbuffer MBS-8K (for Use in Epson Printers)
Port: RS-232   Pin Configuration: P08

Pin	Function	Direction
2	Transmit data	From MBS
3	Receive data	To MBS
7	Signal ground	N/A
11	Reverse channel	From MBS
20	Data terminal ready	From MBS

Note: Pin 4 is active if software flow control is used. However, if hardware flow control is selected, pins 11 or 20 may be used to provide the busy signal.

Company: Printek, Inc.
Product: 910/920 Printers
Port: RS-232   Pin Configuration: P05

Pin	Function	Direction
1	Chassis ground	N/A
2	Transmitted data	From printer
3	Received data	To printer
4	Request to send	From printer
5	Clear to send	To printer
6	Data set ready	To printer
7	Signal ground	N/A
8	Carrier detect	To printer
11	Busy	From printer
20	Data terminal ready	From printer

Notes: (a) XON/XOFF and ETX/ACK are supported. (b) Pin 11 is used for hardware flow control.

Company: Printronix
Product: Printronix 300 Printer
Port: RS-232   Pin Configuration: P05

Pin	Function	Direction
1	Protective ground	N/A
3	Received data (in)	To 300
4	Request to send (out)	From 300
6	Data set ready (in)	To 300
7	Signal ground	N/A
8	Carrier detect (in)	To 300
11	Reverse channel (out)	From 300
20	Data terminal ready (out)	From 300
25	External clock (in)	To 300

App. B RS-232 Pin Assignments for PC Boards, Terminals, and Peripherals

Company: Prometheus Products, Inc.
Product: VERSAcard
Port: Serial   Pin Configuration: C01

Pin	Function	Direction
1	Protective ground	N/A
2	Transmitted data	From Versacard
3	Received data	To Versacard
4	Request to send	From Versacard
5	Clear to send	To Versacard
6	Data set ready	To Versacard
7	Signal ground	N/A
20	Data terminal ready	From Versacard

Notes: (a) Pin 5 should be used for flow control. (b) Pin 6 must be on before VERSAcard will receive data.

Company: Quantex Division of North Atlantic Industries
Product: Series 6000 Printer
Port: Serial   Pin Configuration: P07

Pin	Function	Direction
1	Chassis ground	N/A
2	Transmitted data (out)	From 6000
3	Received data (in)	To 6000
7	Signal ground	N/A
11	Busy	From 6000
14	Busy	From 6000
20	Ready	From 6000

Notes: (a) XON/XOFF is supported. (b) Pin 11 or pin 14 may be used for hardware flow control. (c) Pin 20 indicates the status of "hold."

Company: Qume Corporation
Product: Sprint 5
Port: Serial   Pin Configuration: P03

Pin	Function	Direction
1	Chassis/frame ground	N/A
2	Transmitted data	From Sprint 5
3	Received data	To Sprint 5
4	Request to send	From Sprint 5
5	Clear to send	To Sprint 5
6	Data set ready	To Sprint 5
7	Signal ground	N/A
8	Carrier detect	To Sprint 5
20	Data terminal ready	From Sprint 5

Notes: (a) Pins 20 and 4 both serve the same function of hardware flow control. (b) Pin 5 must be high for data transmission. (c) Pin 6 must be high for data reception.

Company: Qume Corporation
Product: Sprint 9/45 and 9/55
Port: RS-232-C   Pin Configuration: P03

Pin	Function	Direction
1	Chassis ground	N/A
2	Transmitted data	From Sprint
3	Received data	To Sprint
4	Request to send	From Sprint
5	Clear to send	To Sprint
6	Data set ready	To Sprint
7	Signal ground	N/A
8	Carrier detect	To Sprint
20	Data terminal ready	From Sprint

Notes: (a) Pin 20 can be used for hardwired handshaking. (b) XON/XOFF handshaking is supported for flow control.

App. B RS-232 Pin Assignments for PC Boards, Terminals, and Peripherals

Company: Radio Shack
Product: DT-1 CRT
Port: EIA   Pin Configuration: T01

Pin	Function	Direction
1	Protective ground	N/A
2	Transmitted data	From DT-1
3	Received data	To DT-1
4	Request to send	From DT-1
5	Clear to send	To DT-1
6	Data set ready	To DT-1
7	Signal ground	N/A
8	Data carrier detect	To DT-1
20	Data terminal ready	From DT-1

Company: Radio Shack
Product: Line Printer VII/VIII
Port: RS-232-C   Pin Configuration: P14

Pin	Function	Direction
2	Transmitted data	To printer
7	Signal ground	N/A
8	Data carrier detect	From printer

Note: The printers come with a DIN connector that should first be wired to an RS-232-size plug. Pin 8 may then be used for flow control.

Company: Radio Shack
Product: TRS-80 Model II
Port: Channels A and B   Pin Configuration: C01

Pin	Function	Direction
1	Protective ground	N/A
2	Transmitted data	From TRS-80
3	Received data	To TRS-80
4	Request to send	From TRS-80
5	Clear to send	To TRS-80
6	Data set ready	To TRS-80
7	Signal ground	N/A
8	Carrier detect	To TRS-80
15	I/O transmit S.E.T.	To TRS-80
17	Receive clock	To TRS-80
20	Data terminal ready	From TRS-80
24	Transmit clock	From TRS-80

Note: Channel A allows asynchronous or synchronous transmission. Channel B has the same signals but lacks pins 15 and 24 and consequently supports only asynchronous transmission.

Company: Radio Shack
Product: TRS-80 Model III
Port: P1   Pin Configuration: C01

Pin	Function	Direction
1	Protective ground	N/A
2	Transmitted data	From TRS-80
3	Received data	To TRS-80
4	Request to send	From TRS-80
5	Clear to send	To TRS-80
6	Data set ready	To TRS-80
7	Signal ground	N/A
8	Carrier detect	To TRS-80
20	Data terminal ready	From TRS-80
22	Ring indicator	To TRS-80

Company: Radio Shack
Product: Model 16 Computer
Port: Channels A and B   Pin Configuration: C11

Pin	Function	Direction
1	Protective ground	N/A
2	Transmitted data	From Model 16
3	Received data	To Model 16
4	Request to send	From Model 16
5	Clear to send	To Model 16
7	Signal ground	N/A
8	Carrier detect	To Model 16
15	I/O transmit timing	To Model 16
17	Receive timing	To Model 16
20	Data terminal ready	From Model 16
24	Transmit clock	From Model 16

Note: Channel A allows asynchronous or synchronous transmission. Channel B has the same signals but lacks pins 15 and 24 and consequently supports only asynchronous transmission.

App. B   RS-232 Pin Assignments for PC Boards, Terminals, and Peripherals

Company: Rogers Products Company, Inc.
Product: Typrinter
Port: Serial   Pin Configuration: P10

Pin	Function	Direction
1	Protective ground	N/A
2	Transmitted data	From printer
3	Received data	To printer
4	Request to send	From printer
5	Clear to send	To printer
6	Data set ready	To printer
7	Signal ground	N/A
8	Carrier detect	To printer
20	Data terminal ready	From printer

Notes: (a) This is the DTE connector. A DCE connector is available that reverses most of the leads. (b) XON/XOFF is supported.

Company: Santec Corp.
Product: Variflex Printer
Port: RS-232   Pin Configuration: P05

Pin	Function	Direction
1	Protective ground	N/A
2	Transmitted data	From Variflex
3	Received data	To Variflex
4	Request to send	From Variflex
5	Clear to send	To Variflex
6	Data set ready	To Variflex
7	Signal ground	N/A
8	Carrier detect	To Variflex
11	Busy	From Variflex
20	Data terminal ready	From Variflex

Notes: (a) The Variflex supports XON/XOFF or ETX/ACK pacing. (b) Either pin 11 or pin 20 may be used for hardware flow control.

Company: Siemens Corporation
Product: 2712 and PT 80 I2 Printers
Port: EIA   Pin Configuration: P15

Pin	Function	Direction
1	Common return	N/A
2	Transmitted data	From printer
3	Received data	To printer
4	Request to send	From printer
5	Clear to send	To printer
6	Data set ready	To printer
7	Signal ground	N/A
8	Rec. line signal detector	To printer
20	Data terminal ready	From printer
25	Busy	From printer

Notes: (a) Pin 25 could be used for flow control. (b) These devices do support XON/XOFF.

Company: Siemens Corporation
Product: OEM Ink-jet Printer Models 2712 and PT 80 I2
Port: RS-232   Pin Configuration: P15

Pin	Function	Direction
1	Common return	N/A
2	Transmitted data	From printer
3	Received data	To printer
4	Request to send	From printer
5	Clear to send	To printer
6	Data set ready	To printer
7	Signal ground	N/A
8	Data channel RLSD	To printer
20	Data terminal ready	From printer
25	Busy	From printer

Notes: (a) Pin 25 can be used for hardware flow control. (b) XON/XOFF capability exists.

Company: Smith-Corona
Product: TP-1 Printer
Port: Serial   Pin Configuration: P09

Pin	Function	Direction
3	Received data	To TP-1
4	Request to send	From TP-1
7	Signal ground	N/A
20	Data terminal ready	From TP-1

Note: Pin 4 or 20 may be used as the busy signal for flow control.

App. B RS-232 Pin Assignments for PC Boards, Terminals, and Peripherals   235

Company: Silver-Reed
Product: Silver-Reed
Port: RS-232   Pin Configuration: P03

Pin	Function	Direction
1	Protective ground	N/A
2	Transmitted data	From printer
3	Received data	To printer
4	Request to send	From printer
5	Clear to send	To printer
7	Signal ground	N/A
20	Data terminal ready	From printer

Notes: (a) Pin 20 is used for hardware flow control. (b) This interface is the DTF01S, manufactured by Wilker, Inc.

Company: Star Micronics, Inc.
Product: DP-8480 Printer
Port: RS-232   Pin Configuration: P04

Pin	Function	Direction
1	Protective ground	N/A
3	Received data	To DP-8480
4	Request to send	From DP-8480
7	Signal ground	N/A
11	Busy status output	From DP-8480
20	Data terminal ready	From DP-8480

Notes: (a) This interface is for printers with serial numbers 20004833 and higher. (b) These printers use pin 11 for hardware flow control.

Company: Star Micronics, Inc.
Product: Gemini 10/15
Port: RS-232   Pin Configuration: P05

Pin	Function	Direction
1	Frame ground	N/A
2	Transmit data	From Gemini
3	Receive data	To Gemini
4	Request to send	From Gemini
5	Clear to send	To Gemini
6	Data set ready	To Gemini
7	Signal ground	N/A
8	Data carrier detect	To Gemini
11	Reverse channel	From Gemini
20	Data terminal ready	From Gemini

Note: XON/XOFF is supported. Pin 11 is used for hardware flow control.

Company: STB Systems, Inc.
Product: Super RIO Board
Port: Serial   Pin Configuration: C01

Pin	Function	Direction
2	Transmit data	From board
3	Receive data	To board
4	Request to send	From board
5	Clear to send	To board
6	Data set ready	To board
7	Signal ground	N/A
8	Data carrier detect	To board
20	Data terminal ready	From board
22	Ring indicator	To board

Company: Techland Systems Inc.
Product: Synchronous Communication Board
Port: RS-232   Pin Configuration: C01

Pin	Function	Direction
2	Transmit data	From board
3	Receive data	To board
4	Request to send	From board
5	Clear to send	To board
6	Data set ready	To board
7	Signal ground	N/A
8	Receive line signal detector	To board
15	Transmit timing	To board
17	Receive timing	To board
20	Data terminal ready	From board
22	Ring indicator	To board

App. B RS-232 Pin Assignments for PC Boards, Terminals, and Peripherals

Company: Tektronix, Inc.
Product: 4050 CRT Series
Port: RS-232-C   Pin Configuration: T01

Pin	Function	Direction
1	Protective ground	N/A
2	Transmitted data	From 4050
3	Received data	To 4050
4	Request to send	From 4050
5	Clear to send	To 4050
6	Data set ready	To 4050
7	Signal ground	N/A
8	Data carrier detect	To 4050
11	Secondary request to send	From 4050
12	Secondary RLSD	To 4050
19	Secondary request to send	From 4050
20	Data terminal ready	From 4050

Note: Models 4052 and 4054 allow for external clocking on pins 24 and 25.

Company: Tektronix, Inc.
Product: 4643 Printer
Port: Serial   Pin Configuration: P03

Pin	Function	Direction
1	Protective ground	N/A
2	Transmitted data	From 4643
3	Received data	To 4643
4	Request to send	From 4643
7	Signal ground	N/A
8	Rec. line signal detector	To 4643
20	Data terminal ready	From 4643

Note: Pin 20 may be used for hardware flow control.

Company: Teletype Corp.
Product: DataSpeed 40/2 Terminal
Port: Comm.   Pin Configuration: T01

Pin	Function	Direction
1	Protective ground	N/A
2	Transmitted data	From 40/2
3	Received data	To 40/2
4	Request to send	From 40/2
5	Clear to send	To 40/2
6	Data set ready	To 40/2
7	Signal ground	N/A
8	Rec. line signal detector	To 40/2
11	Secondary request to send	From 40/2
12	Secondary RLSD	To 40/2
19	Secondary request to send	From 40/2
20	Data terminal ready	From 40/2
22	Ring indicator	To 40/2

Note: If this port is optioned for full-duplex, pins 4, 11, and 19 are not present.

Company: Teletype Corp.
Product: DataSpeed 40 Printer
Port: RS-232   Pin Configuration: P05

Pin	Function	Direction
1	Protective ground	N/A
2	Transmitted data	From 40
3	Received data	To 40
4	Request to send	From 40
5	Clear to send	To 40
6	Data set ready	To 40
7	Signal ground	N/A
8	Data carrier detect	To 40
11	Supervisory transmitted data	From 40
12	Supervisory received data	To 40
20	Data terminal ready	From 40
22	Ring indicator	To 40
23	Alarm	

App. B   RS-232 Pin Assignments for PC Boards, Terminals, and Peripherals

Company: Teletype Corp.
Product: DataSpeed 4420 Terminal
Port: Modem   Pin Configuration: T01

Pin	Function	Direction
1	Frame ground	N/A
2	Transmitted data	From 4420
3	Received data	To 4420
4	Request to send	From 4420
5	Clear to send	To 4420
6	Data set ready	To 4420
7	Signal ground	N/A
8	Rec. line signal detector	To 4420
11	Secondary request to send	From 4420
12	Secondary RLSD	To 4420
15	Transmit timing	To 4420
17	Receive timing	To 4420
19	Secondary request to send	From 4420
20	Data terminal ready	From 4420
22	Ring indicator	To 4420

Company: Teletype Corp.
Product: DataSpeed AP200 Printer
Port: EIA   Pin Configuration: P11

Pin	Function	Direction
1	Frame ground	N/A
3	Received data	To AP200
6	Data set ready	To AP200
7	Signal ground	N/A
11	Secondary transmitted data	From AP200
14	Device next character	From AP200
19	Secondary request to send	From AP200
20	Data terminal ready	From AP200

Notes: (a) Pins 11 and 20 are equivalent in function: Both indicate that the printer is able to receive. (b) Pin 14 has a positive voltage when the buffer is less than 3/4 full and a negative voltage when buffer is more than 3/4 full.

Company: Teletype Corp.
Product: Model 43 Teleprinter
Port: EIA   Pin Configuration: P03

Pin	Function	Direction
1	Protective ground	N/A
2	Transmitted data	From 43
3	Received data	To 43
4	Request to send	From 43
5	Clear to send	To 43
6	Data set ready	To 43
7	Signal ground	N/A
8	Carrier detect/RLSD	To 43
20	Data terminal ready	From 43
22	Ring indicator	To 43

Note: Pin 20 is affected by the paper supply.

Company: Televideo Systems, Inc.
Product: Model 910, 925, and 950 CRTs
Port: P3 Connector   Pin Configuration: T01

Pin	Function	Direction
1	Frame ground	N/A
2	Transmitted data (out)	From CRT
3	Received data (in)	To CRT
4	Request to send	From CRT
5	Clear to send	To CRT
6	Data set ready	To CRT
7	Signal ground	N/A
8	Data carrier detect	To CRT
20	Data terminal ready	From CRT

App. B RS-232 Pin Assignments for PC Boards, Terminals, and Peripherals

Company: Texas Instruments, Inc.
Product: 810 Printer
Port: Serial   Pin Configuration: P07

Pin	Function	Direction
1	Chassis ground	N/A
2	Transmitted data	From printer
3	Received data	To printer
6	Data set ready	To printer
7	Signal ground	N/A
8	Carrier detect	To printer
11	Reverse channel	From printer
20	Data terminal ready	From printer

Notes: (a) Pins 6 and 8 must be on for the printer to receive data. (b) Pin 11 can be used for flow control on the standard printer, whereas pin 20 is used on the DNB version for flow control.

Company: Texas Instruments, Inc.
Product: 820/840 Printers
Port: EIA   Pin Configuration: P05

Pin	Function	Direction
1	Protective ground	N/A
2	Transmitted data	From printer
3	Received data	To printer
4	Request to send	From printer
5	Clear to send	To printer
6	Data set ready	To printer
7	Signal ground	N/A
8	Rec. line signal detector	To printer
11	Ready/busy	From printer
12	Secondary RLSD	To printer
20	Data terminal ready	From printer
22	Ring indicator	To printer
23	Data signal rate selector	From printer

Notes: (a) Pin 22 is not used on the 840 printer. (b) Pins 5 and 6 must be on for transmission to occur. (c) Pins 6 and 8 must be on for reception to occur. (d) Pin 23 is held on to indicate 1200 bps speed on a dual-speed modem. (e) Pin 11 is used for flow control.

Company: Texas Instruments, Inc.
Product: TI940 Terminal
Port: COMM   Pin Configuration: T01

Pin	Function	Direction
1	Protective ground	N/A
2	Transmitted data	From 940
3	Received data	To 940
4	Request to send	From 940
5	Clear to send	To 940
6	Data set ready	To 940
7	Signal ground	N/A
8	Rec. line signal detector	To 940
11	Reverse channel transmit	From 940
12	Secondary RLSD	To 940
15	Transmit signal timing	To 940
17	Recive signal timing	To 940
19	Secondary request to send	From 940
20	Data terminal ready	From 940
21	Signal quality detector	To 940
22	Ring indicator	To 940
23	Data signal rate selector	From 940
24	Transmit signal timing	From 940

Notes: (a) The 940 will not transmit data unless pin 6 is on. (b) The 940 will not receive data unless pins 6 and 8 are on. (c) Pin 11 may be used for ready/busy indicator.

Company: Texas Instruments, Inc.
Product: 820 RO
Port: EIA   Pin Configuration: P05

Pin	Function	Direction
1	Protective ground	N/A
2	Transmitted data	From 820
3	Received data	To 820
4	Request to send	From 820
5	Clear to send	To 820
6	Data set ready	To 820
7	Signal ground	N/A
8	Rec. line signal detector	To 820
11	Secondary request to send	From 820
12	Secondary RLSD	To 820
20	Data terminal ready	From 820
23	Data signal rate selector	From 820

Notes: (a) Pins 5, 6, and 8 must be on for the 820 to transmit data. (b) Pin 6 must be on for the 820 to receive data. (c) Pin 23 is used by the 820 to select data rates when used with dual-speed modems. (d) Pin 11 is used for printer busy status.

Company: Texas Instruments, Inc.
Product: Silent 745 Printer
Port: EIA   Pin Configuration: P01

Pin	Function	Direction
1	Protective ground	N/A
2	Transmitted data	From printer
3	Received data	To printer
4	Request to send	From printer
7	Signal ground	N/A
8	Data carrier detect	To printer
20	Data terminal ready	From printer

Note: Because this printer supports only 110/300-bps operation and prints at 10/30 cps, no flow control is required.

Company: Texas Instruments, Inc.
Product: Silent 781/783/785/787 Printers
Port: EIA   Pin Configuration: P05

Pin	Function	Direction
1	Protective ground	N/A
2	Transmitted data	From printer
3	Received data	To printer
4	Request to send	From printer
5	Clear to send	To printer
6	Data set ready	To printer
7	Signal ground	N/A
8	Rec. line signal detector	To printer
11	Secondary request to send	From printer
12	Secondary RLSD	To printer
20	Data terminal ready	From printer
22	Ring indicator	To printer
23	Data signal rate selector	From printer

Notes: (a) XON/XOFF is supported by the printers. (b) Pin 11 may be used for hardware flow control.

244 RS-232 Pin Assignments for PC Boards, Terminals, and Peripherals   App. B

Company: Toshiba America Inc.
Product: P1350 Printer
Port: RS-232   Pin Configuration: P03

Pin	Function	Direction
1	Protective ground	N/A
2	Transmit data	From P1350
3	Receive data	To P1350
4	Request to send	From P1350
5	Clear to send	To P1350
6	Data set ready	To P1350
7	Signal ground	N/A
8	Data carrier detect	To P1350
20	Data terminal ready	From P1350

Note: Pin 20 is used for hardware flow control.

Company: WallData Inc.
Product: DCF Protocol Converter
Port: RS-232   Pin Configuration: C01

Pin	Function	Direction
1	Protective ground	N/A
2	Transmit data	From DCF
3	Receive data	To DCF
4	Request to send	From DCF
5	Clear to send	To DCF
6	Data set ready	To DCF
7	Signal ground	N/A
15	Transmit timing	To DCF
17	Receive timing	To DCF
20	Data terminal ready	From DCF
24	Transmit timing	From DCF

App. B RS-232 Pin Assignments for PC Boards, Terminals, and Peripherals 245

Company: Xerox Corporation
Product: 1700 Printer
Port: Serial   Pin Configuration: P10

Pin	Function	Direction
1	Protective ground	N/A
2	Transmitted data	From 1700
3	Received data	To 1700
4	Request to send	From 1700
5	Clear to send	To 1700
6	Data set ready	To 1700
7	Signal ground	N/A
8	Data carrier detect	To 1700
20	Data terminal ready	From 1700

Notes: (a) Pin 5 must be on to enable the 1700 to transmit. (b) Pin 6 must be on to enable the 1700 to receive. (c) Uses XON/XOFF for flow control.

Company: Xerox Corporation
Product: 1730 Printer
Port: Serial   Pin Configuration: P05

Pin	Function	Direction
1	Protective ground	N/A
2	Transmitted data	From 1730
3	Received data	To 1730
4	Request to send	From 1730
5	Clear to send	To 1730
6	Data set ready	To 1730
7	Signal ground	N/A
8	Rec. line signal detector	To 1730
11	Printer ready	From 1730
20	Data terminal ready	From 1730

Notes: (a) Pin 20 can be optioned for printer ready function. (b) Pin 6 must be on to receive data.

Company: Xerox Corporation
Product: 1740/1750 Printers
Port: Serial   Pin Configuration: P03

Pin	Function	Direction
1	Protective ground	N/A
2	Transmitted data	From printer
3	Received data	To printer
4	Request to send	From printer
5	Clear to send	To printer
6	Data set ready	To printer
7	Signal ground	N/A
8	Data carrier detect	To printer
20	Data terminal ready	From printer

Notes: (a) Pin 6 must be on to receive data. (b) Pin 5 must be on to send data. (c) Pin 20 can provide printer ready signal.

Company: Zenith Data Systems, Inc.
Product: Z-25 Printer
Port: Serial   Pin Configuration: P12

Pin	Function	Direction
1	Protective ground	N/A
2	Serial output	From Z-25
3	Serial input	To Z-25
4	Busy	From Z-25
7	Signal common	N/A

Notes: (a) Pin 4 should be used for flow control. (b) The cable supplied with the printer provides pins 1–7, 11, and 20 straight through.

APPENDIX C

interconnections between the IBM PC/XT and peripherals

Appendix C outlines the connections of computers, terminals, and printers through an RS-232 port. When used in conjunction with Appendix B, the proper cables may be constructed to allow data exchange between devices.

The following displays the step-by-step procedure for determining how the pins of RS-232 cables should be connected.

1. In Appendix B, locate the appropriate devices to be connected, noting their corresponding pin configuration. (If your device is not listed, compare its RS-232 pin assignments with devices in Appendix B until a match is found. Then, use that pin configuration as a surrogate.)
2. Proceed to the appropriate table in this appendix. Figure C-1 is for connecting the IBM to printers. Figure C-2 is for connecting computers to terminals (CRTs), to the PC/XT. As multiuser operating systems are used on the IBM, terminal connectivity will become important. Figure C-3 is for connecting the PC/XT to other computers for file transfers.

Printer															
Computer	P01	P02	P03	P04	P05	P06	P07	P08	P09	P10	P11	P12	P13	P14	P15
C01	G01	G02	G03	G04	G04	G05	G06	G05	G07	G08	G05	G07	G01	G09	G10

Figure C-1

Terminal (CRT)		
Computer	T01	T04
C01	G01	G03

Figure C-2

3. Find the pin configuration for the PC board in the column labeled "Computer" at the left of the table.
4. Find the proper pin configuration for the printer, terminal, or computer across the top of the table.
5. Note the diagram number at the intersection of the row and column.
6. Find the appropriately labeled graph in this appendix for a display of the cross connections necessary in the RS-232 cable. Construct the cable accordingly.

App. C   Interconnections between the IBM PC/XT and Peripherals   **249**

For example, to connect an ACA (C01), to an Okidata Pacemaker 2410 printer (P05), use graph G04.

It is important to note that when building RS-232 cables, many different combinations of pin configurations exist for a connection. The diagrams point out only one of many ways in which RS-232 leads may be connected. Neither the author nor the publisher claims responsibility for the accuracy of the diagrams or charts, as they were constructed from information supplied by the vendors. The vendors of these products often provide similar information for device connections. Use their recommendations when possible, as they have been thoroughly tested. This should be done also because, in some cases, more leads are present in the diagrams than are actually needed. They are provided for completeness.

For example, often pin 19, 20, or 4 may be used to hold a given lead, such as data set ready, on or off. The choice may be dictated by a factor such as flow control. If hardware flow control will not be used, pin 4 or 20 would be selected, in which case pin 19 would not even be used. The selection should be based on the options for the particular installation.

Furthermore, different configurations may be possible for ports. The way a port is configured affects the cable to be used. If a port may be set up to emulate either data communications equipment or data terminal equipment, choose the configuration that allows for the most flexibility in your configuration.

Once the cable has been built, the options should be reviewed as described in Chapter 6. They are as follows:

Speed	Flow control
Parity	Character length
Number of stop bits	Mode
Echoplex	Line feeds
Transmission control	Polarity
Interface	Online/offline
Wraparound	Lines/characters per inch

Double-check to ensure that these are properly set. Once set, attach the cable between the devices, power up the devices, enable the ports, and test your system for proper operation.

Computer					
IBM	C01	C02	C05	C09	C11
C01	G03	G02	G02	G12	G03

Figure C-3

250   Interconnections between the IBM PC/XT and Peripherals   App. C

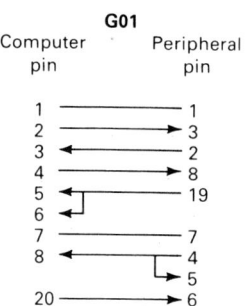

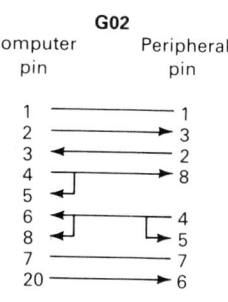

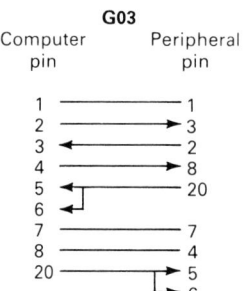

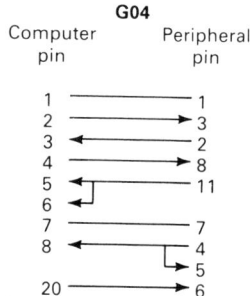

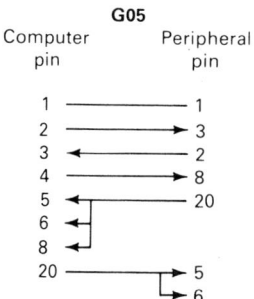

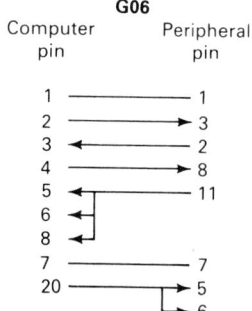

App. C   Interconnections between the IBM PC/XT and Peripharals   **251**

G07

Computer pin	Peripheral pin
1	1
2	→ 3
3	← 2
4	→ 8
5 ←	4
6 ←	↳ 5
8 ←	
7	7
20	→ 6

G08

Computer pin	Peripheral pin
1	1
2	→ 3
3 ←	2
4	→ 8
5 ←	20
6 ←	
7	7
8 ←	4
20	→ 5
	↳ 6

G09

Computer pin	Peripheral pin
1	1
2	2
5 ←	8
6 ←	
8 ←	
20 ←	
7	7

G10

Computer pin	Peripheral pin
1	1
2	→ 3
3 ←	2
4	→ 8
5 ←	25
6 ←	
7	7
8 ←	4
	↳ 5
	↳ 6

G11

Computer pin	Peripheral pin
1	1
2	2
3	3
4	4
5	5
6	6
7	7
8	8
	11
20 ←	19
12	12

G12

Computer pin	Peripheral pin
1	1
2	2
3	3
4	4
5	5
6	6
7	7
8	8
11	11
12	12
15	15
17	17
19	19
20	20
22	22

APPENDIX

D

centronics parallel interface standard

Signal Name	Pin(s)	Source	Category	Description
Data strobe	1, 19	IBM	Timing	A 1-microsecond pulse used to clock data from the IBM to the printer.
Data 1 Data 2 Data 3 Data 4 Data 5 Data 6 Data 7 Data 8	2, 20 3, 21 4, 22 5, 23 6, 24 7, 25 8, 26 9, 27	IBM IBM IBM IBM IBM IBM IBM IBM	Data Data Data Data Data Data Data Data	Each one of these leads provides for a single bit of a data character. A high represents a 1; a low represents a 0.
Acknowledge	10, 28	Ptr	Control	This pulse indicates either the reception of a character or the end of a functional operation.
Busy	11, 29	Ptr	Control	A signal level indicating that the printer cannot receive any more data. This is caused by a paper-out or other fault condition. Consult the manual for a list of the conditions affecting this control lead.
PE	12	Ptr	Control	A control lead indicating that the printer is out of paper.
Select	13	Ptr	Control	A control lead indicating that the printer is selected by the IBM.
0 volts	14	Ptr	Ground	A signal ground reference for other signals.
OSCXT	15	Ptr	—	A 100/200-kHz signal, varying among printers.
0 volts	16	N/A	Ground	A signal ground reference.
Chassis ground	17	Ptr	—	A frame ground for electrical protection.
+5 volts	18	Ptr	—	Positive voltage.
Input prime	31, 30	IBM	Control	A signal that clears the printer buffer and reinitializes the control logic.
Fault	32	Ptr	Control	A signal that indicates a printer fault condition.

Notes: (a) The second pin number indicates the twisted-pair return or signal reference lead. The IBM interface uses pins 18 to 25 on the DB25 connector for this purpose. See the following table for crossovers between the two types of connectors. (b) Pins 1, 10, 31, and 32 are active or on when they are low. All others are high to indicate an on condition.

Centronics Parallel Interface Standard   App. D

Typical Pin Crossovers between the PC and the Centronics Parallel Connectors

IBM DB25S	Amphenol
1 ←→	1
2 ←→	2
3 ←→	3
4 ←→	4
5 ←→	5
6 ←→	6
7 ←→	7
8 ←→	8
9 ←→	9
10 ←→	10
11 ←→	11
12 ←→	12
13 ←→	13
14 ←→	14
15 ←→	32
16 ←→	31
17 ←→	36
18 ←→	33
19 ←→	19
20 ←→	21
21 ←→	23
22 ←→	25
23 ←→	27
24 ←→	29
25 ←→	30

APPENDIX E

escape sequences for controlling popular printers

Often, the user of a PC/XT with a printer must set up the hard-copy device for print control. For example, when using a spreadsheet or word processor, a control sequence must be entered to compress the print to 17 characters per inch. The printer user's manual should be consulted for this but is not always available. The following charts serve as a quick reference for such printer control sequences, recognizing that most printers offer more capabilities than listed.

Feature	Anadex DP-6500	Anadex DP-9000/9500B	Anadex DP-9001/9501B
10 CHARACTERS/INCH	ESC Q	ESC Q	ESC Q
12 CHARACTERS/INCH	ESC T	ESC R	ESC T
17 CHARACTERS/INCH	ESC R	N/A	ESC R
ITALICS ON	ESC t	N/A	N/A
ITALICS OFF	ESC u	N/A	N/A
6 LINES/INCH	ESC H	ESC H	ESC H
8 LINES/INCH	ESC l	ESC l	ESC l
10 LINES/INCH	N/A	N/A	N/A
12 LINES/INCH	N/A	N/A	N/A
LETTER QUALITY	ESC r	N/A	N/A
DP QUALITY	N/A	N/A	N/A
DRAFT QUALITY	N/A	N/A	N/A
EXPANDED PRINT ON	ESC 5	SO	SO
EXPANDED PRINT OFF	ESC 6	SI	SI
SUBSCRIPT ON	ESC (	N/A	N/A
SUBSCRIPT OFF	ESC :	N/A	N/A
SUPERSCRIPT ON	ESC)	N/A	N/A
SUPERSCRIPT OFF	ESC :	N/A	N/A
UNDERLINE ON	ESC 8	RS	RS
UNDERLINE OFF	ESC 9	US	US
EXPANDED PRINT-ONE LINE ONLY	N/A	N/A	N/A
EMPHASIZED ON	ESC p	N/A	N/A
EMPHASIZED OFF	ESC q	N/A	N/A
DOUBLESTRIKE ON	ESC x	N/A	N/A
DOUBLESTRIKE OFF	ESC Q	N/A	N/A
RESET	N/A	N/A	N/A

Notes: (a) N/A indicates not available. In some cases special fonts or upgrades can be used for these capabilities. (b) From a BASIC program, the CHAR$ function should be used to generate these escape sequences [e.g., CHAR$(14) should be used for the SO sequence]. (c) LETTER QUALITY on dot matrix printers refers to near-letter quality or correspondence-quality print. (d) Consult the ASCII chart in Appendix G for decimal equivalents to these sequences.

App. E Escape Sequences for Controlling Popular Printers

Feature	Anadex DP-9625B	Anadex WP-6000	Apple Dot Matrix
10 CHARACTERS/INCH	ESC Q	ESC J0	ESC N
12 CHARACTERS/INCH	ESC T	ESC J2	ESC E
17 CHARACTERS/INCH	ESC R	ESC J7	ESC Q
ITALICS ON	N/A	ESC X	N/A
ITALICS OFF	N/A	ESC Y	N/A
6 LINES/INCH	ESC H	ESC E	ESC A
8 LINES/INCH	ESC I	ESC F	ESC B
10 LINES/INCH	N/A	N/A	N/A
12 LINES/INCH	N/A	ESC !	ESC T12
LETTER QUALITY	ESC r	ESC I5	N/A
DP QUALITY	N/A	ESC I6	N/A
DRAFT QUALITY	N/A	N/A	N/A
EXPANDED PRINT ON	ESC 5	ESC N	SO
EXPANDED PRINT OFF	ESC 6	ESC O	SI
SUBSCRIPT ON	ESC (	ESC I4	N/A
SUBSCRIPT OFF	ESC :	?	N/A
SUPERSCRIPT ON	ESC)	ESC I3	N/A
SUPERSCRIPT OFF	ESC :	?	N/A
UNDERLINE ON	ESC 8	ESC :	ESC X
UNDERLINE OFF	ESC 9	ESC ;	ESC Y
EXPANDED PRINT-ONE LINE ONLY	N/A	N/A	N/A
EMPHASIZED ON	ESC p	N/A	ESC !
EMPHASIZED OFF	ESC q	N/A	ESC "
DOUBLESTRIKE ON	ESC x	N/A	N/A
DOUBLESTRIKE OFF	ESC Q	N/A	N/A
RESET	N/A	N/A	N/A

Notes: (a) N/A indicates not available. In some cases special fonts or upgrades can be used for these capabilities. (b) From a BASIC program, the CHAR$ function should be used to generate these escape sequences [e.g., CHAR$(14) should be used for the SO sequence]. (c) LETTER QUALITY on dot matrix printers refers to near-letter quality or correspondence-quality print. (d) Consult the ASCII chart in Appendix G for decimal equivalents to these sequences.

Feature	Axiom IMP	Centronics 351	C. Itoh Prowriter
10 CHARACTERS/INCH	ESC 6	ESC[1w	ESC N
12 CHARACTERS/INCH	ESC ⟨	ESC[2w	ESC E
17 CHARACTERS/INCH	ESC 7	ESC[4w	ESC Q
ITALICS ON	N/A	N/A	N/A
ITALICS OFF	N/A	N/A	N/A
6 LINES/INCH	ESC 4	ESC[1z	ESC A
8 LINES/INCH	N/A	ESC[2z	ESC B
10 LINES/INCH	N/A	N/A	ESC T nn
12 LINES/INCH	ESC 5	N/A	ESC T nn
LETTER QUALITY	N/A	N/A	N/A
DP QUALITY	N/A	N/A	N/A
DRAFT QUALITY	N/A	N/A	N/A
EXPANDED PRINT ON	ESC SO	ESC[5w	SO
EXPANDED PRINT OFF	ESC SI	ESC[1w	SI
SUBSCRIPT ON	N/A	ESC K	N/A
SUBSCRIPT OFF	N/A	ESC L	N/A
SUPERSCRIPT ON	N/A	ESC L	N/A
SUPERSCRIPT OFF	N/A	ESC K	N/A
UNDERLINE ON	N/A	ESC[4m	ESC X
UNDERLINE OFF	N/A	ESC[0m	ESC Y
EXPANDED PRINT-ONE LINE ONLY	N/A	N/A	N/A
EMPHASIZED ON	N/A	N/A	ESC !
EMPHASIZED OFF	N/A	N/A	ESC "
DOUBLESTRIKE ON	N/A	N/A	N/A
DOUBLESTRIKE OFF	N/A	N/A	N/A
RESET	N/A	N/A	N/A

Notes: (a) N/A indicates not available. In some cases special fonts or upgrades can be used for these capabilities. (b) From a BASIC program, the CHAR$ function should be used to generate these escape sequences [e.g., CHAR$(14) should be used for the SO sequence]. (c) LETTER QUALITY on dot matrix printers refers to near-letter quality or correspondence-quality print. (d) Consult the ASCII chart in Appendix G for decimal equivalents to these sequences.

App. E Escape Sequences for Controlling Popular Printers

Feature	DATASOUTH 180	DATASOUTH 220	DEC LA 100
10 CHARACTERS/INCH	ESC [1w	ESC $10M	ESC [0w
12 CHARACTERS/INCH	ESC [2w	ESC $12M	ESC [2w
17 CHARACTERS/ INCH	ESC [4w	ESC $16M	ESC [4w
ITALICS ON	N/A	N/A	N/A
ITALICS OFF	N/A	N/A	N/A
6 LINES/INCH	ESC [1z	ESC [1z	ESC [0z
8 LINES/INCH	ESC [2z	ESC [2z	ESC [2z
10 LINES/INCH	N/A	N/A	N/A
12 LINES/INCH	N/A	N/A	ESC [3z
LETTER QUALITY	N/A	ESC $1M	ESC [3"z
DP QUALITY	N/A	ESC $10M	ESC [1"z
DRAFT QUALITY	N/A	ESC $13M	ESC [2"z
EXPANDED PRINT ON	ESC $5	ESC $5	ESC [5w
EXPANDED PRINT OFF	ESC $6	ESC $6	ESC [0w
SUBSCRIPT ON	N/A	N/A	N/A
SUBSCRITP OFF	N/A	N/A	N/A
SUPERSCRIPT ON	N/A	N/A	N/A
SUPERSCRIPT OFF	N/A	N/A	N/A
UNDERLINE ON	N/A	N/A	ESC [4m
UNDERLINE OFF	N/A	N/A	ESC [0m
EXPANDED PRINT-ONE LINE ONLY	N/A	ESC $5	N/A
EMPHASIZED ON	N/A	N/A	N/A
EMPHASIZED OFF	N/A	N/A	N/A
DOUBLESTRIKE ON	N/A	N/A	N/A
DOUBLESTRIKE OFF	N/A	N/A	N/A
RESET	N/A	N/A	N/A

Notes: (a) N/A indicates not available. In some cases special fonts or upgrades can be used for these capabilities. (b) From a BASIC program, the CHAR$ function should be used to generate these escape sequences [e.g., CHAR$(14) should be used for the SO sequence]. (c) LETTER QUALITY on dot matrix printers refers to near-letter quality or correspondence-quality print. (d) Consult the ASCII chart in Appendix G for decimal equivalents to these sequences.

Feature	Epson FX-80	Epson Graphtrax 80	Epson MX-80
10 CHARACTERS/INCH	DC2	ESC Q	DC2
12 CHARACTERS/INCH	ESC M	N/A	N/A
17 CHARACTERS/INCH	SI	ESC P	SI
ITALICS ON	ESC 4	ESC 4	N/A
ITALICS OFF	ESC 5	ESC 5	N/A
6 LINES/INCH	ESC 2	ESC 2	ESC 2
8 LINES/INCH	ESC 0	ESC 0	ESC 0
10 LINES/INCH	ESC 1	ESC 1	ESC 1
12 LINES/INCH	N/A	N/A	N/A
LETTER QUALITY	N/A	N/A	N/A
DP QUALITY	N/A	N/A	N/A
DRAFT QUALITY	N/A	N/A	N/A
EXPANDED PRINT ON	ESC W	ESC S	SO
EXPANDED PRINT OFF	DC4	ESC T	DC4
SUBSCRIPT ON	ESC S1	N/A	N/A
SUBSCRIPT OFF	ESC T	N/A	N/A
SUPERSCRIPT ON	ESC SO	N/A	N/A
SUPERSCRIPT OFF	ESC T	N/A	N/A
UNDERLINE ON	ESC-1	N/A	N/A
UNDERLINE OFF	ESC-0	N/A	N/A
EXPANDED PRINT-ONE LINE ONLY	SO	CHR$(14)	SO
EMPHASIZED ON	ESC E	ESC E	ESC E
EMPHASIZED OFF	ESC F	ESC F	ESC F
DOUBLESTRIKE ON	ESC G	ESC G	ESC G
DOUBLESTRIKE OFF	ESC H	ESC H	ESC H
RESET	ESC @	ESC @	N/A

Notes: (a) N/A indicates not available. In some cases special fonts or upgrades can be used for these capabilities. (b) From a BASIC program, the CHAR$ function should be used to generate these escape sequences [e.g., CHAR$(14) should be used for the SO sequence]. (c) LETTER QUALITY on dot matrix printers refers to near-letter quality or correspondence-quality print. (d) Consult the ASCII chart in Appendix G for decimal equivalents to these sequences.

App. E Escape Sequences for Controlling Popular Printers

Feature	Florida Data OSP-130	GE 2030	GE 2120
10 CHARACTERS/INCH	ESC US 13	ESC N	ESC N
12 CHARACTERS/INCH	ESC US 11	ESC M	ESC M
17 CHARACTERS/INCH	ESC US 8	ESC C	ESC C
ITALICS ON	N/A	N/A	N/A
ITALICS OFF	N/A	N/A	N/A
6 LINES/INCH	ESC RS 9	ESC 6	ESC 6
8 LINES/INCH	ESC RS 7	ESC 8	ESC 8
10 LINES/INCH	ESC RS 6	N/A	N/A
12 LINES/INCH	ESC RS 5	ESC G	ESC G
LETTER QUALITY	ESC W	N/A	N/A
DP QUALITY	N/A	N/A	N/A
DRAFT QUALTITY	ESC &	N/A	N/A
EXPANDED PRINT ON	SO	N/A	N/A
EXPANDED PRINT OFF	SI	N/A	N/A
SUBSCRIPT ON	ESC D	N/A	N/A
SUBSCRIPT OFF	ESC U	N/A	N/A
SUPERSCRIPT ON	ESC U	N/A	N/A
SUPERSCRIPT OFF	ESC D	N/A	N/A
UNDERLINE ON	ESC E	N/A	N/A
UNDERLINE OFF	ESC R	N/A	N/A
EXPANDED PRINT-ONE LINE ONLY	SO	N/A	N/A
EMPHASIZED ON	ESC O	N/A	N/A
EMPHASIZED OFF	ESC &	N/A	N/A
DOUBLESTRIKE ON	ESC #2	N/A	N/A
DOUBLESTRIKE OFF	ESC #1	N/A	N/A
RESET	ESC ⟨cr⟩ P	N/A	N/A

Notes: (a) N/A indicates not available. In some cases special fonts or upgrades can be used for these capabilities. (b) From a BASIC program, the CHAR$ function should be used to generate these escape sequences [e.g., CHAR$(14) should be used for the SO sequence]. (c) LETTER QUALITY on dot matrix printers refers to near-letter quality or correspondence-quality print. (d) Consult the ASCII chart in Appendix G for decimal equivalents to these sequences.

Feature	IBM 80 CPS Graphics	IBM 80 CPS Matrix	IDS P80 & P132
10 CHARACTERS/INCH	DC2	DC2	CTRL]
12 CHARACTERS/INCH	N/A	N/A	CTRL \
17 CHARACTERS/INCH	SI	SI	CTRL —
ITALICS ON	N/A	N/A	N/A
ITALICS OFF	N/A	N/A	N/A
6 LINES/INCH	ESC 2	ESC 2	ESC B,8,$
8 LINES/INCH	ESC 8	ESC 0	ESC B,6,$
10 LINES/INCH	ESC 1	ESC 1	N/A
12 LINES/INCH	N/A	N/A	ESC B,4,$
LETTER QUALITY	N/A	N/A	ESC R,1,$
DP QUALITY	N/A	N/A	N/A
DRAFT QUALITY	N/A	N/A	ESC R,2,$
EXPANDED PRINT ON	ESC 1	SO	CTRL A
EXPANDED PRINT OFF	ESC 0	DC4	CTRL B
SUBSCRIPT ON	ESC 1	N/A	CTRL T
SUBSCRIPT OFF	ESC T	N/A	CTRL Y
SUPERSCRIPT ON	ESC O	N/A	CTRL Y
SUPERSCRIPT OFF	ESC T	N/A	CTRL T
UNDERLINE ON	ESC-1	ESC-1	N/A
UNDERLINE OFF	ESC-0	ESC-0	N/A
EXPANDED PRINT-ONE LINE ONLY	SO	SO	N/A
EMPHASIZED ON	ESC E	ESC E	N/A
EMPHASIZED OFF	ESC F	ESC F	N/A
DOUBLESTRIKE ON	ESC G	ESC G	N/A
DOUBLESTRIKE OFF	ESC H	ESC H	N/A
RESET	N/A	N/A	N/A

Notes: (a) N/A indicates not available. In some cases special fonts or upgrades can be used for these capabilities. (b) From a BASIC program, the CHAR$ function should be used to generate these escape sequences [e.g., CHAR$(14) should be used for the SO sequence]. (c) LETTER QUALITY on dot matrix printers refers to near-letter quality or correspondence-quality print. (d) Consult the ASCII chart in Appendix G for decimal equivalents to these sequences.

App. E   Escape Sequences for Controlling Popular Printers

Feature	Infoscribe 1100	Infoscribe 500	Malibu 200
10 CHARACTERS/INCH	ESC 6	ESC 6	ESC E12
12 CHARACTERS/INCH	ESC 8	ESC 8	ESC E10
17 CHARACTERS/INCH	ESC 7	ESC 7	ESC E07
ITALICS ON	ESC A	N/A	N/A
ITALICS OFF	ESC @	N/A	N/A
6 LINES/INCH	ESC 4	ESC 4	ESC LO8
8 LINES/INCH	ESC 5	ESC 5	ESC LO6
10 LINES/INCH	N/A	N/A	N/A
12 LINES/INCH	N/A	N/A	ESC LO4
LETTER QUALITY	ESC 9	ESC 9	ESC @SL
DP QUALITY	ESC 6	N/A	N/A
DRAFT QUALITY	ESC :	N/A	ESC @SD
EXPANDED PRINT ON	CTRL N	SO	ESC @W1
EXPANDED PRINT OFF	CTRL O	SI	ESC @W0
SUBSCRIPT ON	ESC C	ESC C	ESC U
SUBSCRIPT OFF	C-RETURN	ESC R	ESC D
SUPERSCRIPT ON	ESC B	ESC B	ESC D
SUPERSCRIPT OFF	C-RETURN	ESC R	ESC U
UNDERLINE ON	N/A	N/A	N/A
UNDERLINE OFF	N/A	N/A	N/A
EXPANDED PRINT-ONE LINE ONLY	N/A	N/A	N/A
EMPHASIZED ON	N/A	N/A	N/A
EMPHASIZED OFF	N/A 9	N/A	N/A
DOUBLESTRIKE ON	ESC 9	N/A	N/A
DOUBLESTRIKE OFF	ESC 6	N/A	N/A
RESET	ESC R	ESC @	ESC SUB I

Notes: (a) N/A indicates not available. In some cases special fonts or upgrades can be used for these capabilities. (b) From a BASIC program, the CHAR$ function should be used to generate these escape sequences [e.g., CHAR$(14) should be used for the SO sequence]. (c) LETTER QUALITY on dot matrix printers refers to near-letter quality or correspondence-quality print. (d) Consult the ASCII chart in Appendix G for decimal equivalents to these sequences. C-Return is shorthand for carriage return or end of line character.

Feature	Mannesmann Spirit80	MT-160	NEC PC-8023A
10 CHARACTERS/INCH	DC2	ESC [4w	ESC N
12 CHARACTERS/INCH	N/A	ESC [5w	ESC E
17 CHARACTERS/INCH	SI	ESC [6w	ESC Q
ITALICS ON	ESC 4	N/A	N/A
ITALICS OFF	ESC 5	N/A	N/A
6 LINES/INCH	ESC 2	ESC [3z	ESC A
8 LINES/INCH	ESC 0	ESC [4z	ESC B
10 LINES/INCH	ESC 1	N/A	ESCT(1)(5)
12 LINES/INCH	ESC 3 18	N/A	ESCT(1)(2)
LETTER QUALITY	N/A	ESC [1y	N/A
DP QUALITY	N/A	N/A	N/A
DRAFT QUALITY	N/A	ESC [0y	N/A
EXPANDED PRINT ON	ESC W 1	ESC W1	DC2
EXPANDED PRINT OFF	ESC W0	ESC W0	DC4
SUBSCRIPT ON	ESC S 1	ESC [1z	N/A
SUBSCRIPT OFF	ESC T	ESC [2z	N/A
SUPERSCRIPT ON	ESC S 0	ESC [0z	N/A
SUPERSCRIPT OFF	ESC T	ESC [2z	N/A
UNDERLINE ON	ESC −1	ESC [4m	ESC X
UNDERLINE OFF	ESC −0	ESC [0m	ESX Y
EXPANDED PRINT-ONE LINE ONLY	SO	SO	N/A
EMPHASIZED ON	ESC E	ESC [=z	ESC !
EMPHASIZED OFF	ESC F	ESC [)z	ESC "
DOUBLESTRIKE ON	ESC G	N/A	N/A
DOUBLESTRIKE OFF	ESC H	N/A	N/A
RESET	ESC @	ESC [6~	N/A

Notes: (a) N/A indicates not available. In some cases special fonts or upgrades can be used for these capabilities. (b) From a BASIC program, the CHAR$ function should be used to generate these escape sequences [e.g., CHAR$(14) should be used for the SO sequence]. (c) LETTER QUALITY on dot matrix printers refers to near-letter quality or correspondence-quality print. (d) Consult the ASCII chart in Appendix G for decimal equivalents to these sequences.

App. E Escape Sequences for Controlling Popular Printers

Feature	Okidata 2410	Okidata 83A	Panasonic KX-P1090
10 CHARACTERS/INCH	ESC 6	RS	ESC + P + (01)
12 CHARACTERS/INCH	ESC A	N/A	ESC + P + (00)
17 CHARACTERS/INCH	ESC B	GS	N/A
ITALICS ON	N/A	N/A	ESC + 4
ITALICS OFF	N/A	N/A	ESC + 5
6 LINES/INCH	ESC 4	ESC 6	ESC + 2
8 LINES/INCH	ESC 5	ESC 8	ESC + 0
10 LINES/INCH	N/A	N/A	ESC + 1
12 LINES/INCH	N/A	N/A	ESC + A + 6
LETTER QUALITY	ESC 7	N/A	N/A
DP QUALITY	ESC 8	N/A	N/A
DRAFT QUALITY	ESC 9	N/A	N/A
EXPANDED PRINT ON	ESC C	US	ESC + W + (01)
EXPANDED PRINT OFF	ESC Z	RS	ESC + W + (00)
SUBSCRIPT ON	ESC D	N/A	ESC + S + (01)
SUBSCRIPT OFF	ESC E	N/A	ESC + T
SUPERSCRIPT ON	ESC F	N/A	ESC + S + (00)
SUPERSCRIPT OFF	ESC E	N/A	ESC + T
UNDERLINE ON	ESC U	N/A	ESC + − + (01)
UNDERLINE OFF	ESC V	N/A	ESC + − + (00)
EXPANDED PRINT-ONE LINE ONLY	N/A	N/A	N/A
EMPHASIZED ON	N/A	N/A	ESC + E
EMPHASIZED OFF	N/A	N/A	ESC + F
DOUBLESTRIKE ON	N/A	N/A	ESC + G
DOUBLESTRIKE OFF	N/A	N/A	ESC + H
RESET	SI	N/A	ESC +

Notes: (a) N/A indicates not available. In some cases special fonts or upgrades can be used for these capabilities. (b) From a BASIC program, the CHAR$ function should be used to generate these escape sequences [e.g., CHAR$(14) should be used for the SO sequence]. (c) LETTER QUALITY on dot matrix printers refers to near-letter quality or correspondence-quality print. (d) Consult the ASCII chart in Appendix G for decimal equivalents to these sequences.

Feature	Printek 920	Printronix MVP 150B	Star Gemini 10
10 CHARACTERS/INCH	ESC [1w	DC2	DC2
12 CHARACTERS/INCH	ESC [2w	ESC V	ESC B2
17 CHARACTERS/INCH	ESC [4w	SI	SI
ITALICS ON	N/A	N/A	ESC 4
ITALICS OFF	N/A	N/A	ESC 5
6 LINES/INCH	ESC [1x	ESC 2	ESC 2
8 LINES/INCH	ESC [2x	ESC 0	ESC 0
10 LINES/INCH	N/A	ESC 1	ESC 1
12 LINES/INCH	ESC [4x	N/A	N/A
LETTER QUALITY	N/A	ESC P	N/A
DP QUALITY	N/A	ESC R	N/A
DRAFT QUALITY	N/A	N/A	N/A
EXPANDED PRINT ON	SO	SO	ESC W1
EXPANDED PRINT OFF	SI	DC4	ESC W0
SUBSCRIPT ON	ESC [3x	N/A	ESC S1
SUBSCRIPT OFF	ESC [1x	N/A	ESC T
SUPERSCRIPT ON	ESC [3x	N/A	ESC S0
SUPERSCRIPT OFF	ESC [1x	N/A	ESC T
UNDERLINE ON	ESC [4m	ESC-1	ESC-1
UNDERLINE OFF	ESC [m	ESC-0	ESC-0
EXPANDED PRINT-ONE LINE ONLY	N/A	N/A	SO
EMPHASIZED ON	N/A	ESC E	ESC E
EMPHASIZED OFF	N/A	ESC F	ESC F
DOUBLISTRIKE ON	N/A	ESC G	ESC G
DOUBLISTRIKE OFF	N/A	ESC H	ESC H
RESET	ESC c	ESC @	ESC @

Notes: (a) N/A indicates not available. In some cases special fonts or upgrades can be used for these capabilities. (b) From a BASIC program, the CHAR$ function should be used to generate these escape sequences [e.g., CHAR$(14) should be used for the SO sequence]. (c) LETTER QUALITY on dot matrix printers refers to near-letter quality or correspondence-quality print. (d) Consult the ASCII chart in Appendix G for decimal equivalents to these sequences.

App. E Escape Sequences for Controlling Popular Printers

Feature	Toshiba P1350
10 CHARACTERS/INCH	ESC E 12
12 CHARACTERS/INCH	ESC E 10
17 CHARACTERS/INCH	ESC E 07
ITALICS ON	N/A
ITALICS OFF	N/A
6 LINES/INCH	ESC L 08
8 LINES/INCH	ESC L 06
10 LINES/INCH	N/A
12 LINES/INCH	ESC L 04
LETTER QUALITY	ESC*2
DP QUALITY	ESC*0
DRAFT QUALITY	ESC*1
EXPANDED PRINT ON	ESC !
EXPANDED PRINT OFF	ESC "
SUBSCRIPT ON	ESC U
SUBSCRIPT OFF	ESC D
SUPERSCRIPT ON	ESC D
SUPERSCRIPT OFF	ESC U
UNDERLINE ON	ESC I
UNDERLINE OFF	ESC J
EXPANDED PRINT-ONE LINE ONLY	N/A
EMPHASIZED ON	N/A
EMPHASIZED OFF	N/A
DOUBLESTRIKE ON	N/A
DOUBLESTRIKE OFF	N/A
RESET	ESC SUB I

Notes: (a) N/A indicates not available. In some cases special fonts or upgrades can be used for these capabilities. (b) From a BASIC program, the CHAR$ function should be used to generate these escape sequences [e.g., CHAR$(14) should be used for the SO sequence]. (c) LETTER QUALITY on dot matrix printers refers to near-letter quality or correspondence-quality print. (d) Consult the ASCII chart in Appendix G for decimal equivalents to these sequences.

APPENDIX F

escape sequences for controlling popular terminals

When writing application programs for the PC/XT running a terminal emulation package, the programmer must know the specific terminal escape sequence for items such as homing the cursor, erasing the screen, and cursor positioning. The specific terminal user's manual should be consulted for such sequences but is not always available. The following charts may be used for this purpose, recognizing that most terminals offer more capabilities than listed.

Note: These sequences are important to device-dependent applications. For example, TERMCAP is a UNIX feature that capitalizes on terminal screen capabilities. Consequently a PC/XT emulating a given terminal can use device-dependent applications because UNIX will capitalize on features such as those in these charts.

Feature	ADDS Regent 25	ADDS Regent 30	ADDS Viewpoint 60
READ CURSOR POSITION	ESC ?	ESC ENQ	ESC ENQ
CURSOR UP	CTRL Z	CTRL Z	CTRL Z
CURSOR DOWN	CTRL J	CTRL J	CTRL J
CURSOR RIGHT	CTRL F	CTRL F	CTRL F
CURSOR LEFT	CTRL U	CTRL U	CTRL U
HOME CURSOR	CTRL A	CTRL A	CTRL A
CLEAR TO END OF PAGE	ESC y	ESC k	ESC k
CLEAR TO END OF LINE	ESC t	ESC K	ESC K
LINE INSERT	ESC M	ESC M	ESC M
LINE DELETE	ESC 1	ESC 1	ESC 1
CHARACTER INSERT	ESC F	ESC F	ESC F
CHARACTER DELETE	ESC E	ESC E	ESC E
POSITION CURSOR	ESC Y nn	ESC Y r c	ESC Y r c
CLEAR ALL	ESC *	CTRL L	CTRL F
UNDERSCORE	N/A	ESC n '	ESC O '
BLINK	N/A	ESC n B	ESC O B
REVERSE VIDEO	N/A	ESC n P	ESC O P
BLANK VIDEO	N/A	N/A	ESC O D
132 COLUMN MODE	N/A	N/A	N/A
80 COLUMN MODE	N/A	N/A	N/A
HORIZONTAL TAB SET	ESC 1	N/A	N/A
LOCK KEYBOARD	ESC 5	ESC 5	ESC 5
UNLOCK KEYBOARD	ESC 6	ESC 6	ESC 6
NEXT PAGE	N/A	DC1	N/A
PREVIOUS PAGE	N/A	SOH	N/A
PROTECT ON	ESC)	ESC P	ESC O H
PROTECT OFF	ESC (	ESC p	ESC O @
RESET DEVICE	N/A	N/A	N/A

Notes: (a) N/A indicates not available. (b) The letters nn, r, c, pn, and Pn should be substituted with an appropriate number to represent a row, column, or the number of times to perform a sequence. (c) These sequences are important to devise dependent applications. For example, TERMCAP is a UNIX feature that capitalizes on terminal screen capabilities. Consequently a PC/XT emulating a given terminal can use device dependent applications because UNIX will capitalize on features such as those in these charts..

Feature	AT&T4410	AT&T4415	DEC VT52	DEC VT100
READ CURSOR POSITION	ESC [6 n	ESC [6 n	N/A	ESC[6n
CURSOR UP	ESC [pn A	ESC [pn A	ESC A	ESC[Pn A
CURSOR DOWN	ESC [pn B	ESC [pn B	ESC B	ESC[Pn B
CURSOR RIGHT	ESC [pn C	ESC [pn C	ESC C	ESC[Pn C
CURSOR LEFT	ESC [pn D	ESC [pn D	ESC D	ESC[Pn D
HOME CURSOR	ESC [H	ESC [H	ESC H	ESC[H
CLEAR TO END OF PAGE	ESC [J	ESC [OJ	ESC J	ESC[O J
CLEAR TO END OF LINE	ESC [K	ESC [OK	ESC K	ESC[O K
LINE INSERT	ESC [L	ESC [pn L	N/A	N/A
LINE DELETE	ESC [M	ESC [pn M	N/A	N/A
CHARACTER INSERT	ESC [@	ESC [pn @	N/A	N/A
CHARACTER DELETE	ESC [P	ESC [pn P	N/A	N/A
POSITION CURSOR	ESC[:n;pnH	ESC [y;x f	ESCY r+31 c+31	ESC[Pn; Pn H
CLEAR ALL	ESC [2J	ESC [2J	N/A	ESC[2 J
UNDERSCORE	ESC [4m	ESC [?31;4 o	N/A	ESC[4m
BLINK	ESC [5m	ESC [?31;5 o	N/A	ESC[5m
REVERSE VIDEO	ESC [7m	ESC [?31;7 o	N/A	ESC[7m
BLANK VIDEO		ESC [?31;30o	N/A	N/A
132 COLUMN MODE	ESC [?3h	ESC [?3; h	N/A	ESC[?3h
80 COLUMN MODE	ESC [?31	ESC [?3; 1	N/A	ESC[?31
HORIZONTAL TAB SET	N/A	ESC H	N/A	ESC H
LOCK KEYBOARD	N/A	ESC .	N/A	N/A
UNLOCK KEYBOARD	N/A	ESC b	N/A	N/A
NEXT PAGE	N/A	ESC [pn U	N/A	N/A
PREVIOUS PAGE	N/A	ESC [pn V	N/A	N/A
PROTECT ON	N/A	ESC V	N/A	N/A
PROTECT OFF	N/A	ESC W	N/A	N/A
RESET DEVICE	N/A	ESC c	N/A	ESC c

Notes: (a) N/A indicates not available. (b) The letters nn, r, c, pn, and Pn should be substituted with an appropriate number to represent a row, column, or the number of times to perform a sequence.

Feature	Hazeltine 1420
READ CURSOR POSITION	ESC CTRL E
CURSOR UP	ESC CTRL L
CURSOR DOWN	ESC CTRL K
CURSOR RIGHT	CTRL P
CURSOR LEFT	CTRL H
HOME CURSOR	ESC CTRL R
CLEAR TO END OF PAGE	ESC y
CLEAR TO END OF LINE	ESC t
LINE INSERT	ESC CTRL Z
LINE DELETE	ESC CTRL S
CHARACTER INSERT	ESC Q
CHARACTER DELETE	ESC W
POSITION CURSOR	N/A
CLEAR ALL	ESC CTRL L
UNDERSCORE	N/A
BLINK	N/A
REVERSE VIDEO	N/A
BLANK VIDEO	N/A
132 COLUMN MODE	N/A
80 COLUMN MODE	N/A
HORIZONTAL TAB SET	ESC 1
LOCK KEYBOARD	ESC CTRL U
UNLOCK KEYBOARD	ESC CTRL F
NEXT PAGE	N/A
PREVIOUS PAGE	N/A
PROTECT ON	ESC CTRL Y
PROTECT OFF	ESC CTRL _
RESET DEVICE	N/A

Notes: (a) N/A indicates not available. (b) The letters nn, r, c, pn, and Pn should be substituted with an appropriate number to represent a row, column, or the number of times to perform a sequence.

App. F Escape Sequences for Controlling Popular Terminals

Feature	HP 2624	HP 2648	IBM 3101
READ CURSOR POSITION	ESC · DC1	ESC · DC1	ESC 5
CURSOR UP	ESC A	ESC A	ESC A
CURSOR DOWN	ESC B	ESC B	ESC B
CURSOR RIGHT	ESC C	ESC C	ESC C
CURSOR LEFT	ESC D	ESC D	ESC D
HOME CURSOR	ESC H	ESC H	ESC H
CLEAR TO END OF PAGE	ESC J	ESC J	ESC J
CLEAR TO END OF LINE	ESC K	ESC K	ESC I
LINE INSERT	ESC L	ESC L	ESC N
LINE DELETE	ESC M	ESC M	ESC O
CHARACTER INSERT	ESC Q	ESC Q	ESC P
CHARACTER DELETE	ESC P	ESC P	ESC Q
POSITION CURSOR	ESC&a #r#c	ESC&a #r#c	ESC Y xy
CLEAR ALL	ESC g	ESC g	ESC ;
UNDERSCORE	ESC &d D	ESC &d D	N/A
BLINK	ESC &d A	ESC &d A	ESC 3 I
REVERSE VIDEO	ESC &d B	ESC &d B	ESC 3 E
BLINK VIDEO	ESC &d S	ESC &d S	ESC 3 M
132 COLUMN MODE	N/A	N/A	N/A
80 COLUMN MODE	N/A	N/A	N/A
HORIZONTAL TAB SET	N/A	N/A	ESC 0
LOCK KEYBOARD	N/A	N/A	ESC :
UNLOCK KEYBOARD	N/A	N/A	ESC ;
NEXT PAGE	ESC V	ESC V	N/A
PREVIOUS PAGE	ESC U	ESC U	N/A
PROTECT ON	ESC]	ESC &dJ	ESC 3C
PROTECT OFF	ESC [	ESC &d@	ESC 3B
RESET DEVICE	ESC E	ESC E	N/A

Notes: (a) N/A indicates not available. (b) The letters nn, r, c, pn, and Pn should be substituted with an appropriate number to represent a row, column, or the number of times to perform a sequence.

Feature	Lear-Siegler ADM3/5	Teletype 5410	Teletype 5420
READ CURSOR POSITION	ESC ?	N/A	ESC [6 n
CURSOR UP	CTRL K	ESC [A	ESC [pn A
CURSOR DOWN	CTRL J	ESC [B	ESC [pn B
CURSOR RIGHT	CTRL L	ESC [C	ESC [pn C
CURSOR LEFT	CTRL H	ESC [D	ESC [pn D
HOME CURSOR	CTRL ^	ESC [H	ESC [H
CLEAR TO END OF PAGE	ESC y	ESC [J	ESC [OJ
CLEAR TO END OF LINE	ESC t	ESC [K	ESC [OK
LINE INSERT	ESC E	ESC [L	ESC [pn L
LINE DELETE	ESC R	ESC [M	ESC [pn M
CHARACTER INSERT	ESC Q	ESC [@	ESC [pn @
CHARACTER DELETE	ESC M	ESC [P	ESC [pn P
POSITION CURSOR	ESC = r c	ESC[pn;pnH	ESC[y;x f
CLEAR ALL	ESC *	ESC [2J	ESC [2J
UNDERSCORE	N/A	ESC [4m	ESC[?31;4 o
BLINK	N/A	ESC [5m	ESC[?31;5 o
REVERSE VIDEO	N/A	ESC [7m	ESC[?31;7 o
BLANK VIDEO	N/A	ESC [8m	ESC[?31;30o
132 COLUMN MODE	N/A	ESC [?3h	ESC[?3; h
80 COLUMN MODE	N/A	ESC [?31	ESC[?3; l
HORIZONTAL TAB SET	ESC 1	N/A	ESC H
LOCK KEYBOARD	ESC #	N/A	ESC `
UNLOCK KEYBOARD	ESC "	N/A	ESC b
NEXT PAGE	N/A	N/A	ESC [pn U
PREVIOUS PAGE	N/A	N/A	ESC [pn V
PROTECT ON	ESC)	N/A	ESC V
PROTECT OFF	ESC (	N/A	ESC W
RESET DEVICE	N/A	N/A	ESC c

Notes: (a) N/A indicates not available. (b) The letters nn, r, c, pn, and Pn should be substituted with an appropriate number to represent a row, column, or the number of times to perform a sequence.

App. F Escape Sequences for Controlling Popular Terminals

Feature	Televideo 910	Televideo 925
READ CURSOR POSITION	ESC ?	ESC ?
CURSOR UP	CTRL K	CTRL K
CURSOR DOWN	CTRL V	CTRL V
CURSOR RIGHT	CTRL L	CTRL L
CURSOR LEFT	CTRL H	CTRL H
HOME CURSOR	CTRL ^	CTRL ^
CLEAR TO END OF PAGE	ESC y	ESC y
CLEAR TO END OF LINE	ESC T	ESC T
LINE INSERT	ESC E	ESC E
LINE DELETE	ESC R	ESC R
CHARACTER INSERT	ESC Q	ESC Q
CHARACTER DELETE	ESC W	ESC W
POSITION CURSOR	ESC = r c	ESC = r c
CLEAR ALL	ESC *	ESC *
UNDERSCORE	ESC G8	ESC G8
BLINK	ESC G2	ESC G2
REVERSE VIDEO	ESC G4	ESC G4
BLANK VIDEO	ESC G1	ESC G1
132 COLUMN MODE	N/A	N/A
80 COLUMN MODE	N/A	N/A
HORIZONTAL TAB SET	ESC 1	ESC 1
LOCK KEYBOARD	ESC #	ESC #
UNLOCK KEYBOARD	ESC "	ESC "
NEXT PAGE	N/A	ESC K
PREVIOUS PAGE	N/A	ESC J
PROTECT ON	ESC& ESC)	ESC& ESC)
PROTECT OFF	ESC' ESC(	ESC' ESC(
RESET DEVICE	N/A	N/A

Notes: (a) N/A indicates not available. (b) The letters nn, r, c, pn, and Pn should be substituted with an appropriate number to represent a row, column, or the number of times to perform a sequence.

APPENDIX G

ASCII character set

App. G ASCII Character Set

B7 B6 B5			0 0 0	0 0 1	0 1 0	0 1 1	1 0 0	1 0 1	1 1 0	1 1 1
BITS B4 B3 B2 B1		COLUMN ROW	0	1	2	3	4	5	6	7
0 0 0 0	0	NUL CTRL @	0 0 0	DLE 20 CTRL p 16 10	SP 40 CTRL 32 (sp) 20	0 60 48 30	100 @ 64 40	P 120 80 50	` 140 96 60	p 160 112 70
0 0 0 1	1	SOH CTRL a	1 1 1	DC1 21 (XON) 17 CTRL q 11	! 41 33 21	1 61 49 31	A 101 65 41	Q 121 81 51	a 141 97 61	q 161 113 71
0 0 1 0	2	STX CTRL b	2 2 2	DC2 22 CTRL r 18 12	" 42 34 22	2 62 50 32	B 102 66 42	R 122 82 52	b 142 98 62	r 162 114 72
0 0 1 1	3	ETX CTRL c	3 3 3	DC3 23 (XOFF) 19 CTRL s 13	# 43 35 23	3 63 51 33	C 103 67 43	S 123 83 53	c 143 99 63	s 163 115 73
0 1 0 0	4	EOT CTRL d	4 4 4	DC4 24 CTRL t 20 14	$ 44 36 24	4 64 52 34	D 104 68 44	T 124 84 54	d 144 100 64	t 164 116 74
0 1 0 1	5	ENQ CTRL e	5 5 5	NAK 25 CTRL u 21 15	% 45 37 25	5 65 53 35	E 105 69 45	U 125 85 55	e 145 101 65	u 165 117 75
0 1 1 0	6	ACK CTRL f	6 6 6	SYN 26 CTRL v 22 16	& 48 38 26	6 66 54 36	F 106 70 46	V 126 86 56	f 146 102 66	v 166 118 76
0 1 1 1	7	BEL CTRL g	7 7 7	ETB 27 CTRL w 23 17	' 47 39 27	7 67 55 37	G 107 71 47	W 127 87 57	g 147 103 67	w 167 119 77
1 0 0 0	8	BS CTRL h	10 8 8	CAN 30 CTRL x 24 18	(50 40 28	8 70 56 38	H 110 72 48	X 130 88 58	h 150 104 68	x 170 120 78
1 0 0 1	9	HT CTRL i	11 9 9	EM 31 CTRL y 25 19	) 51 41 29	9 71 57 39	I 111 73 49	Y 131 89 59	i 151 105 69	y 171 121 79
1 0 1 0	10	LF CTRL j	12 10 A	SUB 32 CTRL z 26 1A	* 52 42 2A	: 72 58 3A	J 112 74 4A	Z 132 90 5A	j 152 106 6A	z 172 122 7A
1 0 1 1	11	VT CTRL k	13 11 B	ESC 33 CTRL [27 1B	+ 53 43 2B	; 73 59 3B	K 113 75 4B	[133 91 5B	k 153 107 6B	{ 173 123 7B
1 1 0 0	12	FF CTRL l	14 12 C	FS 34 CTRL \ 28 1C	, 54 44 2C	< 74 60 3C	L 114 76 4C	\ 134 92 5C	l 154 108 6C	| 174 124 7C
1 1 0 1	13	CR CTRL m	15 13 D	GS 35 CTRL] 29 1D	- 55 45 2D	= 75 61 3D	M 115 77 4D	] 135 93 5D	m 155 109 6D	} 175 125 7D
1 1 1 0	14	SO CTRL n	16 14 E	RS 36 CTRL 30 1E	. 56 46 2E	> 76 62 3E	N 116 78 4E	136 94 5E	n 156 110 6E	~ 176 126 7E
1 1 1 1	15	SI CTRL o	17 15 F	US 37 CTRL - 31 1F	/ 57 47 2F	? 77 63 3F	O 117 79 4F	_ 137 95 5F	o 157 111 6F	DEL CTRL (bs) 177 127 7F

*Keyboard-generated characters.

APPENDIX H

vendor peripheral comparisons

Boards for the PC/XT

Vendor	Product	Memory (K = 1000)	Serial port	Parallel port	Graphics	Clock	Light port	Game port	Monitor support	Ram disk	Print spooler
Amdek	MAI Board	128K	—	Yes	—	—	Yes	—	Yes	—	—
Apparat Inx.	Print Spooler Board	64K	—	Yes	—	—	—	—	—	—	—
Apstek, Inc.	PIC-1 Board	—	—	Yes	—	Yes	—	—	—	—	Yes
	Multi-function Card	256K	Yes	Yes	—	Yes	—	—	—	Yes	Yes
	SIC-1	—	Yes	—	—	Yes	—	—	—	—	—
AST Research Inc.	Advanced Comm. Card CC-232	—	Yes	—	—	—	—	—	—	—	—
	Comboplus	256K	Yes	Yes	—	Yes	—	—	—	Yes	Yes
	Megaplus	512K	Yes	Yes	—	Yes	—	—	—	Yes	Yes
	I/O Plus II	—	Yes	Yes	—	Yes	—	Yes	—	Yes	Yes
	Expansion Memory	256K	—	—	—	—	—	—	—	Yes	Yes
	SixPakPlus	384K	Yes	Yes	—	Yes	—	—	—	Yes	Yes
California Computer Systems	SuperVision Board	—	—	—	—	—	—	—	Yes	—	—
California Micro Computer	Switchport Board	256K	Yes	Yes	—	Yes	—	—	—	—	—
Conographic Corp.	Cono#Color Board	128K	—	—	—	—	Yes	—	Yes	—	—
Control Systems	Parallel Interface Adapter	—	—	Yes	—	—	—	—	—	—	—
Datamac Computer Systems	DMS-1/2	—	Yes	—	—	—	—	—	—	—	—
Davong Systems, Inc.	Async + RAM Board	256K	Yes	—	—	—	—	—	—	—	—
Daystar Systems	Ultra55 Board	256K	Yes	Yes	—	Yes	—	Yes	—	—	—
Easitech Corp.	Easiboard	256K	Yes	Yes	—	Yes	—	—	—	Yes	Yes
GM Enterprises, Inc.	Parallel I/O Adapter	—	—	Yes	—	—	—	—	—	—	—

Boards for the PC/XT (continued)

Vendor	Product	Memory (K = 1000)	Serial port	Parallel port	Graphics	Clock	Light pen	Game port	Monitor support	Ram disk	Print spooler
Hercules Computer Tech.	Graphics Card	64K	—	Yes	—	—	—	—	Yes	—	—
IBM Corporation	Color/Graphics Adapter	—	—	—	—	—	—	—	Yes	—	—
	Printer Adapter	—	—	Yes	—	—	—	—	—	—	—
	Async Communication Adapter	—	Yes	—	—	—	—	—	—	—	—
Ideassociates, Inc.	Ideaboard	256K	Yes	Yes	—	Yes	—	—	—	Yes	—
	Ideaplus Card	256K	Yes	Yes	—	Yes	—	—	—	Yes	Yes
	Ideamini I/O Card	—	Yes	Yes	—	Yes	—	—	—	Yes	Yes
Indigo Data Systems	PC Multipak	256K	Yes	Yes	—	Yes	—	—	—	—	Yes
Maynard Electronics	SandStar Multifunction Card	640K	Yes	Yes	—	Yes	—	Yes	—	—	—
Memory Technologies	Versa-Ram Plus II	256K	Yes	Yes	—	Yes	—	—	—	—	Yes
Micro Synergy, Inc.	Pro Series 5 Board	1024K	Yes	Yes	—	Yes	—	Yes	—	—	—
Microcomputer Bus. Ind.	Monte Carlo Card	1000K	Yes	Yes	—	Yes	—	Yes	—	—	—
Microsoft	The Systemcard	256K	Yes	Yes	—	—	—	—	—	Yes	Yes
Microtek, Inc.	HAL Board	256K	Yes	Yes	—	Yes	—	—	—	Yes	Yes
Paso Com	Professional 1 Series	256K	Yes	Yes	—	Yes	—	Yes	—	—	—
	Professional 11 Series	—	Yes	Yes	—	Yes	—	—	—	—	—
	Professional 111 Series	—	Yes	Yes	—	Yes	—	—	—	—	—
PC Ware, Inc.	Serial Comm. Adapter	—	Yes	—	—	—	—	—	—	—	—
	Parallel Printer Adapter	—	—	Yes	—	—	—	—	—	—	—
Personal Data	Pack-780 Board		Yes								

Company	Product	Memory									
Personal Systems Tech.	Pack-RAM+Combo Card	256K	Yes	Yes	—	Yes	—	—	—	—	—
	Async Communication Ports	—	Yes	—	—	—	—	—	—	—	—
Plantronics	Time-Spectrum Board	256K	Yes	—	—	Yes	—	—	—	—	—
	Colorplus	—	—	—	—	—	—	Yes	—	—	—
Quadram Corp.	Quadlink Board	—	—	—	—	—	Yes	—	—	—	—
	Quadboard	256K	Yes	Yes	—	Yes	—	—	—	—	Yes
	IPIC	—	—	Yes	—	—	—	—	—	—	—
	RS-232C Async/Adapter	—	Yes	—	—	—	—	—	—	—	—
Raytronics	RAMPLUS Board	256K	Yes	—	—	Yes	—	—	—	Yes	—
	RAMPLUS!	1024K	Yes	Yes	—	Yes	—	—	—	Yes	—
Seattle Computer	RAM+3	256K	Yes	Yes	—	Yes	—	—	—	—	—
Sigma Designs, Inc.	Enhanced Support Card	256K	Yes	Yes	—	Yes	Yes	—	—	—	Yes
	Stack Board	256K	—	—	—	—	—	—	—	—	—
	SDI-ESC+Memory Board	512K	Yes	Yes	—	Yes	Yes	—	—	—	—
STB Systems, Inc.	STB "Super RIO" card	256K	Yes	Yes	—	Yes	Yes	—	—	—	Yes
Tava Corp.	Trump Card	256K	Yes	Yes	—	—	Yes	—	—	—	—
Tecmar	PC-Mate Board	256K	Yes	Yes	—	Yes	—	Yes	—	Yes	Yes
	Graphics Master	128K	—	—	—	—	—	Yes	—	—	—
USI Computer Products	Multidisplay Card	32K	—	Yes	Yes	—	—	—	—	—	—
Vista Computer Co.	Multicard	256K	Yes	Yes	—	Yes	—	—	—	—	—
	PC Master	—	Yes	Yes	—	Yes	—	—	—	—	—
	Maxicard	256K	—	—	—	Yes	—	—	—	Yes	—
	PC Clock I/O	—	Yes	Yes	—	Yes	—	—	—	—	—
Wesper Microsystems, Inc.	Wizard-Spooler S/P	16 K	Yes	Yes	—	—	—	Yes	—	—	—
Zen/Tek	Dual Com Card	—	Yes	—	—	—	—	—	—	—	—
Zobek	2SP Board	—	Yes	—	—	—	—	—	—	—	—

Communication Software

Vendor	Product	ASCII file transfer	Binary file transfer	XMODEM protocol	XON/XOFF	Error-checking protocol	Remote operation	Terminal emulation
Coefficient Systems Corp.	VTERM	Yes	—	—	Yes	—	—	Yes
Hayes Microcomputer Products	Smartcom II Software	Yes	Yes	—	Yes	Yes	Yes	—
IBM Corporation	IBM Async. Comm. Support	Yes	Yes	—	Yes	—	—	Yes
Inner Loop Software	VDTE 2	Yes	Yes	—	Yes	—	—	Yes
Intl. Software Alliance	LYNC Comm. Software	—	—	—	—	—	—	—
Mark of the Unicorn	PC/Intercomm	Yes	Yes	Yes	Yes	—	—	Yes
Microstuf, Inc.	Crosstalk	Yes	Yes	—	Yes	Yes	Yes	Yes
Persoft, Inc.	SmarTerm TE100-FT	Yes	Yes	—	Yes	Yes	—	Yes
Persoft, Inc.	SmarTerm TE400-FT	Yes	Yes	—	Yes	Yes	—	Yes
Solution Software Systems	PCMODEM	—	—	—	—	—	—	—
Southeastern Software	Data Capture/PC	Yes	—	—	Yes	—	—	—
The Headlands Press, Inc.	PC-Talk III	Yes	Yes	Yes	Yes	—	—	—
Tymlabs Corp.	HP2621 Terminal Emulator	Yes	—	—	Yes	—	—	Yes

Note: Refer to the terminal emulation chart for specifics.

Local Area Networks

Vendor	Product	Access method	Media	Printer type	Dedicated terminal	Dedicated file server
3Com Corporation	Etherseries	CSMA/CD	Coaxial	Serial	Yes	Yes
Corvus Systems, Inc.	Omninet	CSMA/CD	Twisted pair	Parallel	No	Yes
Novell, Inc.	Sharenet S	TOKEN	Twisted pair	Serial	Yes	Yes
	Sharenet X	CSMA/CD	Coaxial	Ser/par	—	Yes
ORCHID Technology	PCnet	CSMA/CD	Coaxial	Ser/par	—	—
Percom Data Corp.	Vision Network	TOKEN	Coaxial	Ser/par	—	—
Santa Clara Systems, Inc.	SCS PCnet	CSMA/CD	Coaxial	Ser/par	—	—
Tecmar, Inc.	Elan	CSMA/CD	Coaxial	Ser/par	—	—
XCOMP, Inc.	XNET	CSMA/CD	Twisted pair	Ser/par	—	—

Modem Comparisons

Company	Modem	Board	Dial-up	PVT-line	Async	Sync	Hayes-mode	Pulse	T-tone	Auto-answer	Kybd dial
AT & T Information Systems	Local Area Data Set	—	—	Yes	Yes	Yes	—	Yes	Yes	Yes	—
	103J Data Set	—	Yes	—	Yes	—	—	Yes	Yes	Yes	—
	201C/2024 Data Sets	—	—	Yes	Yes	—	—	—	—	—	—
	201C (DDD) Data Sets	—	Yes	—	—	Yes	—	Yes	Yes	Yes	—
	208A/2048 Data Sets	—	—	Yes	—	Yes	—	—	—	—	—
	208B Data Set	—	Yes	—	—	Yes	—	Yes	Yes	Yes	—
	209A/2096 Data Sets	—	—	Yes	—	Yes	—	—	—	—	—
Bizcomp	212A Data Set	—	Yes	—	Yes	Yes	—	Yes	Yes	Yes	—
	PC:Intellimodem	Yes	Yes	—	Yes	—	—	Yes	Yes	Yes	Yes
Black Box Catalog	SHM-NPR Short Haul Modem	—	—	Yes	Yes	—	—	—	—	—	—
	Limited Distance Modem	—	—	Yes	Yes	Yes	—	—	—	—	—
Bytcom, Inc.	212AD Modem	—	Yes	—	Yes	Yes	—	Yes	Yes	Yes	Yes
Comdata	212A	—	Yes	Yes	Yes	—	—	—	—	Yes	—
Gandalf Data, Inc.	MLDS 122 Short-Haul Modem	—	—	Yes	Yes	—	—	—	—	—	—
Hayes Microcomputer Products	Smartmodem 1200B	Yes	Yes	—	Yes	—	Yes	Yes	Yes	Yes	Yes
	Smartmodem 1200	—	Yes	—	Yes	—	Yes	Yes	Yes	Yes	Yes

Company	Product										
Ideassociates, Inc.	Ideacomm 1200 Modem	Yes	Yes	—	Yes	—	—	—	Yes	Yes	—
Microcom, Inc.	PCS Modem	—	—	—	Yes	—	—	—	Yes	Yes	Yes
Microperipheral Corp.	PConnection Modem	Yes	—	—	—	—	—	—	—	—	—
Prometheus Products, Inc.	Pro-Modem 1200	—	Yes	—	Yes	—	Yes	Yes	Yes	Yes	Yes
U.S. Robotics Inc.	Password Modem	—	Yes	—	Yes	—	Yes	Yes	Yes	Yes	Yes
Ven-Tel Inc.	PC Modem Plus	Yes	Yes	—	Yes	—	Yes	Yes	Yes	Yes	Yes
Ven-Tel Inc.	Ven-Tel 212 Plus II	—	Yes	—	Yes	Yes	—	Yes	Yes	Yes	Yes
Wolfdata, Inc.	Quikcom	Yes	Yes	—	Yes	—	—	—	—	—	Yes

Printer Comparisons

Company	Printer	Speed (bps)	Interface(s)	Print Type
Anacom General Corp.	150/160 Printer	150	Ser/par	Dot matrix
Anadex, Inc.	WP-600 Printer	276	Ser/par	Dot matrix
Axiom Corporation	DP9625A Printer	?	Ser/par	Dot matrix
C. Itoh/Leading Edge	IMP Printer	100	Ser/par	Dot matrix
	Starwriter F-10 Printer	40	Ser/par	Letter quality
	Starwriter I Printer	25	Ser/par	Letter quality
Dataproducts	M-100 Printer	140	Ser/par	Dot matrix
DATASOUTH Computer Corp.	DS-220 Printer	220	Ser/par	Dot matrix
	DS 180 Matrix Printer	180	Ser/par	Dot matrix
Diablo Systems, Inc.	620 Printer	25	Serial	Letter quality
	KSR1640 Printer	45	Serial	Letter quality
	KSR1650 Printer	45	Serial	Letter quality
Digital Equipment Corp.	LA-100PC Printer	240	Serial	Dot matrix
	LA120 Printer	120	Ser/par	Dot matrix
Docutel/Olivetti	JETT-i Printer	110	?????	Dot matrix
Dynax, Inc.	DX-15 Printer	?	?????	Letter quality
	Brother HR-25 Printer	23	?????	Letter quality
Envision	430 Printer	300	Ser/par	Dot matrix
Epson America, Inc.	RX/FX Printer(s)	100	Ser/par	Dot matrix
Florida Data Corp.	OSP-130 Printer	600	Ser/par	Dot matrix
Fujitsu America, Inc.	SP830 Printer	80	Serial	Letter quality
General Electric	2030 Printer	60	Ser/par	Dot matrix
	2120 Printer	120	Ser/par	Dot matrix
	3404 Printer	300	Ser/par	Dot matrix
HI-G Printers Corp.	9/80 PS Printer	150	Ser/par	Dot matrix
Howard Industries	Typrinter 221 Printer	20	Serial	Letter quality
Inforunner Corp.	Riteman Printer	?	?????	Dot matrix
Infoscribe, Inc.	1100 Printer	200	Ser/par	Dot matrix
	500 Printer	150	Ser/par	Dot matrix

Company	Model	Price	Interface	Type
Mannesmann Tally Corp.	MT-160 Printer	160	Ser/par	Dot matrix
	Spirit MT-80 Printer	80	Ser/par	Dot matrix
NEC Information Systems	PC-8023A-C Printer	120	Ser/par	Dot matrix
	5510 Printer	55	Serial	Letter quality
	5530 Printer	55	Parallel	Letter quality
	3510 Printer	35	Serial	Letter quality
	3530 Printer	35	Parallel	Letter quality
	7700 Printers	55	Serial	Letter quality
Okidata Corp.	2410 Printer	350	Ser/par	Dot matrix
	Microline 83A Printer	120	Ser/par	Dot matrix
Olivetti Periph. Eqpt.	DY-211 Printer	20	Serial	Letter quality
	DY-311 Printer	32	Ser/par	Letter quality
	DY-811 Printer	65	Ser/par	Letter quality
Pertec Computer Company	Stylist 360 Printer	17	Ser/par	Dot matrix
Printek, Inc.	920 Printer	340	Ser/par	Dot matrix
Printronix	MVP 150B Printer	180	Parallel	Dot matrix
Qume Corp.	Sprint 11 Plus Printer	40	Ser/par	Letter quality
	Sprint 5/45 Printer	45	Ser/par	Letter quality
	Sprint 5/55 Printer	55	Serial	Letter quality
	Sprint 9/55 Printer	55	Ser/par	Letter quality
Silver-Reed America, Inc.	EXP550 Printer	16	Serial	Letter quality
Smith-Corona	TP-1 Printer	12	Serial	Letter quality
Star Micronics, Inc.	Gemini-10X	120	Ser/par	Dot matrix
Systemed Corporation	Typrinter	12	Parallel	Letter quality
Texas Instruments, Inc.	810-LQ Printer		Serial	Dot matrix
	TI-855 Printer	150	Ser/par	Dot matrix
Toshiba America, Inc.-ISD	P-1350 Printer	160	Ser/par	Dot matrix
	1730 Printer	32	Ser/par	Letter quality
Xerox Corp.	1740/50 Printers	45	Serial	Letter quality
Xymec, Inc.	HY-Q 1000 Printer	20	Ser/par	Letter quality

Terminal Emulation Packages

Company	Package	Adds	Data General 100/200/400	Dec VT52	Dec VT100	HP 2600	IBM 3101	Televideo 900 Series	2780/3780 BSC	3270 BSC	3270 SDLC	3278/9 Coaxial	5251 SDLC
AST Research, Inc.	AST-3780 RJE Emulator	—	—	—	—	—	—	—	Yes	—	—	—	—
	PC 3270	—	—	—	—	—	—	—	—	—	Yes	Yes	—
	AST 5251	—	—	—	—	—	—	—	—	—	—	—	Yes
BARR Systems, Inc.	BARR/HASP	—	—	—	—	—	—	—	Yes	—	—	—	—
Coefficient Systems Corp.	VTERM	—	—	Yes	Yes	—	—	—	—	—	—	—	—
CXI, Inc.	PCOX	—	—	—	—	—	—	—	—	—	—	Yes	—
IBM Corporation	IBM Async Comm Support	—	—	—	—	—	Yes	—	—	—	—	—	—
	IBM Bisynchronous Comm.	—	—	—	—	—	—	—	—	Yes	—	Yes	—
Information Technologies	Linkup	—	—	Yes	Yes	—	Yes	—	Yes	—	—	—	—
Inner Loop Software	VDTE 2	—	—	Yes	—	Yes	—	—	—	—	—	—	—
Intelligent Technologies	PC Express	—	—	Yes	Yes	—	—	—	—	—	Yes	—	—
Mark of the Unicorn	PC/Intercomm	—	—	Yes	Yes	—	—	—	—	—	—	—	—
Microlog, Inc.	Babytalk	—	—	Yes	Yes	—	Yes	—	Yes	Yes	Yes	—	—
Microsoft Corp.	The Systemcard	—	—	—	—	—	—	—	—	—	—	—	Yes
Microstuf, Inc.	Crosstalk	Yes	—	Yes	Yes	—	Yes	Yes	—	—	—	—	—

Vendor	Product	1	2	3	4	5	6	7	8	9	10	11	12
Persoft, Inc.	SmarTerm TE100-FT	—	—	Yes	Yes	—	—	—	—	—	—	—	—
	SmarTerm TE400-FT	—	Yes	—	—	—	—	—	—	—	—	—	—
Phone 1, Inc.	CLEO-3270	—	—	—	—	—	—	Yes	Yes	Yes	—	—	—
	CLEO-3780	—	—	—	—	—	—	Yes	—	—	—	—	—
Software Dynamics, Inc.	SDI-3780	—	—	—	—	—	—	Yes	—	—	—	—	—
Techland Systems, Inc.	BLUE LYNX 5251	—	—	—	—	—	—	—	—	—	—	—	Yes
	BLUE LYNX 3276	—	—	—	—	—	—	—	Yes	Yes	—	Yes	—
	BLUE LYNX 3276/5	—	—	—	—	—	—	—	—	—	—	—	—
Tymlabs Corp.	HP2621 Terminal Emulator	—	—	—	—	Yes	—	—	—	—	—	—	—

Miscellaneous Add-Ons

Vendor	Product	Category
Advanced Systems Concepts	ASCI Switch	Code-activated switch
Applied Dynamics	Keytops	Keyboard/keytops
B&B Electronics	RS-232 Wiring Adapter	Break-out box
Bejed, Inc.	BJ-1208 EIA Mini-Switch	Serial ABC switch
Black Box Catalog	X Switch	Serial ABC switch
	ABC-Centronics Switch	Parallel ABC switch
	SAM+ Centronics	Break-out box
	Sam+232	Break-out box
	BOB-Centronics	Break-out box
	AME	Null-modem cable/async modem eliminator
	SME-3	Synchronous modem eliminator
	ABC Switch	Serial ABC switch
California Computer Systems	Z/Plus	Operating system software/board
Intracomputer	Printer Switch	Parallel ABC switch
	ANM-1	Null-modem cable/async modem eliminator
IQ Technologies, Inc.	SC821 SmartCable	Null-modem cable/async modem eliminator
Jaxon, RVR Systems	OWL	Break-out box
	LBS-1	Null-modem cable/async modem eliminator
Key Tronic	KB 5150 Keyboard	Keyboard/keytops
Microlog, Inc.	Baby Blue Board	Operating system software/board
Microsoft Corp.	Microsoft Mouse	Mouse
Mouse Systems	PC Mouse	Mouse
Percom Data Corp.	PHD	Hard disk storage
Personal Data Systems	Pack-Z80 Board	Operating system software/board
Princeton Graphic Systems	HX-12 Monitor	Monitor
Quadram Corp.	Quadlink Board	Operating system software/board
	Quadchrome Monitor	Monitor
Vertex Systems	Keyfixer	Keyboard/keytops

APPENDIX I

vendor addresses

Vendor	P.O. box	St. address	City	St	Zip	Phone number
3Com Corporation	P.O. Box 7390	1390 Shorebird Way	Mountain View	CA	94039	415 961 9602
Advanced Systems Concepts		435 N. Lake Ave., Dept. B	Pasadena	CA	91101	213 793 8971
Amdek		2201 Lively Blvd.	Elk Grove Village	IL	60007	312 364 1180
Anacom General Corp.		1116 Vallencia Dr.	Fullerton	CA	92631	714 992 0223
Anadex, Inc.		20732 Lassen St.	Chatsworth	CA	91311	213 998 8010
Apparat Inx.		4401 S. Tamarac Pkwy.	Denver	CO	80237	303 741 1778
Applied Dynamics	P.O. Box 1810					
Apstek, Inc.		2636 Walnut Hill Ln.	Cottonwood	AZ	86326	602 634 7148
AST Research, Inc.		2372 Morse Ave.	Dallas	TX	75229	214 357 5288
AT & T Information Systems		One Speedwell Ave.	Irvine	CA	92714	714 540 1333
			Morristown	NJ	07960	201 898 2000
Axiom Corporation		1014 Griswold Ave.	San Fernando	CA	91340	213 365 9521
B&B Electronics			Mendota	IL	61342	815 539 5827
Barr Systems, Inc.	P.O. Box 475B	2500 Blue Ridge Rd.	Raleigh	NC	27607	800 227 7797
Bejed, Inc.		4824 Northeast 42nd	Portland	OR	97218	503 281 8153
Bizcomp		532 Weddell Dr.	Sunnyvale	CA	94086	408 745 1616
Black Box Catalog	P.O. Box 12800		Pittsburgh	PA	15241	412 746 2910
Bytcom, Inc.		2169 Francisco Blvd.	San Rafael	CA	94901	800 227 3254
California Computer Systems		250 Caribbean Dr.	Sunnyvale	CA	94086	408 734 5811
California Micro Computer		17791 Jamestown Ln.	Huntington Beach	CA	92647	714 847 4141
C. Itoh/Leading Edge		225 Turnpike St.	Canton	MA	02021	800 343 3436
Coefficient Systems Corp.		611 Broadway	New York	NY	10012	212 777 6707
Comdata		7900 N. Nagle	Morton Grove	IL	60053	312 470 9600
Conographic Corp.		2268 Golden Circle	Newport Beach	CA	92660	714 650 2666
Control Systems		2855 Anthony Ln.	Minneapolis	MN	55418	612 789 2421

Company	Address		City	State	Zip	Phone
Corvus Systems, Inc.	2029 O'Toole Ave.		San Jose	CA	95131	408 946 7700
CXI, Inc.	10011 N. Foothill		Cupertino	CA	95014	408 725 1881
Datamac Computer Systems	680 Almanor Ave.		Sunnyvale	CA	94086	408 735 0323
Dataproducts	6200 Canoga Ave.	P.O. Box 3400	Woodland Hills	CA	91365	213 887 8489
DATASOUTH Computer Corp.		P.O. Box 240947	Charlotte	NC	28224	800 438 5050
Davong Systems, Inc.	217 Humboldt Ct.		Sunnyvale	CA	94086	408 734 4900
Daystar Systems	10511 Church Rd.		Dallas	TX	75238	214 341 8136
Diablo Systems, Inc.	24500 Industrial		Hayward	CA	94545	800 824 7888
Digital Equipment Corp.	2 MT. Royal Ave., UP		Marlboro	MA	1752	800 DIGITAL
Digitronics	53 John St.		Cumberland	RI	2864	401 724 8500
Docutel/Olivetti	1909 E. Cornell St.		Peoria	IL	61614	800 447 4700
Dynax, Inc.	5698 Bandini Blvd.		Bell	CA	90201	213 260 7121
Easitech Corp.	2215 Perimeter Pk., 22		Atlanta	GA	30341	404 452 7576
Electronic Specialists	171 S. Main St.	P.O. Box 389	Natick	MA	01760	800 225 4876
Envision	631 River Oaks Pkwy.		San Jose	CA	95134	408 946 9755
Epson America, Inc.	3415 Kashiwa St.		Torrance	CA	90505	213 539 9140
Florida Data Corp.	600 D. John Rodes Blvd.		Melbourne	FL	32935	305 259 4700
Fujitsu America, Inc.	2945 Oakmead Village		Santa Clara	CA	90505	714 558 8757
Gandalf Data, Inc.	1019 S. Noel Ave.		Wheeling	IL	60090	312 541 6060
General Electric Company	G.E. Drive		Waynesboro	VA	22980	703 949 1188
GM Enterprises, Inc.	485 E. Granville Ave.		Roselle	IL	60172	312 893 1171
Hayes Microcomputer Prod.	5923 Peachtree Blvd.		Norcross	GA	30092	404 449 8791
Hercules Computer Tech.	3200 Adeline St.		Berkeley	CA	94703	415 654 2476
Hewlett-Packard	16399 W. Bernardo Dr.		San Diego	CA	92127	800 547 3400
HI-G Printers Corp.	96 W. Dudley Town Rd.		Bloomfield	CT	06002	203 522 8600
Howard Industries	2031 E. Cerritos Ave.		Anaheim	CA	92806	714 778 3443
IBM Corporation		P.O. Box 1328	Boca Raton	FL	33432	800 462 3333

Vendor	P.O. box	St. address	City	St	Zip	Phone number
IBM Instruments, Inc.	P.O. Box 332		Danbury	CT	6810	800 243 7054
I-Bus Systems		8863 Balboa Ave.	San Diego	CA	92123	800 382 4229
Ideassociates, Inc.		7 Oak Park Dr.	Bedford	MA	01730	800 257 5027
Indigo Data Systems		100 E. Nasa Rd. 1,	Webster	TX	77598	800 231 9480
Information Technologies		7850 East Evans Rd.	Scottsdale	AZ	85260	602 998 1033
Inforunner Corp.		1621 Stanford St.	Santa Monica	CA	90404	213 453 6688
Infoscribe, Inc.		2720 S. Croddy Way	Santa Ana	CA	92704	714 641 8595
Inner Loop Software	P.O. Box 45857-A		Los Angeles	CA	90045	213 645 5162
Intek		780 Charcot Ave.	San Jose	CA	95131	408 946 9041
Intelligent Technologies		151 University Ave.	Palo Alto	CA	94301	415 328 2411
Intl. Software Alliance		1835 Mission Ridge	Santa Barbara	CA	93103	805 966 3077
Intra Computer		101 W. 31st St.	New York	NY	10001	212 947 5533
IQ Technologies, Inc.		1181 NE First St.	Bellevue	WA	98005	206 451 0232
Jaxon, RVR Systems	P.O. Box 265		Dewitt	NY	13214	
Key Tronic	P.O. Box 1468		Spokane	WA	99214	800 262 6006
Mannesmann Tally Corp.		8301 S. 180th St.	Ken	WA	98032	206 251 5524
Mark of the Unicorn	P.O. Box 423		Arlington	MA	02174	617 489 1387
Maynard Electronics		400 Semoran Blvd.	Casselberry	FL	32707	305 331 6402
Memory Technologies		4343 Grand Prix Dr.	Logansport	IN	46947	800 348 3377
Microcom, Inc.		1400A Providence Hwy.	Norwood	MA	2062	617 762 9310
Microcomputer Bus. Ind.		1019 8th St.	Golden	CO	80401	303 279 8438
Microlog, Inc.		222 Rte. 59	Suffern	NY	10901	914 368 0353
Microperipheral Corp.		2565 152nd Ave, NE	Redmond	WA	98052	206 881 7544
Microsoft Corp.		10700 Northup Way	Bellevue	WA	98004	206 828 8080
Microstuf, Inc.		1845 The Exchange #140	Atlanta	GA	30339	404 952 0267
Micro Synergy, Inc.		187 Ulmerton Rd.	Largo	FA	33544	813 584 2488
Microtek, Inc.		4750 Viewridge Ave.	San Diego	CA	92123	800 854 1081

Company	Address		City	State	ZIP	Phone
Mouse Systems		2336H Walsh Ave.	Santa Clara	CA	95051	408 988 0211
NEC Information Systems, Inc.		5 Militia Dr.	Lexington	MA	02173	800 343 4418
Novell, Inc.	P.O. Box 2603	1170 N. Industrial Pk.	Orem	UT	84057	801 226 8202
Okidata Corp.		111 Gaither Dr.	Mt. Laurel	NJ	08054	609 235 2600
Olivetti Periph. Eqpt.		505 White Plains Rd.	Tarrytown	NY	10591	914 631 3000
ORCHID Technology		487 Sinclair Fr. Rd.	Milpitas	CA	95035	408 942 8660
Paso Com			Mission Viejo	CA	92690	714 552 0130
PC Ware, Inc.		4883 Tonino Dr.	San Jose	CA	95136	408 978 8626
Percom Data Corp.		11220 Pagemill Rd.	Dallas	TX	75243	214 340 7081
Persoft, Inc.		2740 Ski Ln.	Madison	WI	53713	608 233 1000
Personal Data Systems		1110 Wrigley Way	Milpitas	CA	95035	408 262 7880
Personal Systems Tech.		15801 Rockfield	Irvine	CA	92714	714 859 8871
Pertec Computer Corporation		12910 Culver Blvd.	Los Angeles	CA	90066	714 660 0488
Phone 1, Inc.		461 N. Mulford Rd.	Rockford	IL	61107	815 397 8110
Plantronics	P.O. Box 502	7630 Hayward Rd.	Frederick	MD	21701	800 638 6211
Princeton Graphic Systems		1101-1 State Rd.	Princeton	NJ	08540	800 221 1490
Printek, Inc.		1517 Townline Rd.	Benton Harbor	MI	49022	616 925 3200
Printronix	P.O. Box 19559	17500 Cartwright Rd.	Irvine	CA	92713	800 556 1234
Prometheus Products, Inc.		45277 Fremont Blvd.	Fremont	CA	94538	415 490 2370
Protocol Computers, Inc.		6150 Canoga Ave.	Woodland Hills	CA	91367	800 423 5904
Quadram Corp.		4357 Park Dr.	Norcross	GA	30093	404 923 6666
Qume Corporation		2350 Qume Dr.	San Jose	CA	95131	408 942 4000
Raytronics		4901 Morena, Bldg. 900	San Diego	CA	92117	800 854 1085
Santa Clara Systems, Inc.		1860 Hartog Dr.	San Jose	CA	95131	408 287 4640
Seattle Computer		1114 Industry Dr.	Seattle	WA	98188	800 426 8936
Sigma Designs, Inc.		2990 Scott Blvd.	Santa Clara	CA	95050	408 496 0536
Silver-Reed America, Inc.		8665 Hayden Pl.	Culver City	CA	90230	213 837 6104
Smith-Corona		65 Locust Ave.	New Canaan	CT	06840	203 972 1471
Software Dynamics, Inc.	P.O. Box 247		Dunedin	FL	34296	813 733 8784

Vendor	P.O. box	St. address	City	St	Zip	Phone number
Solution Software Systems		117 S. Main	Mt. Prospect	IL	60056	312 893 5111
Southeastern Software		7743 Briarwood Dr.	New Orleans	LA	70128	504 246 8438
Star Micronics, Inc.		2803 NW 12th St.	Dallas/Fort Worth Airport	TX	75261	214 456 0052
STB Systems, Inc.	P.O. Box 1811		Richardson	TX	75080	214 234 8750
Systemed Corporation	P.O. Box 18		Mountain City	TN	37683	615 727 6000
Tallgrass Technologies		11667 W. 90th	Overland Park	KS	66214	913 492 6002
Tava Corp.		1711 Corinthian	Newport Beach	CA	92660	714 261 0200
Techland Systems, Inc.		25 Waterside Plaza	New York	NY	10010	212 684 7788
Tecmar, Inc.		6225 Cochran Rd.	Solon	OH	44139	216 464 7410
Texas Instruments, Inc.	P.O. Box 1444		Houston	TX	77011	713 373 1050
The Headlands Press, Inc.	P.O. Box 862		Tiburon	CA	94920	415 435 9775
Topaz Electronics Div.		3855 Ruffin Rd.	San Diego	CA	92123	619 279 0831
Toshiba America, Inc.-ISD		2441 Michelle Dr.	Tustin	CA	92680	714 730 5000
TPS Electronics		4047 Transport St.	Palo Alto	CA	94303	415 856 6833
Tymlabs Corp.		211 East 7 St.	Austin	TX	78701	512 478 8611
USI Computer Products		71 Park Ln.	Brisbane	CA	94005	415 468 4900
U.S. Robotics, Inc.		1123 West Washington	Chicago	IL	60607	312 733 0497
Ven-Tel, Inc.		2342 Walsh Ave.	Santa Clara	CA	95051	800 538 5121
Vertex Systems		7950 W. Fourth St.	Los Angeles	CA	90048	231 938 0857
Vista Computer Co.		1317 E. Edinger Ave.	Santa Ana	CA	92705	800 854 8017
Votrax, Inc.		500 Stephenson Hwy.	Troy	MI	48084	800 521 1350
WALLDATA, Inc.		14828 NE 95th St.	Redmond	WA	98052	206 883 4777
Wesper Microsystems, Inc.		14321 Myford Rd.	Tustin	CA	92680	800 854 8737
Wolfdata, Inc.		187 Billerica Rd.	Chelmsford	MA	01824	617 250 1500
XCOMP, Inc.		7566 Trade St.	San Diego	CA	92121	619 271 8730
Xerox Corporation		Xerox Square	Rochester	NY	14644	716 427 5400
Xymec, Inc.		17905 J Sky Park Cir.	Irvine	CA	92714	714 423 3411
Zen/Tek		455 Whitepine Dr.	Salt Lake City	UT	84107	801 263 3925
Zobek		7343 J. Ronson Rd.	San Diego	CA	92111	714 571 6971

Index

201C modem, 59
209 modem, 66
212A modem, 21
2024 modem, 59
2780/3780 BSC:
  ASCII, 63
  BARR/HASP, 63
  EBCDIC, 63
  Job Entry Subsystem, JES, 60
  Linkup, 62
  picture, 62
  point-to-point, 61
  protocol converters, 72
  protocols, 60
  Remote Job Entry, RJE, 60
  space compression, 61
3270 BSC:
  3270 PC, 157
  3278/79 Adapter, 158
  Binary Synchronous Adapter, 66
  Binary Synchronous Comm., 64
  cluster controllers, 64
  devices, 64
  modems, 66
  multipoint BSC, 64
  PCOX interface, 67
  picture, 66
  polling, 64
  polling address, 65
  protected fields, 65
  protocol converters, 72
  selection, 65
  selection address, 65
  system generation, 65
3270 PC, 157
3270 BSC, 157
  synchronous environments. 157
3278/79 Adapter:
  3270 BSC, 158
  coaxial cable, 158
3B2/5, 150
5251 Remote Work Station:
  BLUE LYNX, 69
  picture, 69
  protocol converters, 72
  Synchronous Data Link Control, 69

ABC switches, 128
ACA, 28
Alternatives to keyboard, 139
Amphenol connector, 120
AppleDOS:
  operating systems, 150
  Quadlink, 154
AppleDOS to PC-DOS:
  APPLE-IBM Connection, 154
  cabling, 153
  Crosstalk XVI, 152
  file transfers, 151
  Quadlink, 154
APPLE-IBM Connection:
  AppleDOS to PC-DOS, 154
  file transfers, 154

ASCII:
  2780/3780 BSC, 63
  protocol converters, 71
AST-3780, 62
Asynchronous Comm. Adapter:
  ACA, 28
  COM1 port, 28
  COM2 port, 28
  current loop, 28
  DB25P, 28
  MODE command, 29
  picture, 28
  RS-232, 28
  straight-through cable, 29
  wrap plug, 117
Asynchronous pass-through, 72
Asynchronous transmission:
  dial-up, 20
  protocol converters, 70
  start/stop bit, 16
Auto-answer, 46

Bar code readers, 141
BARR/HASP 2780/3780 BSC, 63
Battery backup for clocks, 30
Binary files, 39
Binary Synchronous Adapter, 66
Binary Synchronous Comm.:
  3270 BSC, 64
  protocols, 60
Binary Synchronous Comm., BSC, 60
Bit-mapped graphics, 102
Bits:
  data bits, 14
  one bit, 13
  parity bit, 15
  start bit, 14
  stop bit, 14
  zero bit, 13
BLACK BOX SAM+ RS232 TRI-State, 110
Blind dialing, 22
Block check character, 59
Block-mode graphics, 102
BLUE LYNX 5251 Work Station, 69
Board-level modems:
  advantages, 23
  disadvantages, 24
  intelligent modems, 23
  RS-232, 23
  slot requirement, 24
Booting:
  DIR/W, 3
  POST, 3
Breakout boxes:
  cabling, 113
  DTE/DCE emulation, 110
  hardware flow control, 113–14
  how-to-use, 112–15
  parallel interface, 123
  printers, 110
  SAM+ RS232 TRI-State, 110
Buffers:
  printer server, 91
  RAM buffer, 125
  RS-232, 74
  standalone buffer, 126
Bus interface unit, 88
Bus networks:
  Carrier-Sense Multiple Access, 86
  topology, 86
Bus topology, 87

Cabling:
  AppleDOS to PC-DOS, 153
  breakout boxes, 113
  Extended Distance Data Cables, 27
  shielded cables, 27
  SmartCable, 116
  stand-alone modems, 27
  wiring adapter, 117
  wrap plug, 117
Carrier-sense multiple access, 86
CCITT V.24, 51
CCS SuperVision monitor board, 42
Centronics parallel interface, 117
Champ connector, 120
Character length, 131
Clear to send:
  modems, 50
  printers, 105
  RS-232, 50–51
Clock:
  battery backup, 30
  multifunction boards, 30
Cluster controllers, 64
Coaxial cable:
  media, 83
  3278/79 adapter, 158
Code-activted switch:
  intelligent switches, 129
  optimizations, 160
  switches, 129
Collision detection, 87
Color/Graphics Adapter:
  monitors, 144
  pin assignments, 144
COM1 port:
  Asynchronous Comm. Adapter, 28
  intelligent modems, 23
COM2 port:
  Asynchronous Comm. Adapter, 28
  intelligent modems, 23
COMM.Bas program, 22
Communication server, 90
Communication software:
  Crosstalk XVI, 40
  End-of-file, EOF, 37
  file transfer programs, 35
  function keys, 38
  intelligent modems, 37
  PC-TALK III, 36
  printers, 40
  Smartcom II, 36
  teletype transmission, 36
  terminal emulation, 35
  VisiTerm, 152

Index

Compressed printing, 101
Control leads:
  null-modem cables, 106–9
  parallel interface, 119
  printers, 105
Conversion:
  parallel interface, 160
  RS-232, 160
CP/M, 148
Cross connections, 104–8
Crosstalk XVI:
  AppleDOS to PC-DOS, 152
  communication software, 40
  protocol converters, 72
  terminal emulation, 43
CSMA/CD:
  carrier sensing, 86
  collision detection, 87
  Ethernet, 87
Current loop, 28

Data bits, 14
Data carrier detect:
  modems, 50
  printers, 105
  RS-232, 49
Data communication equipment, 30
Data leads:
  null-modem cables, 105
  parallel interface, 118
  printers, 104
  RS-232, 44
Data set ready:
  modems, 47
  printers, 105
  RS-232, 47
Data terminal equipment, 30
Data terminal ready:
  hardware flow control, 107
  modems, 45
  printers, 105
  RS-232, 45
Database management systems, 4
DB25 to champ cable, 122
DB25P, 28
DBASE II:
  database management systems, 4
  file transfers, 154
DCE, 18
DEC VT100:
  protocol converters, 71
  terminal emulation, 41
DEC VT52, 41
Dialing, 21
Dial-up:
  asynchronous transmission, 20
  half-duplex, 50
  point-to-point, 58
  RS-232, 47
  The Source, 20
  Telenet, 20
  Tymnet, 20

DIR/W, 3
Disconnecting line, 47
DOS, 148
Dot matrix, 98
Dot matrix impact printers, 97
Double-strike printing, 101
Dow Jones, 4
DTE, 18
DTE/DCE emulation:
  breakout boxes, 110
  emulation, 103
  printers, 103
DTE-DCE interaction, 50

EBCDIC:
  2780/3780 BSC, 63
  protocol converters, 71
Echoplex printer option, 131
EIA standard, 5
Emulation:
  DTE/DCE emulation, 103
  intelligent modems, 25
  printers, 102
End-of-file, EOF, 37
ENQ/ACK, 39
EtherLink:
  Ethernet, 93
  local area networks, 89
Ethernet:
  bus topology, 87
  CSMA/CD, 87
  EtherLink, 93
  local area networks, 87
  PC Interface, 150
Exclusion key, 21
Expanded printing, 101
Extended Distance Data Cables, 27

Fiber optics, 83
File locking, 89
File server:
  file locking, 89
  local area networks, 89
  server, 89
File transfer:
  AppleDOS to PC-DOS, 151
  APPLE-IBM Connection, 154
  binary files, 39
  communication software, 35
  DBASE II, 154
  ENQ/ACK, 39
  flow control, 38
  print files, 153
  Quadlink, 155
  Visifile, 153
  XON/XOFF, 38
Flow control:
  file transfer, 38
  modems, 53
  paper-out condition, 53

Flow control: (*cont.*)
  printer options, 130
  printers, 107
  RS-232, 53
  secondary data carrier detect, 54
  secondary request to send, 54
  secondary signals, 53
  XON/XOFF, 54
Frame ground, 51
Friction feed printers, 99
Front-end processor, 48
Full-character impact printers, 97
Full-duplex, 51
Function keys, 38

Game paddles, 142
Game ports, 30
Gateways, 85
GE Tymshare, 4
Graphics printers, 101
Ground leads:
  null-modem cables, 105
  parallel interface, 118
  printers, 104

Half-duplex:
  dial-up, 50
  DTE-DCE interaction, 50
  RS-232, 49
Hardware flow control:
  breakout boxes, 113–14
  data terminal ready, 107
  parallel interface, 119
  picture, 108
  printers, 107
  request to send, 107
  RS-232, 55
  secondary request to send, 108
Hayes-compatible mode, 25
Hayes Smartmodem 1200B:
  intelligent modems, 22
  picture, 24
Hewlett-Packard 2621, 41
Hewlett-Packard 7475A plotter, 145

IBM parallel connector, 120
IBM 3101:
  protocol converters, 71
  terminal emulation, 41
  XT/370, 157
Impact printers:
  dot matrix, 97
  full-character, 97
  printers, 97
Information Systems Network, 88
Intelligent modems:
  blind dialing, 22
  board-level modems, 23
  COM1 port, 23
  COM2 port, 23

COMM.BAS program, 22
communication software, 37
dialing, 21
emulation, 25
Hayes-compatible mode, 25
Hayes Smartmodem, 1200B, 22
keyboard dialing, 21
lights, 25
number linking, 21
options, 25
RS-232, 46
redial, 21
rotary dialing, 22
stand-alone modems, 25
touch-tone dialing, 22
Intelligent switches:
  code-activated switch, 129
  local area networks, 83
Interfaces:
  printer options, 133
  printers, 99, 103
ISO model protocol, 87

Job Entry Subsystem, JES, 60

Keyboard dialing, 21
Keytops:
  alternatives to keyboard, 139
  Synchronous Data Link Control, 70

LAN, 81
Lear Siegler ADMs, 41
Light-pens, 30
Line feed printer option, 132
Lines/character per inch, 133
Linkup:
  2780/3780 BSC, 62
  terminal emulation, 43
Local area networks:
  bus interface unit, 88
  EtherLink, 89
  Ethernet, 87
  file server, 89
  gateways, 85
  Information Systems Network, 88
  intelligent switches, 83
  media, 83
  network adapter, 88
  optimizations, 160
  PCnet, 93
  private branch exchanges, 83
  resource sharing, 82
  server, 88
  topology, 83
  transporter, 88
  User PCs, 89
  XNET, 92
Loopback switch, LBS, 115
Lotus 1-2-3 spreadsheet, 4

Index   **301**

Magnetic card readers, 142
Mean time to repair:
  printers, 102
  reliability, 102
Media:
  coaxial cable, 83
  fiber optics, 83
  local area networks, 83
  twisted pair, 83
Memory:
  multifunction boards, 30
  RAM disk, 32
Mini-Print Spooler, 126
MODE command:
  Asynchronous Comm. Adapter, 29
  positional parameters, 29
Mode printer option, 131
Modems:
  201C modem, 59
  209 modem, 66
  212A modem, 21
  2024 modem, 59
  3270 BSC, 66
  clear to send, 50
  data carrier detect, 50
  data set ready, 47
  data terminal ready, 45
  dialing, 21
  exclusion key, 21
  flow control, 53
  optimizations, 160
  receive data, 44
  request to send, 50
  reverse channel, 54
  ring indicator, 45
  secondary signals, 52
  short-haul modems, 33
  timing out, 46
  transmit data, 44
Monitors, 143
  Color/Graphics Adapter, 144
  RGB monitors, 143
Mouse:
  PC Mouse, 140
  RS-232, 140
Multifunction boards:
  advantages, 33
  clock, 30
  disadvantages, 33
  game ports, 30
  light-pens, 30
  memory, 30
  parallel interface, 30
  picture, 31
  RS-232, 30
  serial ports, 30
MultiPlan spreadsheet, 4
Multipoint BSC, 64

Network adapter, 88
Null-modem cables:
  control leads, 106-9
  cross connections, 104-8
  data leads, 105
  ground leads, 105
  Loopback switch, LBS, 115
  picture, 108, 110
  printers, 104
  receive timing, 109
  synchronous modem eliminator, 109
  timing leads, 108-9
  transmit timing, 109
Number linking, 21

One bit, 13
On-line/off-line option, 133
Open Systems Interconnection, 87
Operating systems:
  AppleDOS, 150
  CP/M, 148
  optimizations, 160
  PC-DOS, 148
  PCDOS and AppleDOS differences, 151
  UNIX, 149
  VM/CMS, 156
  XENIX, 149
Optimizations:
  code-activated switch, 160
  local area networks, 160
  modems, 160
  operating systems, 160
  PC Interface, 160
  parallel switches, 127
  picture, 160
  plotters, 160
  printers, 160
  serial ABC switches, 128
  short-haul modems, 160
  switches, 160
Options:
  intelligent modems, 25
  printers, 99

Page length printer option, 134
Paper-out condition, 53
Parallel interface:
  acquiring parallel port, 124
  amphenol connector, 120
  breakout boxes, 123
  Centronics, 117
  champ connector, 120
  control leads, 119
  conversion, 160
  data leads, 118
  DB25 to champ cable, 122
  ground leads, 118
  hardware flow control, 119
  IBM parallel connector, 120
  multifunction boards, 30
  pinout, 121
  printers, 117
  RS-232, 120

Parallel interface: (cont.)
   switches, 128
   transmit timing, 120
Parallel switches, 127
Parity:
   bit, 15
   check, 15
   error, 16
   printer options, 131
PCDOS and AppleDOS differences, 151
PC-DOS operating system, 148
PC/InterComm software, 42
PC Interface:
   Ethernet, 150
   optimizations, 160
   RS-232, 150
   UNIX, 149
PC Mouse, 140
PCnet:
   local area networks, 93
   remote execution, 93
PCOX interface:
   3270 BSC, 67
   picture, 68
PC-TALK III software, 36
Performance, 99
Phone-line suppressors, 138
Pin assignments for Adapter, 144
Pin feed printers, 99
Pinout for parallel interface, 121
Pitches for printers, 100
Plotters, 145
   Hewlett-Packard 7475A, 145
   optimizations, 160
Point-to-point:
   dial-up, 58
   2780/3780 BSC, 61
Polarity printer option, 132
Polling, 64
Polling address, 65
Port sharing, 26
Positional parameters, 29
Power-on self test, POST, 3
Power supplies, 138
print files, 153
Printer options:
   character length, 131
   echoplex, 131
   flow control, 130
   interfaces, 133
   line feeds, 132
   lines/character per inch, 133
   mode, 131
   on-line/off-line, 133
   page length, 134
   parity, 131
   polarity, 132
   speeds, 130
   stop bit, 131
   transmission mode, 132
   wraparound, 134
Printer server:
   buffers, 91
   server, 90

Printers:
   bit-mapped graphics, 102
   block-mode graphics, 102
   breakout boxes, 110
   clear to send, 105
   communication software, 40
   compressed printing, 101
   control leads, 105
   DTE/DCE emulation, 103
   data carrier detect, 105
   data leads, 104
   data set ready, 105
   data terminal ready, 105
   double-strike printing, 101
   emulation, 102
   expanded printing, 101
   flow control, 107
   friction feed, 99
   graphics, 101
   ground leads, 104
   hardware flow control, 107
   impact printers, 97
   interfaces, 99, 103
   mean time to repair, 102
   null-modem cables, 104
   optimizations, 160
   options, 99
   parallel interface, 117
   performance, 99
   pin feed, 99
   pitches, 100
   proportional space printing, 101
   protective ground, 104
   RAM buffer, 125
   RS-232, 104
   receive data, 104
   reliability, 102
   request to send, 105
   reverse channel, 107
   signal ground, 104
   sprocket feed, 99
   tractor feed, 99
   transmit data, 104
Private branch exchanges:
   local area networks, 83
   protocol converters, 71
Programmable comm. boards:
   data communication equipment, 30
   data terminal equipment, 30
Proportional space printing, 101
Protected fields, 65
Protective ground:
   printers, 104
   RS-232, 51
Protocol converters:
   2780/3780 BSC, 72
   3270 BSC, 72
   5251 Remote Work Station, 72
   ASCII, 71
   asynchronous pass-through, 72
   asynchronous transmission, 70
   Crosstalk XVI, 72
   DEC VT100, 71
   EBCDIC, 71

Index

IBM 3101, 71
picture, 73
private branch exchanges, 71
synchronous transmission, 70
Televideo 900 series, 71
WallData DCF, 73
Protocols:
2780/3780 BSC, 60
Binary Synchronous Comm., BSC, 60
Block Check Character, 59
ISO model, 87
Open Systems Interconnection, 87
Synchronous Data Link Control, 67
synchronous environment, 59
synchronous transmission, 16
XMODEM protocol, 39

Quadlink, 154,
AppleDOS, 154
AppleDOS to PC-DOS, 154
file transfers, 155

RAM buffer:
buffers, 125
printers, 125
RAM disk:
disks, 32
memory, 32
Receive data:
modems, 44
printers, 104
RS-232, 44
Receive timing:
null-modem cables, 109
RS-232, 78
timing, 77
Redial, 21
Reliability:
mean time to repair, 102
printers, 102
Remote execution on PCnet, 93
Remote Job Entry, RJE, 60
Request to send:
hardware flow control, 107
modems, 50
printers, 105
RS-232, 50–51
Resource sharing, 82
Reverse channel:
modems, 54
printers, 107
RS-232, 54
RGB monitors, 143
Ring indicator:
modems, 45
RS-232, 45
Ring networks:
token passing, 85
topology, 85
Ring topology, 86
Rotary dialing, 22

RS-232, 4
acquiring serial port, 27
Asynchronous Comm. Adapter, 28
auto-answer, 46
board-level modem, 23
buffers, 74
CCITT V.24, 51
clear to send, 50–51
conversion, 160
data carrier detect, 49
data leads, 44
data set ready, 47
data terminal ready, 45
dial-up, 47
disconnecting line, 47
EIA standard, 5
flow control, 53
frame ground, 51
front-end processor, 48
full-duplex, 51
half-duplex, 49
hardware flow control, 55
intelligent modems, 46
mouse, 140
multifunction boards, 30
parallel interface, 120
PC Interface, 150
port sharing, 26
printers, 104
protective ground, 51
received data, 44
receiver timing, 78
request to send, 50–51
reverse channel, 54
ring indicator, 45
secondary data carrier detect, 54
secondary request to send, 54
secondary signals, 52
signal ground, 51
slave timing, 78
software flow control, 54
standalone modems, 26
switches, 128
timing, 75
timing out, 46
transmit data, 44
transmit timing, 76
wrap plug, 117

SAMPLES program, 3
Secondary data carrier detect:
flow control, 54
RS-232, 54
Secondary request to send:
flow control, 54
hardware flow control, 108
RS-232, 54
Secondary signals:
flow control, 53
modems, 52
RS-232, 52
Selection, 65
Selection address, 65

304

Serial ABC switches, 128
Serial ports, 30
Server:
  communication server, 90
  file server, 89
  local area networks, 88
  printer server, 90
Service bureaus:
  Dow Jones, 4
  GE Tymshare, 4
Shielded cables, 27
Short-haul modems:
  distance, 34
  modems, 33
  optimizations, 160
  picture, 35
  speeds, 34
Signal ground:
  printers, 104
  RS-232, 51
Slave timing:
  RS-232, 78
  timing, 78
SmartCable, 116
Smartcom II comm. software, 36
SmarTerm/PC terminal emulation, 42
Software flow control:
  RS-232, 54
  XON/XOFF, 54
The Source, 20
Space compression, 61
Speeds:
  printer options, 130
  short-haul modems, 34
Spreadsheets:
  Lotus 1-2-3, 4
  MultiPlan, 4
  VisiCalc, 4
Sprocket feed printers, 99
Stand-alone modems:
  advantages, 25
  cabling, 27
  disadvantages, 26
  intelligent modems, 25
Standalone buffer:
  buffers, 126
  Mini-Print Spooler, 126
Standalone modems, 26
Star topology:
  picture, 84-85
  topology, 83
Start bit, 14
Start/stop bit, 16
Stop bit:
  bits, 14
  printer options, 131
Straight-through cable, 29
Switches:
  ABC, 128
  code-activated switch, 129
  optimizations, 160
  parallel interface, 128
  RS-232, 128
Synchronization, 16

Synchronous Data Link Control:
  5251 Remote Work Station, 69
  keytops, 70
  protocols, 67
  Systems Network Architecture, 67
Synchronous environments:
  3270 PC, 157
  protocols, 59
  XT/370, 156
Synchronous modem eliminator, 109
Synchronous transmission:
  protocol converters, 70
  protocols, 16
  timing, 16, 75
System generation, 65
Systems Network Architecture, 67

Telenet, 20
Teletype transmission, 36
Televideo 900 series:
  protocol converters, 71
  terminal emulation, 41
Terminal emulation:
  CCS SuperVision monitor board, 42
  communication software, 35
  Crosstalk XVI, 43
  DEC VT100, 41
  DEC VT52, 41
  Hewlett-Packard 2621, 41
  IBM 3101, 41
  Lear Siegler ADMs, 41
  Linkup, 43
  PC/InterComm, 42
  SmarTerm/PC, 42
  Televideo 900 series, 41
Timing:
  null-modem cables, 108-9
  picture, 78
  receive timing, 77
  RS-232, 75
  slave timing, 78
  synchronization, 16
  synchronous transmission, 16, 75
  transmit timing, 76
Timing out, 46
Token passing, 85
Topology:
  bus networks, 86
  local area networks, 83
  ring networks, 85
  star topology, 83
Touch-Tone dialing, 22
Tractor feed printers, 99
Transmission mode option, 132
Transmit data:
  modems, 44
  printers, 104
  RS-232, 44
Transmit timing:
  null-modem cables, 109

Index

Transmit timing: (cont.)
   parallel interface, 120
   RS-232, 76
   timing, 76
Transporter, 88
Twisted pair media, 83
Tymnet, 20

UNIX:
   operating systems, 149
   PC Interface, 149
   3B2/5, 150
User PCs within LANs, 89

VisiCalc spreadsheet, 4
Visifile, 153
VisiTerm comm. software, 152
VM/CMS operating system, 156

WallData DCF:
   picture, 73
   protocol converters, 73
Wiring Adapter, 117
Wrap plug:
   Asynchronous Comm. Adapter, 117
   cabling, 117
   RS-232, 117
Wraparound printer option, 134

XENIX operating system, 149
XMODEM protocol, 39
XNET local area network, 92
XON/XOFF:
   file transfer, 38
   flow control, 54
   software flow control, 54
XT/370, 156
   IBM 3101, 157
   synchronous environments, 156